# AROUND WORTHING

## IN OLD PHOTOGRAPHS

To my Bestest Girlfriend Rita
From.
Eddie x Xmas 99.

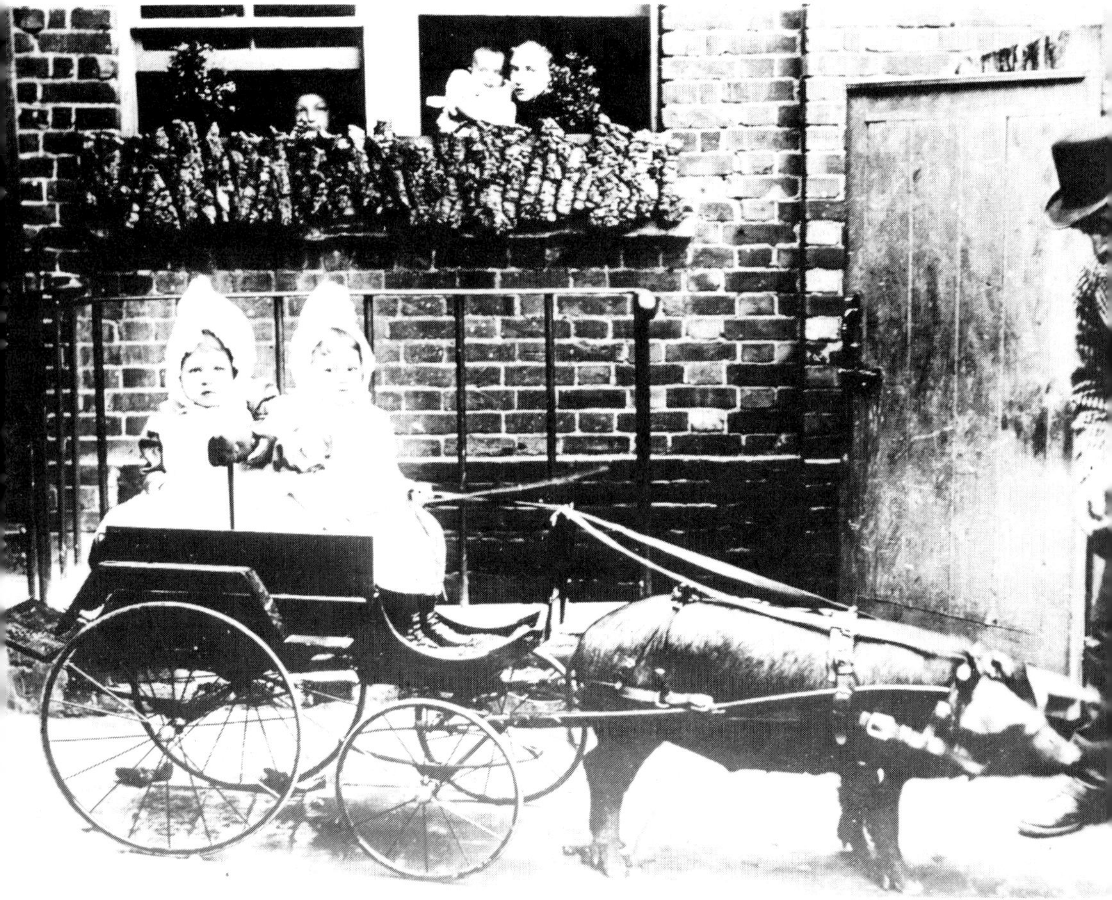

PIGS ARE NOT USUALLY HARNESSED INTO CARTS. The cart in this picture is interesting in itself, with the back-to-back seats for the babies. It is hard to tell whether the babies or the pig look more solemn!

# AROUND WORTHING IN OLD PHOTOGRAPHS

COLLECTED BY
DR SALLY WHITE

Budding BOOKS

A Budding Book

First published in 1991 by Alan Sutton Publishing Limited

This edition published in 1998 by Budding Books,
an imprint of Sutton Publishing Limited
Phoenix Mill · Thrupp · Stroud · Gloucestershire GL5 2BU



A catalogue record for this book is available from the British Library

ISBN 1-84015-031-9

For my mother in gratitude for her unfailing love and understanding

Typesetting and origination by
Sutton Publishing Limited.
Printed in Great Britain by
WBC Limited, Bridgend, Mid-Glamorgan.

# CONTENTS


| | | |
|---|---|---|
| | INTRODUCTION | 6 |
| 1 | THE PIER | 9 |
| 2 | THE SEAFRONT | 15 |
| 3 | SHOPS–COMMERCE–HOTELS | 29 |
| 4 | EDUCATION AND HEALTH | 43 |
| 5 | ENTERTAINMENT | 55 |
| 6 | SPORTS AND PASTIMES | 65 |
| 7 | PARKS AND GARDENS | 75 |
| 8 | WAR AND PEACE | 79 |
| 9 | RELIGIOUS LIFE | 87 |
| 10 | TRANSPORT | 97 |
| 11 | EVENTS | 107 |
| 12 | PEOPLE | 115 |
| 13 | STREETS AND BUILDINGS | 123 |
| 14 | RURAL LIFE | 147 |
| | ACKNOWLEDGEMENTS | 160 |

# INTRODUCTION

Undervalued by many people, Worthing is a town which repays investigation. With familiarity grows affection. Almost hidden among the lesser buildings are delights like Ambrose Place, Bedford Row, Salvington Windmill and the centres of the old villages which combine to form the modern town of Worthing.

The area around Worthing has more history than many people realize, and has been a popular place to live since the New Stone Age. At that time, around six thousand years ago, the South Downs, the hills around Worthing were the site of one of Britain's first industrial complexes. Several hundred mine shafts were dug into the Downs so that high-quality flint could be extracted for tool-making. In the Bronze and Iron Ages settlement continued and was concentrated on the hills. The glorious hillfort at Cissbury is the most impressive evidence of the large-scale construction projects which the local Iron Age population undertook.

Arriving in the first century AD, the Romans preferred to settle on the fertile coastal plain. There they developed successful farming communities which were linked by road to Chichester and other towns. Following the departure of the Roman authorities in the early fifth century, a new group arrived who gave the area its name. Sussex was the kingdom of the South Saxons. We know relatively little about where these Saxons lived, but cemeteries like that at Highdown show that they must have been reasonably rich. The -ing ending of place names like Tarring, Goring and Sompting is a clear indication of the Saxon origin of these villages. Saxon society was essentially rural and these farming communities developed into villages which were still larger than Worthing into the nineteenth century when Worthing was in the parish of Broadwater.

Worthing owes its development and prosperity to the popularity of sea bathing and to its early royal patronage. In 1798 King George III sent his youngest daughter, Princess Amelia, to Worthing to try sea bathing as a cure for her lame knee. Close enough to Brighton for the young princess to be visited by her brother the Prince of Wales, but far enough for her to be thought safe from the influence of his dissolute entourage, Worthing acquired a reputation as a genteel resort which it has enjoyed ever since.

Although mainly flat, Worthing stretches to the Downs to the north and they are visible from many parts of the town. The close proximity of the hills is often credited with some responsibility for Worthing's claim to have an exceptionally sunny and fog-free climate. This claim has been central to the town's marketing campaigns for at least 150 years. Among its other advantages is a gently shelving beach. At low tide there is a wide expanse of sand which is thronged with people throughout the summer. Since sea bathing first became popular, the sea at Worthing has been considered especially safe. Once the town had become established as a resort, its continued popularity can be attributed to its situation, facilities and reputation as a nice place 'for those who delight to embrace the limpid wave', as one Victorian writer put it. Many visitors become loyal, returning to Worthing year after year.

People often picture early bathers enveloped from head to foot in voluminous costumes, slipping, discreetly, into the sea from a bathing machine. This image is far from accurate. In the late eighteenth and early nineteenth centuries bathers were often naked and mixed freely on the beach. Periodic attempts were made to ensure that men and women bathed separately, but this rule was by no means rigorously enforced. During the Victorian period clothes became heavier and more concealing, and seaside wear did not escape this trend. Women were expected to leave only their hands and face uncovered while bathing. Men could leave their head, arms and legs bare. Reducing enjoyment even further, bathing rules stated that men over eight years old could not bathe within fifty yards of a place where 'a person of the female sex' might bathe. Such stringent restrictions were bound to be opposed and broken, but it was only in 1909 that Worthing gave in to the prevailing trend and allowed mixed bathing away from the central part of the town. After the First World War mixed bathing became the rule, and the beaches were crowded with families and groups of friends bathing together.

Although Worthing is not a rowdy resort and has avoided the brasher attractions favoured by many seaside towns, there has never been a shortage of entertainments for visitors when they were not bathing. Sailing, rowing boats, trips on steamers, rides on donkeys, ponies or in the goat cart were available for those who wanted more than a stroll along the promenade or out along the pier. Over the years the town has had an impressive number of theatres, cinemas, libraries and other cultural venues, as well as skating rinks and snooker halls. In the nineteenth century the cultural life of the town was closely linked to the visitor season. The town seemed to doze during the winter in the preparation for the next summer's liveliness. By the early years of the twentieth century there was a strong feeling that entertainment should be provided throughout the year, not only for the residents but also in an attempt to attract winter visitors. When the council had the chance to buy the Beach House Estate the local newspapers were full of the proposals to build a Winter Garden there with a concert hall, bandstand, fountain, sports facilities and gardens. In spite of these grandiose plans the Winter Garden was unfortunately never built.

For years Worthing's only surviving theatre, the Connaught, had a good repertory company, but a few years ago the future of the theatre was in jeopardy. It then came under new management and now seems safe, at least for the time being. Since the Odeon was demolished to make way for the new Montague Shopping Centre, the only cinema in Worthing has been the Dome on the seafront. To go inside the Dome is like stepping back fifty years to the heyday of the cinema. It is a wonderful period piece and its exterior, although sadly neglected, is one of the most attractive on the eastern part of the seafront.

One of the delightful things about Worthing is its position. Between the sea and the Downs, it is only fifty-seven miles from London and just a short distance from a number of villages which have retained many of their old buildings and much of their charm. Since the days of James Town and other Victorian coach owners, plenty of excursions have been available. Bramber and Arundel, with their castles, were popular destinations, as was Chanctonbury Ring which was reached in a horse-drawn coach. There was also a weekly packet boat to Dieppe.

The plain between the Downs and the sea widens along this section of the coast and is extremely fertile. Although Worthing never became a major industrial town it was, until the 1950s, the centre of an enormously productive and successful glasshouse industry. Flowers, although grown in large numbers, were usually a secondary crop. Growers concentrated on fruit and vegetables which were not generally grown in quantity in England, including grapes, tomatoes and cucumbers, most of which were sold in London. During the First World War Worthing cucumbers were in great demand in munitions and other factories, where they were used for refreshing the workers. Considerable value was put on their continued production as a necessity and not a luxury.

In the early years of the twentieth century the Downs were used by the army for training and manoeuvres. The London Scottish VRC were regular visitors, camping at Tarring. The Essex Regiment, the King's Royal Rifles, Rough Riders and even the New South Wales Australian Cadets took their turns. Old photographs show that the troops also paraded through the town and in the parks, attracting large crowds.

Like every other town in the country Worthing made its contribution to the South African, First and Second World Wars. During the First World War streets of about 130 small terraced houses typically sent about 75 men to fight. Since the men and women left behind also made their own contributions, the impact on the town must have been enormous. Being on the south coast, Worthing was in the area where a German invasion was anticipated during the Second World War. The beach and seafront were defended, the pier blown up to hinder a landing and thousands of children were sent to, hopefully, safer areas. Never a prime target itself, Worthing none the less suffered its share of damage from German bombing. The war memorials are a testament to the men who died in the forces, but the women and civilians who died are not mentioned.

In the post-war period it began to seem that the demolition of old and even listed buildings was the rule rather than the exception. In response to this, conservation groups were set up. They, and individual members of the population, have lobbied for the preservation of old buildings and those of special interest, trying to safeguard the town's character. This pressure is paying off and some conservation areas have been established.

To many outsiders Worthing is still best known for its long-standing popularity with older people. They come to the town in large numbers and have earned it the affectionate nickname of 'God's Waiting Room'. However, Worthing should not be dismissed simply because it is a popular retirement town. It has a great deal to offer to residents and visitors of all ages who like tranquility rather than rowdiness. Anyone who takes the time to explore the town and surrounding area will be amply rewarded for their efforts. Many will, like me, agree with broadcaster Ray Gosling who said that he liked Worthing for simply 'being what it is'.

SECTION ONE

# The Pier

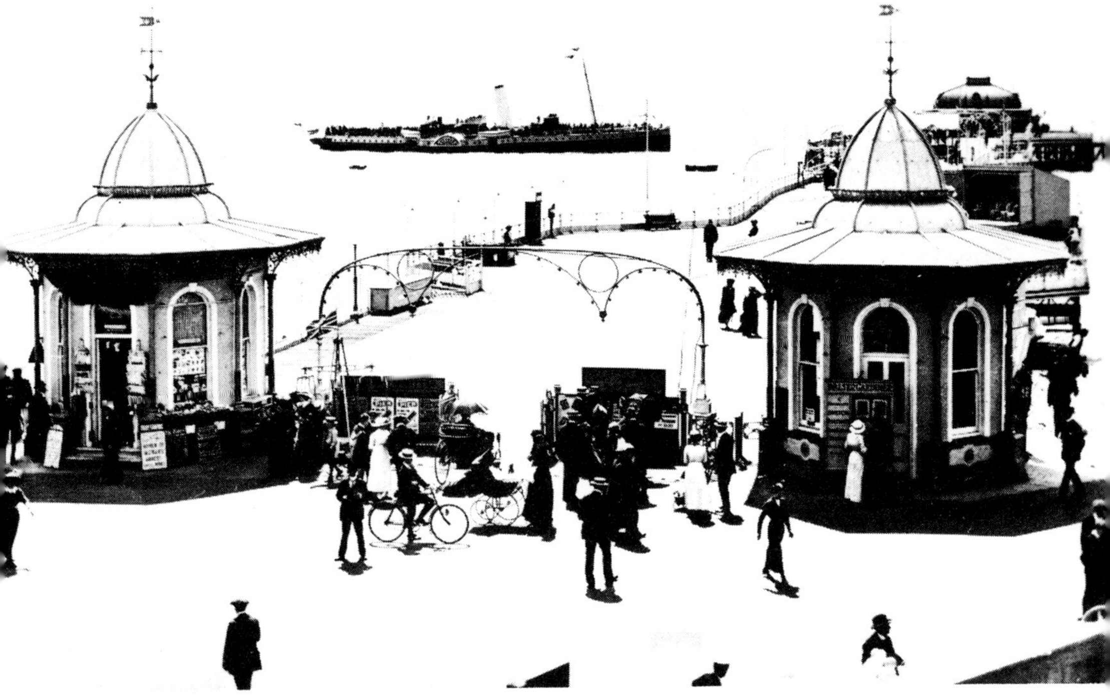

MR LEONARD BENTALL, MAYOR OF WORTHING in 1949, said that only Worthing Pier had been 'blown down, burnt out and blown up'. The first pier, built in 1862, was a simple deck with a landing stage at the pierhead where steamers could tie up. In 1889 the deck was widened, a southern pavilion was built and two kiosks were added at the landward end. One kiosk was a bazaar and the other was used by the pier master, Tom Belton, as a toll-house.

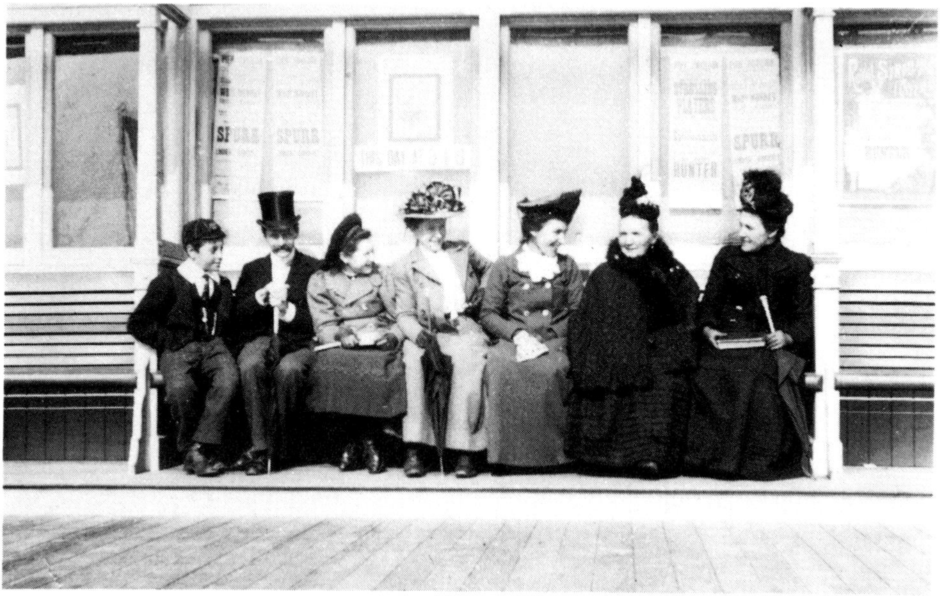

THIS DELIGHTFUL GROUP was photographed on the pier in 1901. They have all squeezed into one of the shelters to get out of the wind. They look like three generations of one family and sport a wonderful variety of hats.

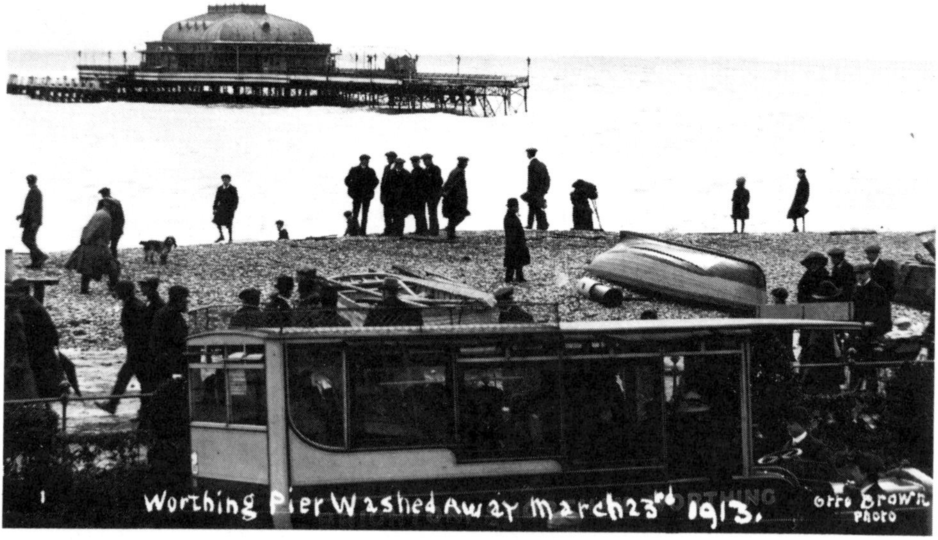


DISASTER FIRST STRUCK THE PIER on the night of Easter Monday 1913. During the evening the wind strengthened to eighty miles per hour and shortly after midnight the pier decking collapsed into the sea. Crowds had gathered to watch the storm and more flocked to the beach in the morning to see the damage. This photograph was taken by the Worthing photographer Otto Brown.

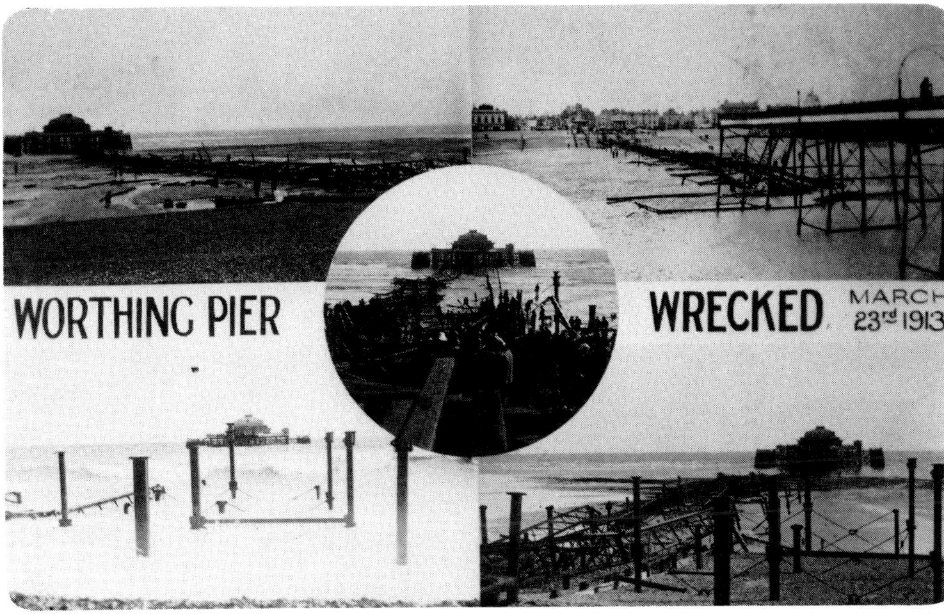


THE EASTER STORM CAUSED DEVASTATION throughout southern England but only Worthing's pier was blown away. Postcard makers were quick to mark the disaster. This multiview shows the extent of the damage, with the jetty and the landward end of the pier being completely destroyed. Steamers took passengers on trips around the pierhead.

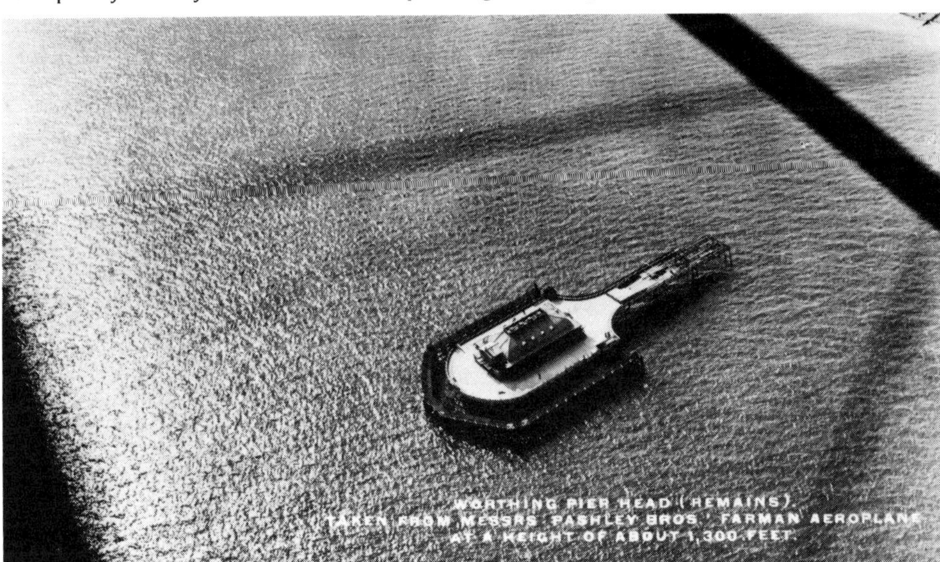


TOURISTS FLOCKED TO WORTHING in record numbers to see the isolated pierhead which was nicknamed 'Easter Island'. This picture was taken by aviation pioneers Cecil and Eric Pashley, who flew their Farman aeroplane from Shoreham airport.

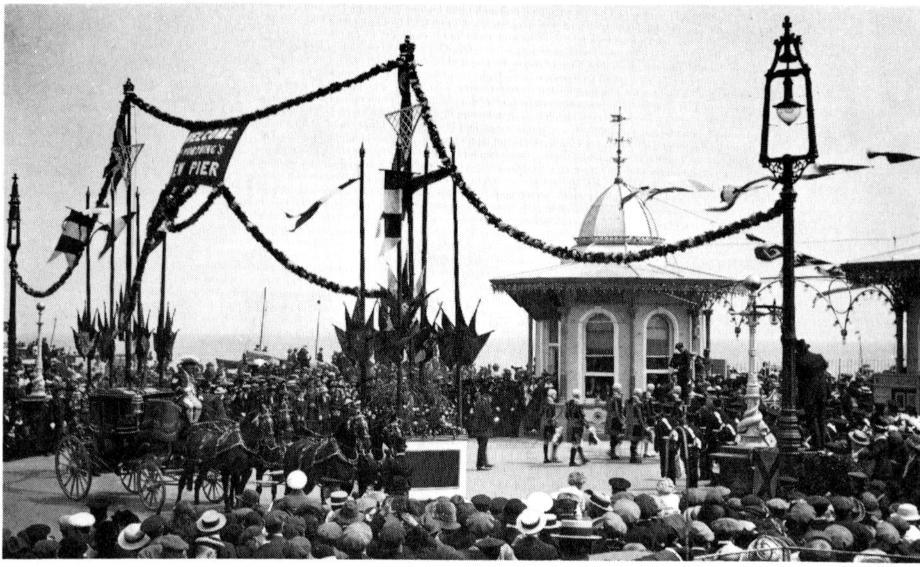

THE PIER WAS REBUILT and opened on 29 May 1914. The general mood of celebration was illustrated by a ditty in the local newspaper which began, 'The Pier is now mended, Our troubles are ended.' The rebuilding cost over £10,000 and the new pier was opened by the lord mayor of London, the Right Honourable Alderman Sir T.V. Bowater who brought his own ceremonial coach down from London for the occasion. The procession led from the station to the pier through decorated streets. A public holiday was called in Worthing to celebrate the event and huge crowds watched the proceedings. The advertising hoardings in the lower picture cover the site of the Sea House Hotel which had burnt down in 1901.

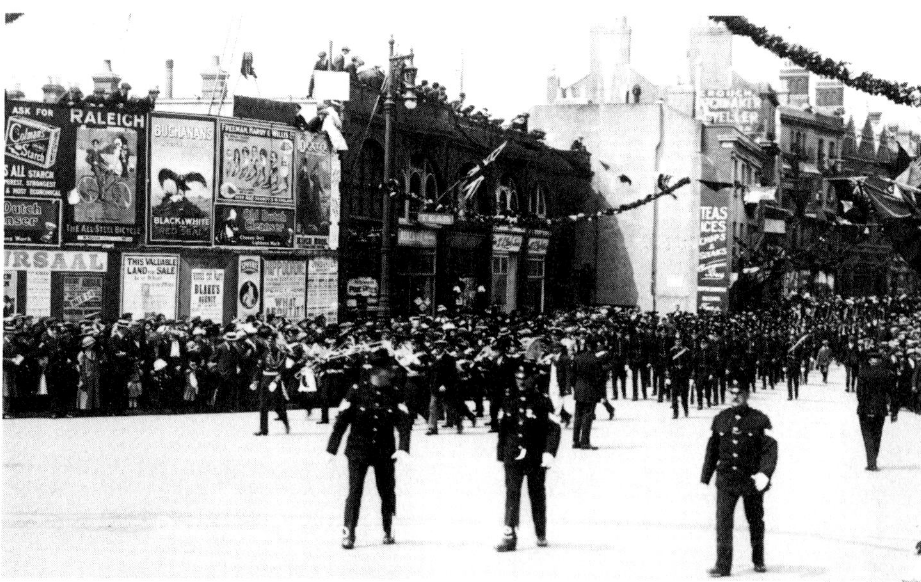

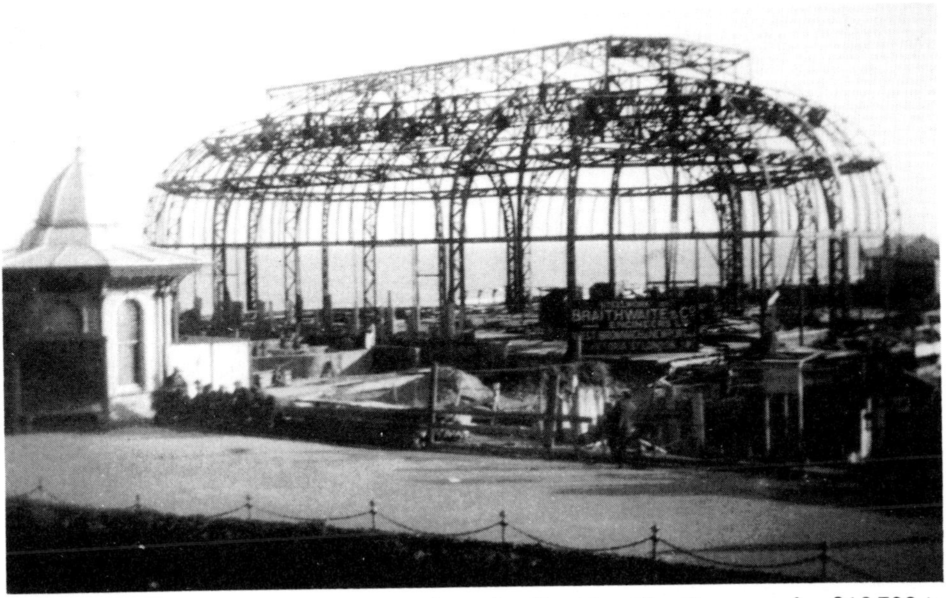

WORTHING CORPORATION BOUGHT THE PIER from the Worthing Pier Company for £18,798 in 1920. During the 1920s concert parties were very popular, but the town lacked a good venue. When repairs needed to be carried out in 1925 the opportunity was taken to build a new pavilion at the shore end. There was considerable controversy over the design chosen by Messrs Adshead and Ramsey. It was opened by the mayor, Mr Walter Gardiner, on 25 June 1926.

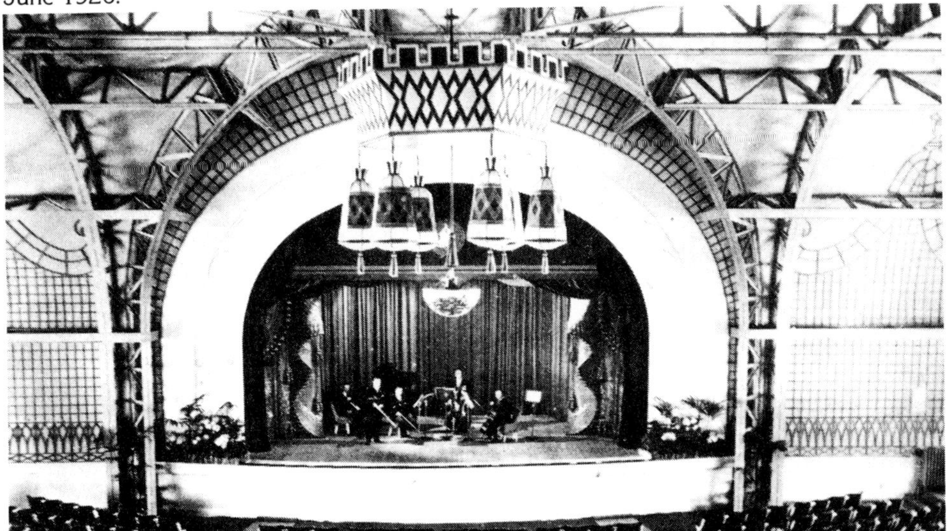

THE INSIDE OF THE NEW PAVILION can be seen on this postcard. Britain's only full-time, all-year-round, municipal orchestra was based there under the direction of H. Joseph Shadwick. In 1935 Herbert Lodge began twenty years as Worthing's musical director.

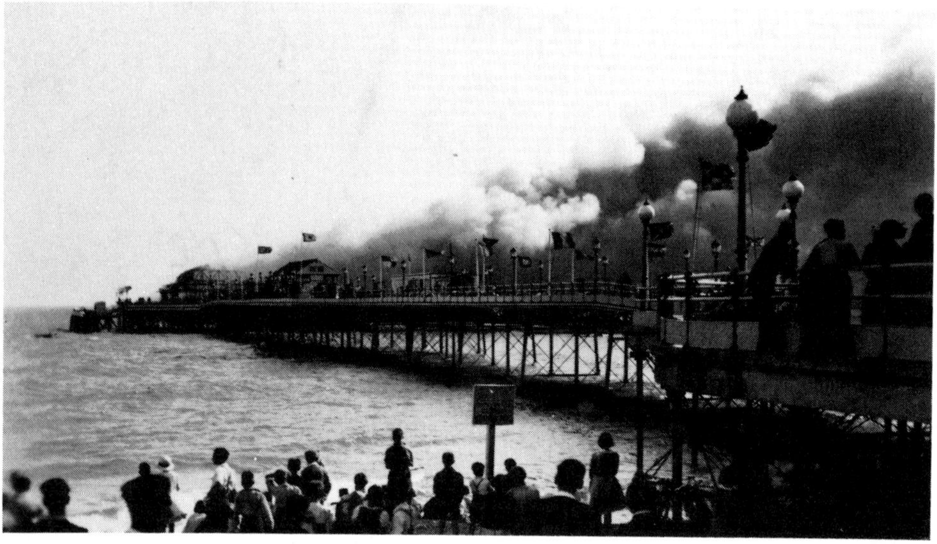

DISASTER STRUCK AGAIN on 10 September 1933. People on the beach noticed wisps of smoke coming from the southern end of the pier, but it was twenty minutes before the alarm was raised. Fanned by a strong wind the fire caught hold and destroyed the South Pavilion and decking. The blaze could be seen from as far away as Beachy Head.

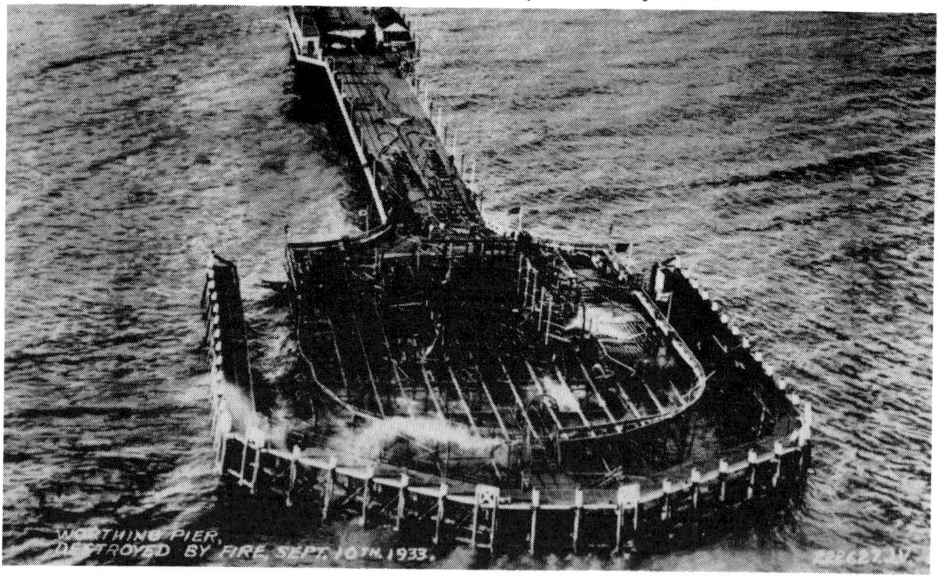


ALTHOUGH GUTTED BY THE BLAZE, the pier had risen from the ashes by July 1935 and was described by the *Daily Mirror* as 'the suntrap of the South Coast'. In 1937 a central windshield and an amusement pavilion were added. During 1940 the authorities blew a large hole in the pier to hinder a possible German landing. The South Pavilion was again isolated. Due to a post-war shortage of steel the pier was not repaired until 1949, when the reopening was marked by a firework display.

SECTION TWO

# The Seafront

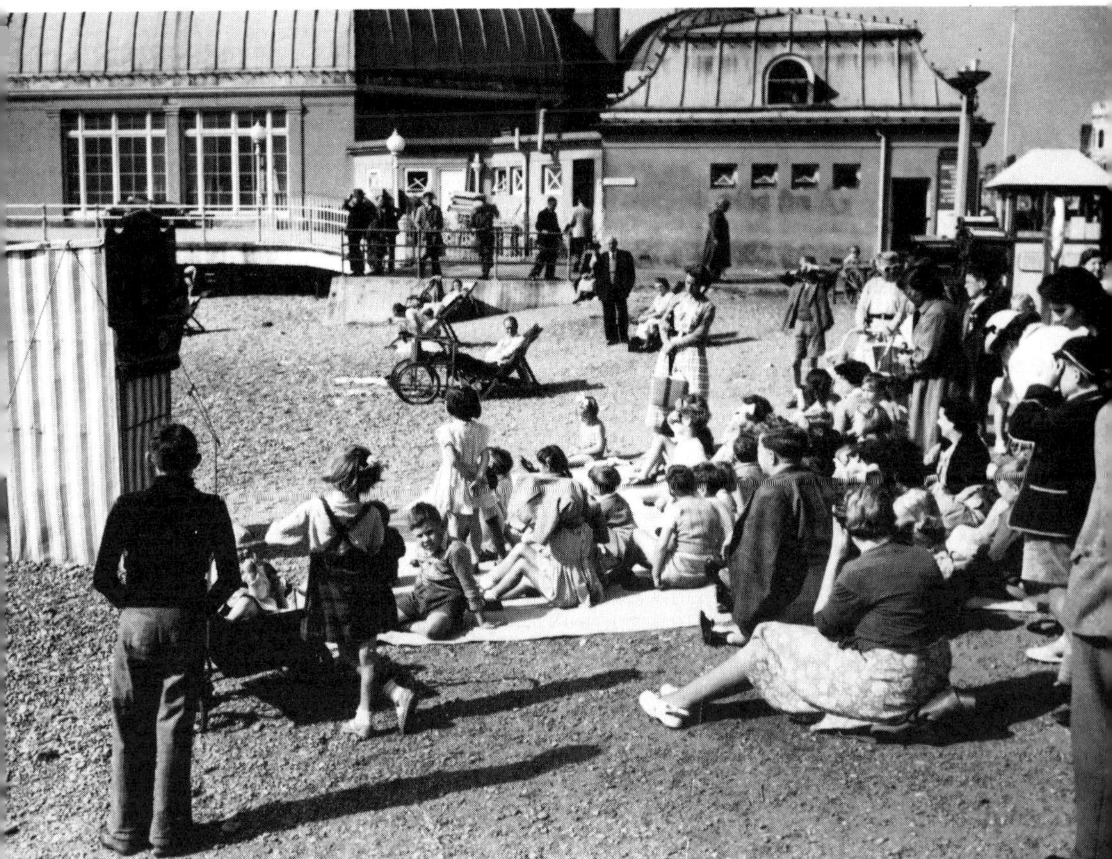

FOR MANY YEARS an English beach in summer was not complete without the striped tent and raucous voices of a Punch and Judy show. This one was set up just to the east of the pier during the 1950s.

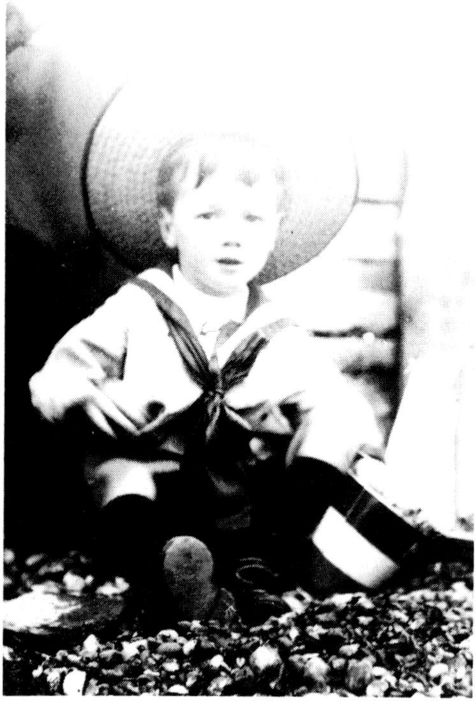

THIS SMALL BOY SEEMS OVERDRESSED to us today but his shoes, socks, sailor suit and hat were fashionable seaside wear for boys at the turn of the century. He is well equipped for a day on the beach with his toy yacht and bucket.

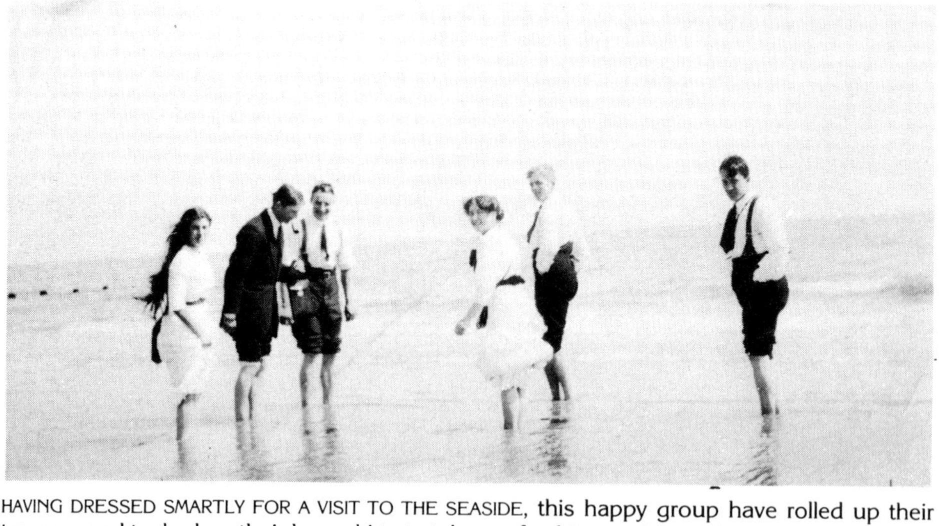

HAVING DRESSED SMARTLY FOR A VISIT TO THE SEASIDE, this happy group have rolled up their trousers and tucked up their long skirts to take a refreshing paddle in the sea. The man with the pipe in his mouth and his jacket firmly buttoned up looks much less at ease than his companions.

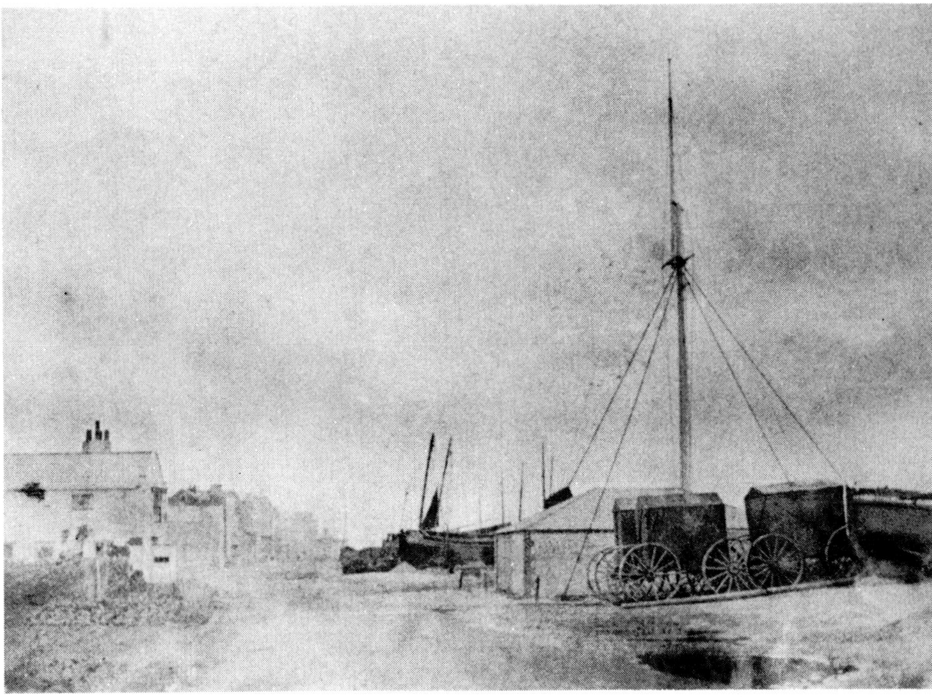

THIS VIEW, LOOKING FROM HEENE TOWARDS WORTHING, was taken in the 1850s, before there had been much development this far west. It is difficult to equate it with the same stretch of seafront today. It shows the coastguard's flagpole on the right and the coastguard's station on the left.

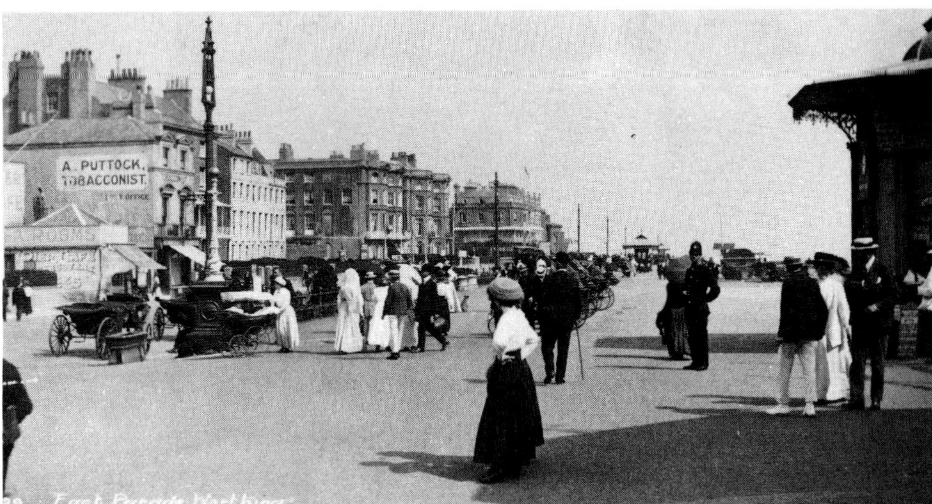


ONE OF THE KIOSKS at the end of the pier is visible to the right of this picture. The woman with her hands on her hips completely hides another who can only be seen by her shadow.

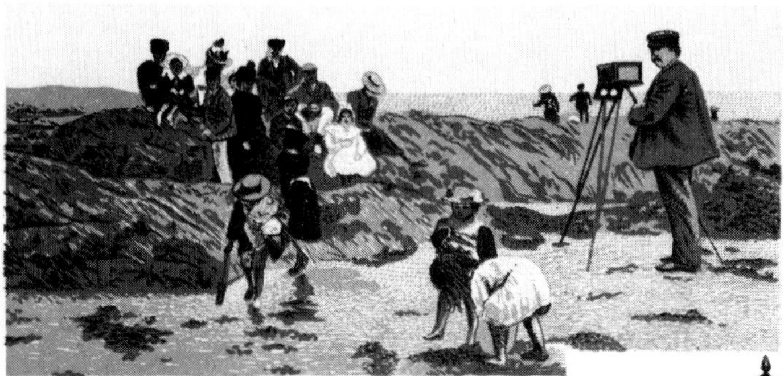

A "SITTING" AT LOW TIDE.

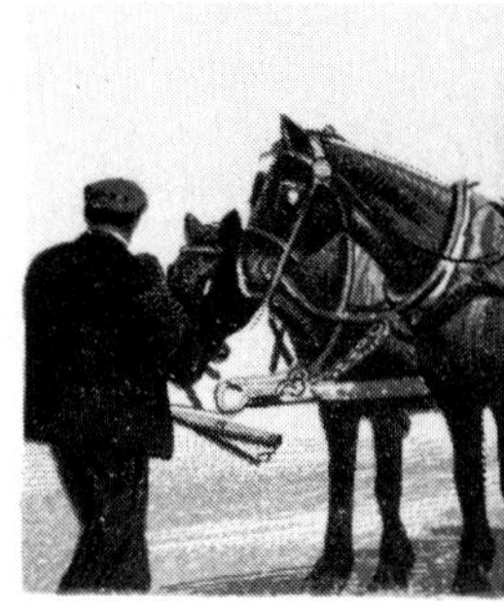

O

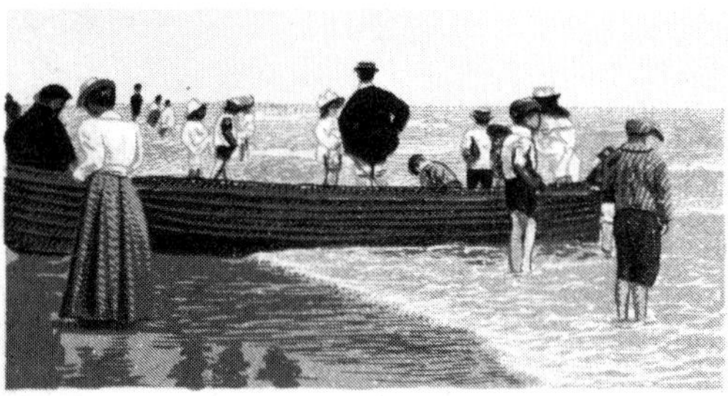

BOATING AT WORTHING.

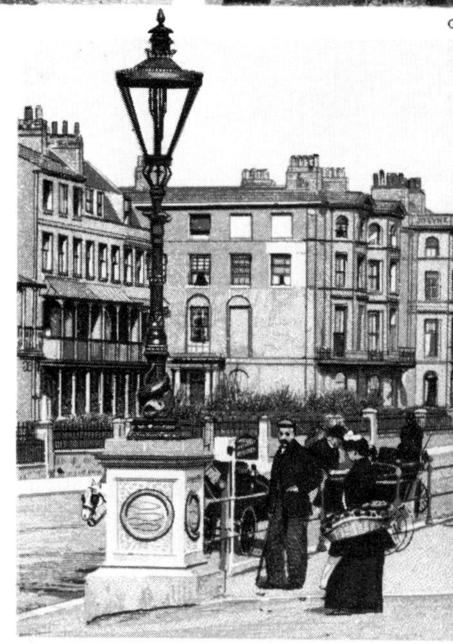

THE PARA

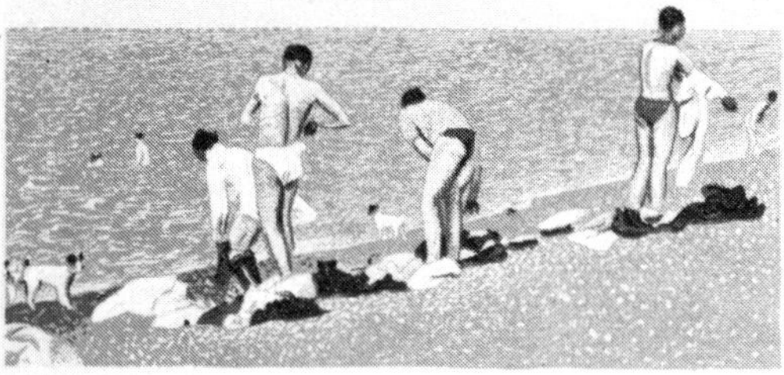

A QUIET DIP

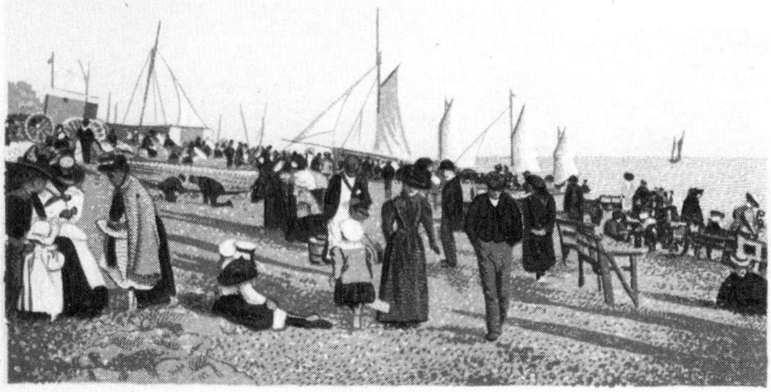

A STROLL ON WORTHING BEACH

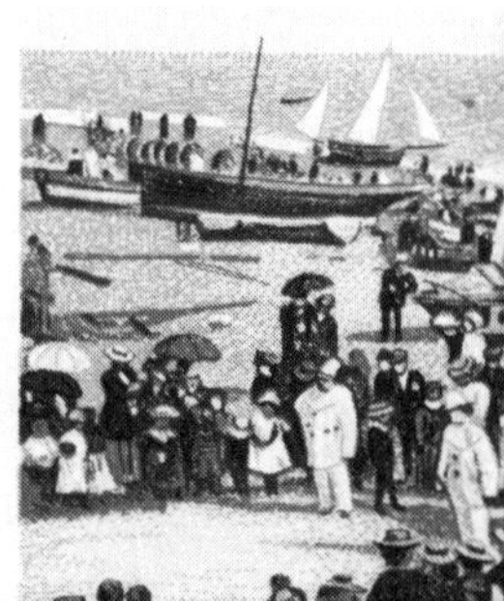

PIERRO

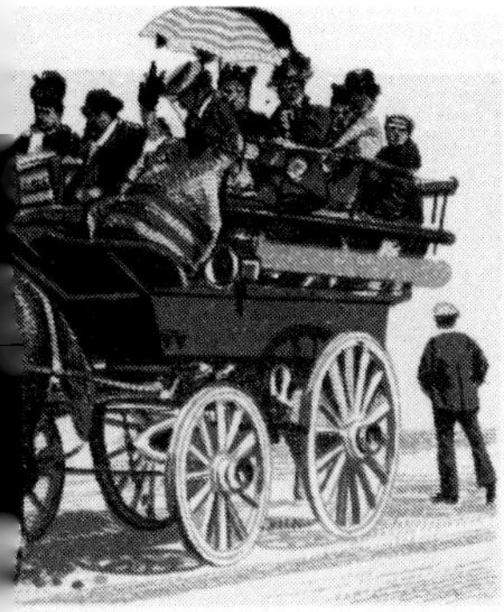

'NDEL

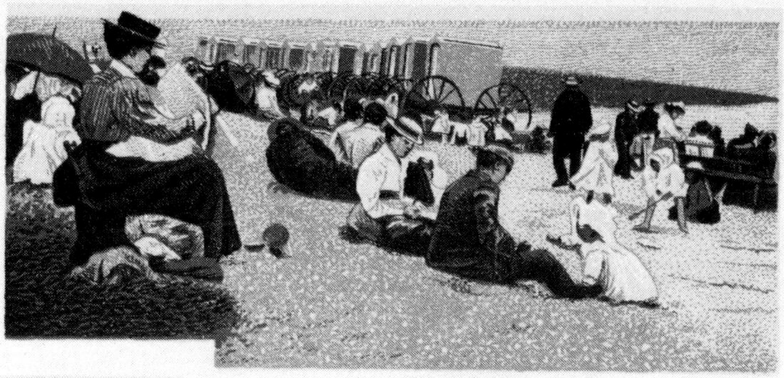

ON WORTHING SANDS.

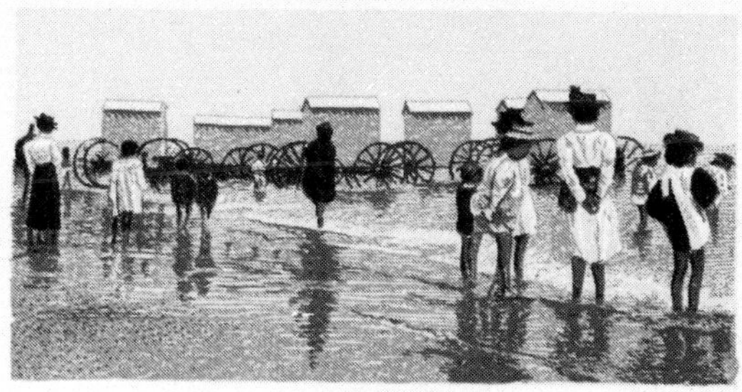

JUVENILE JOYS

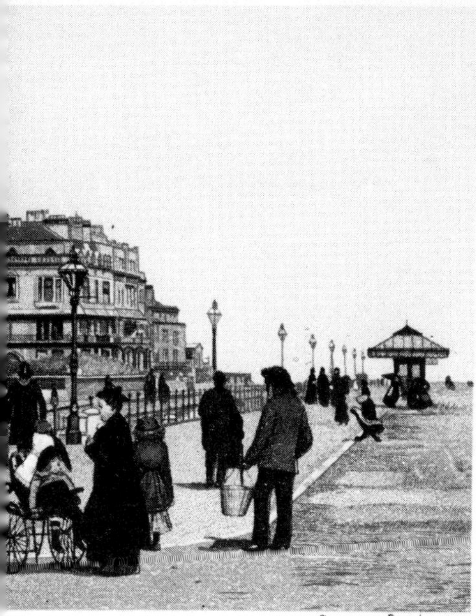

BY POULTON & SON, LONDON

KING EAST

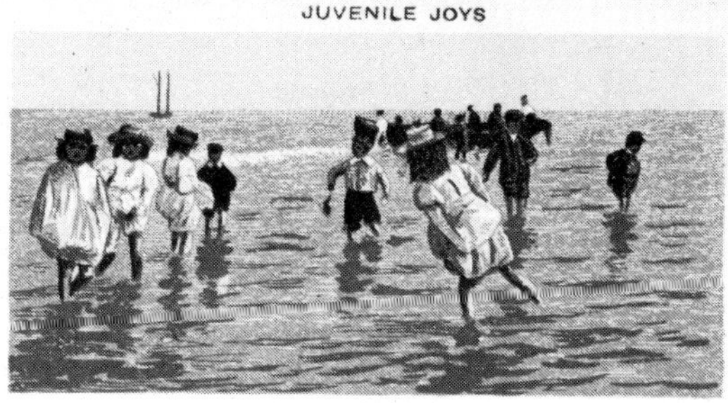

SEASIDE DELIGHTS.

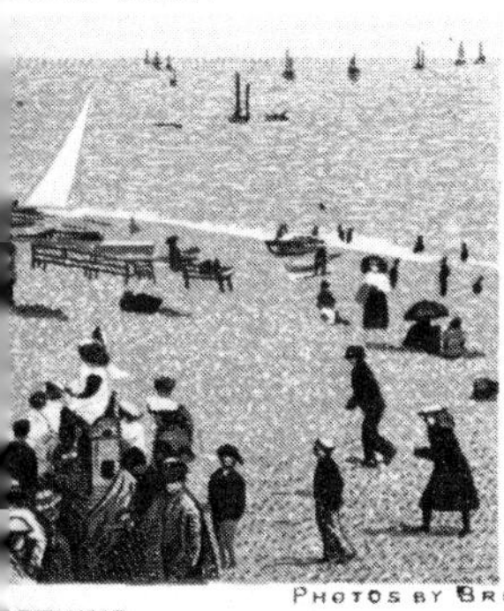

'RTHING.

PHOTOS BY BROWN & RAWCLIFFE LTD.

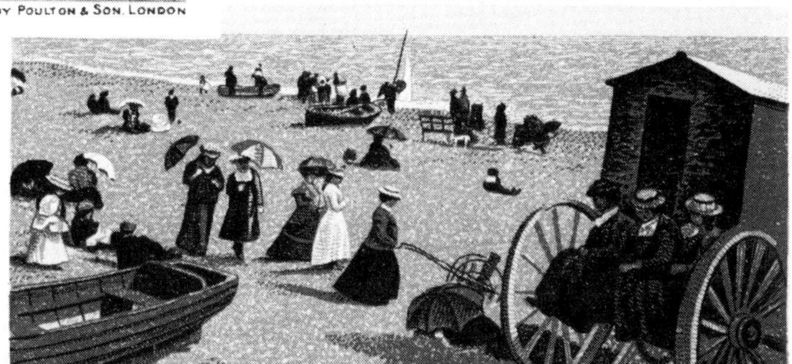

WORTHING, BEACH

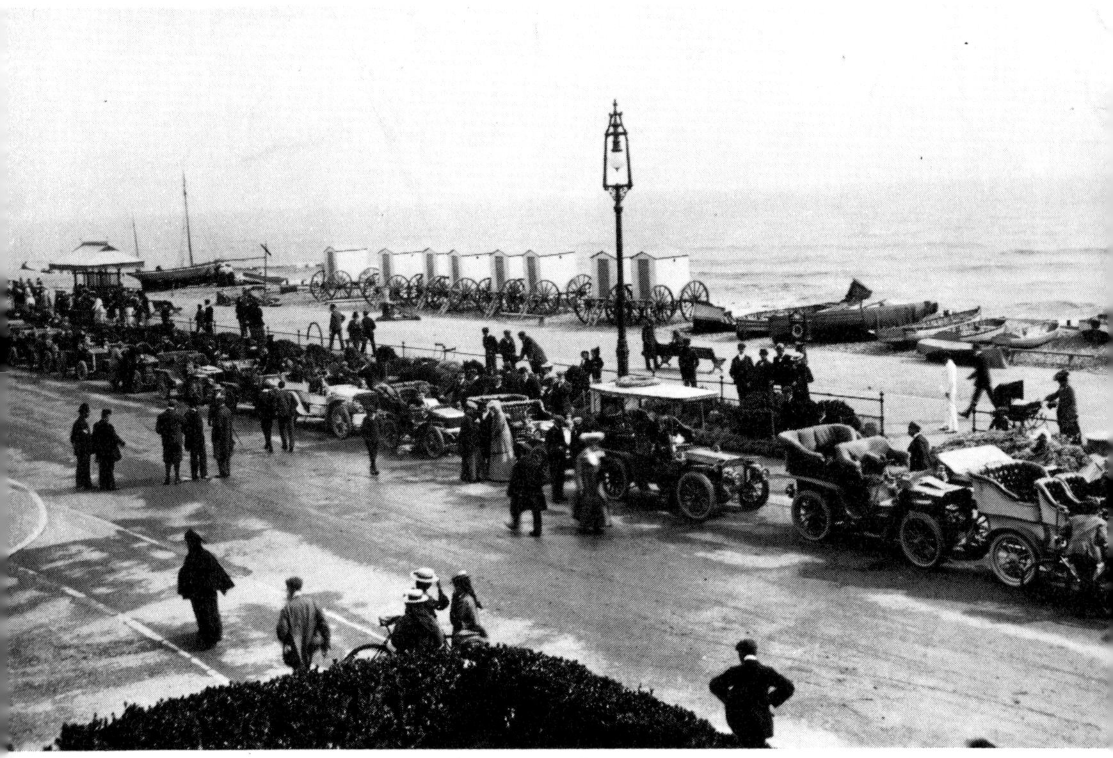

THIS MOTOR RALLY TOOK PLACE *c.* 1905 on Marine Parade. It shows a wide range of motor cars and motoring fashions for the drivers and their companions. The promenade is crowded with bathing machines, boats and people. The cars, still a novelty at this time, are attracting a lot of attention.

Previous Page.

MANY FIRMS PRODUCED ALBUMS of views of seaside towns designed as souvenirs for visitors. These pages of views give a taste of the delights which were available to visitors in 1906.

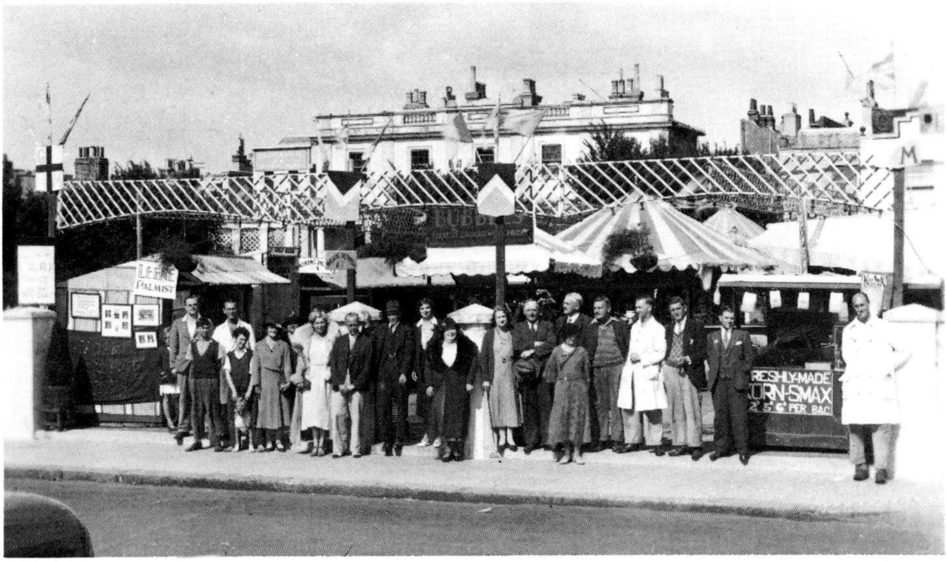


THE 'G' AND 'M' ON THE LAMP-POSTS show that this picture was taken in 1935 when King George V and Queen Mary celebrated their Silver Jubilee. The people lined up on the pavement look like a party of trippers. The house in the background is the elegant Grafton House which was rarely photographed. The site now houses an ugly multi-storey car park and a bowling alley.

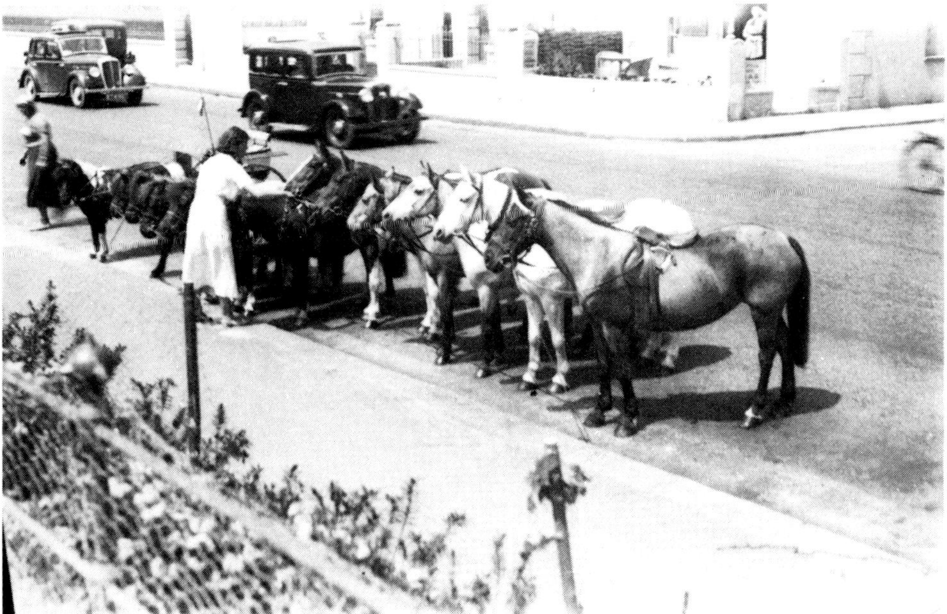

THIS PONY STAND was, for many years, on the seafront at the end of New Street. It was run by Mrs A.H. Booth until 1953, at which time a ride cost 3d ($1\frac{1}{2}$p).

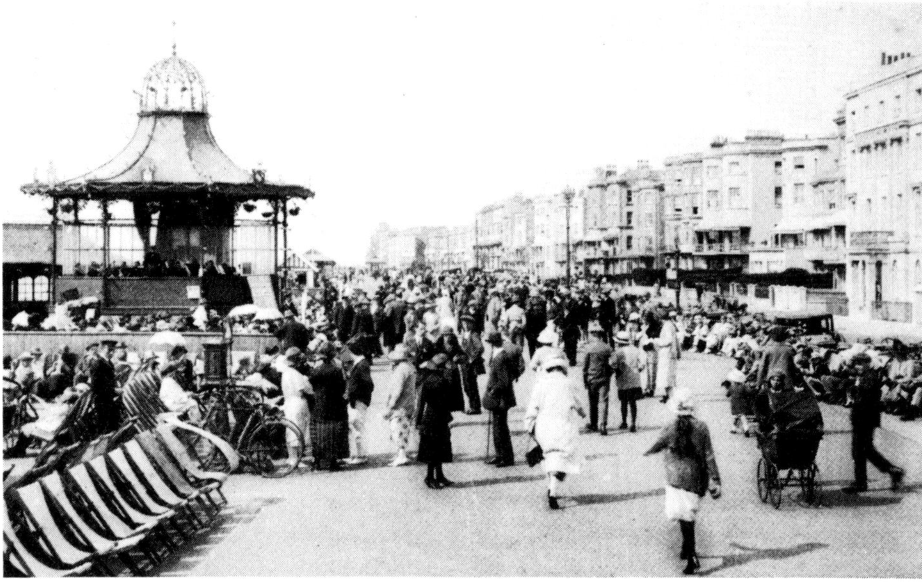

TRIPPERS THRONGED TO WORTHING in the 1920s and '30s, the heyday of British seaside holidays. Concerts in the bandstand regularly drew large audiences as well as more casual attention from passers-by.

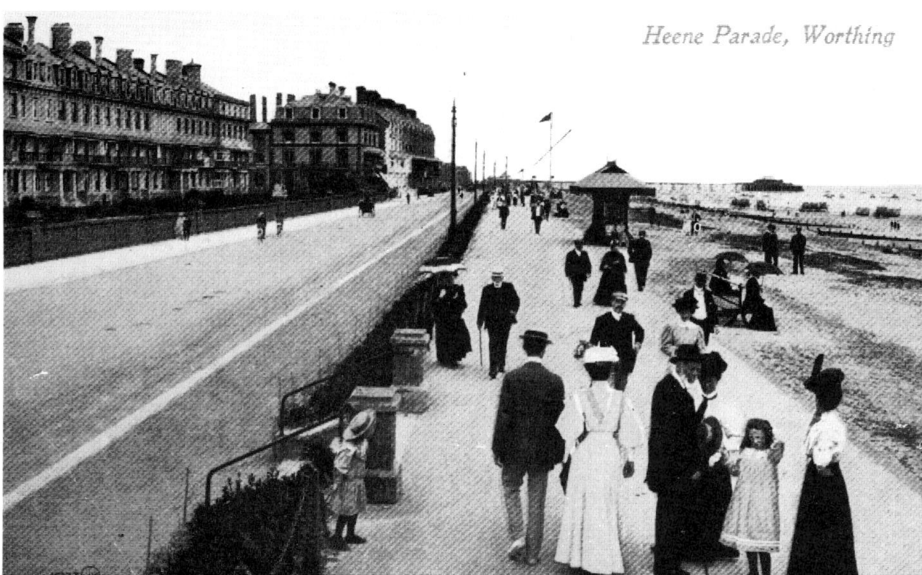


HEENE TERRACE, on the left of this picture, was built in the middle of the nineteenth century when Heene was separate from the main part of Worthing seafront. By the 1890s, when this picture was taken, the seafront had been developed up to Grand Avenue. Bathing machines can be seen on the beach with the pier in the background.

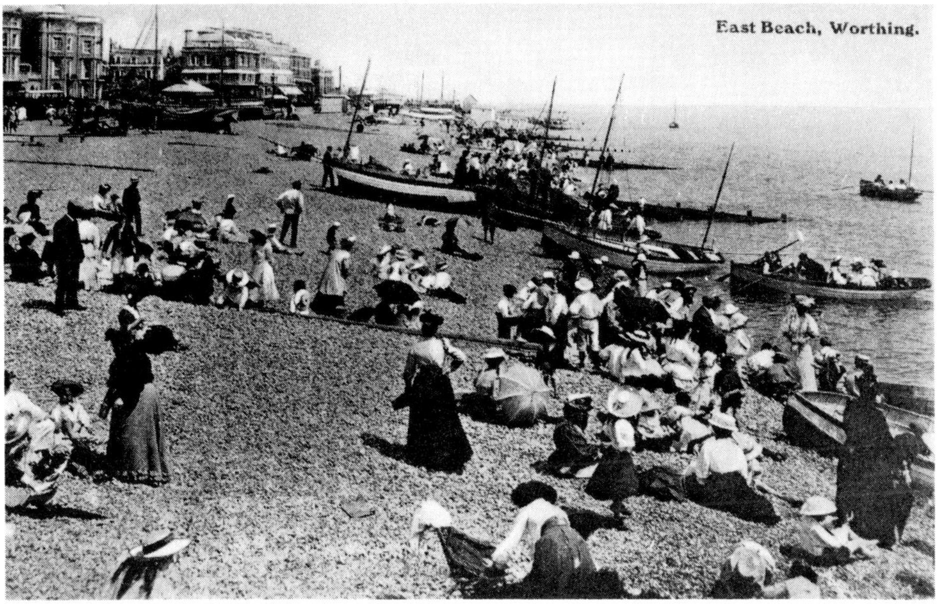


THE EAST BEACH is between the pier and Splash Point. To us these people look overdressed, but they appear to be enjoying themselves. No one is bathing, but some of the boats are taking people for pleasure trips.

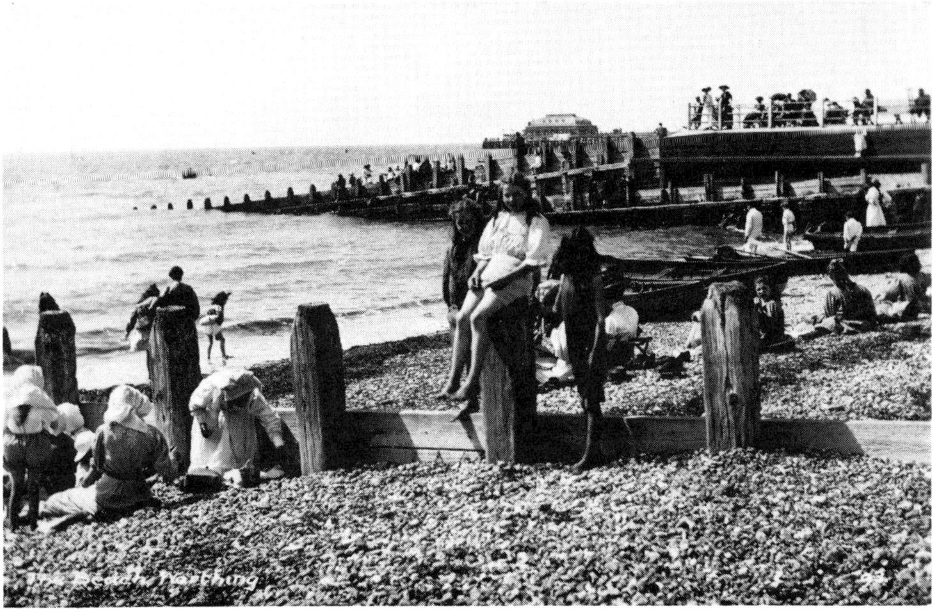

EVEN AT HIGH TIDE the beach is a pleasant place to be in summer.

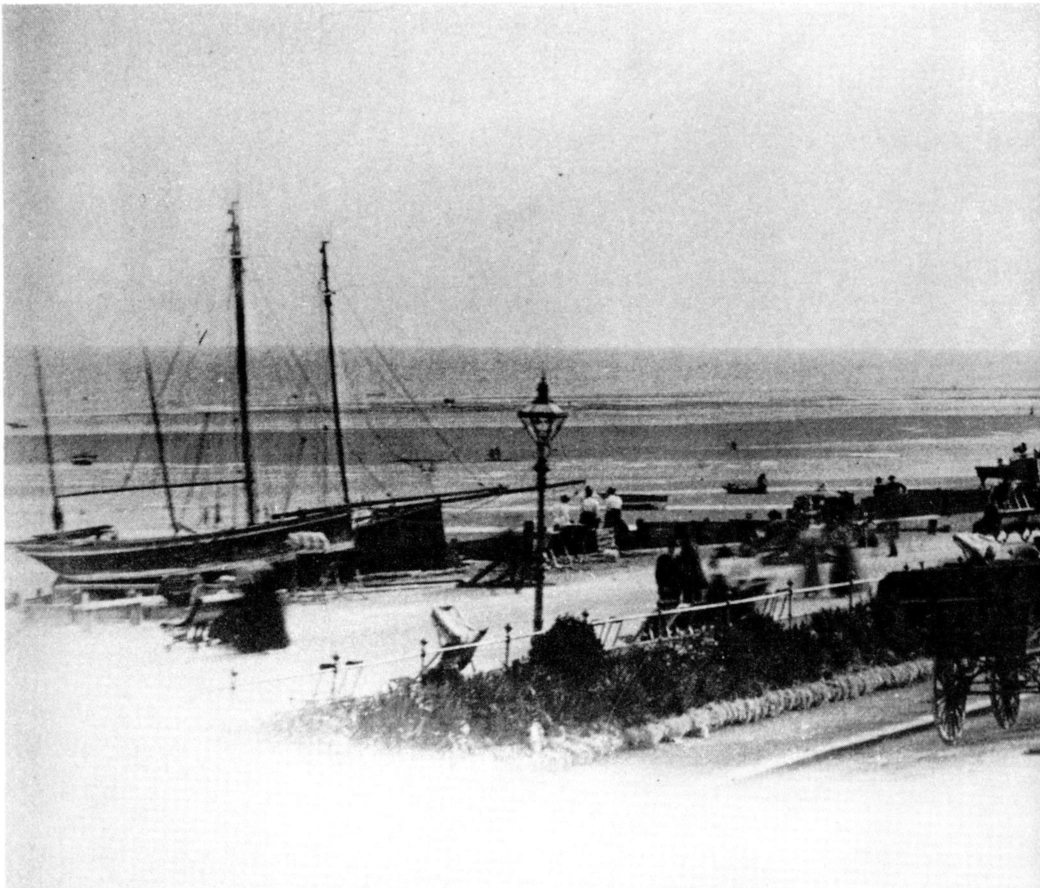

THIS TURN-OF-THE-CENTURY VIEW of the seafront has a pleasantly tranquil air. The bandstand, built in 1897, was very attractive and was a loss to the town when it was demolished in 1925. It was replaced by the band enclosure, now called the Lido. The slight blurring in parts of the picture shows it was not posed. Photographers had to use much longer exposures than we do today and any movement resulted in blurring.

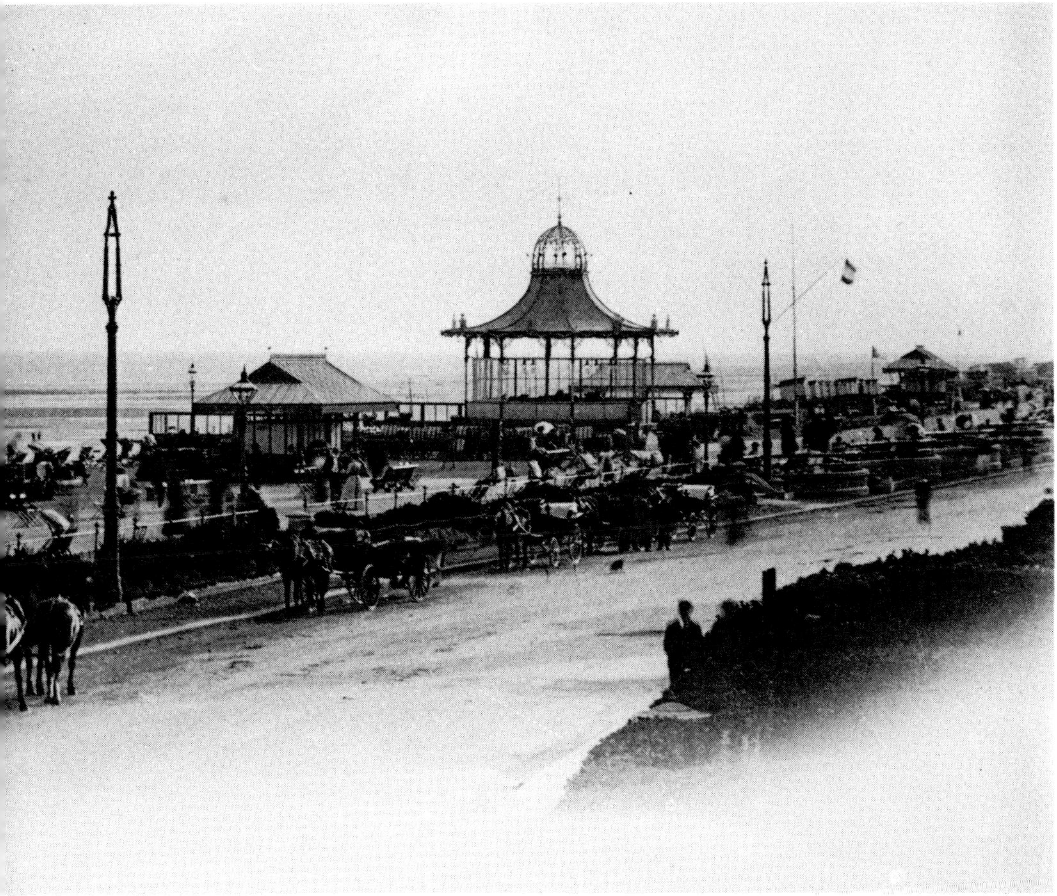

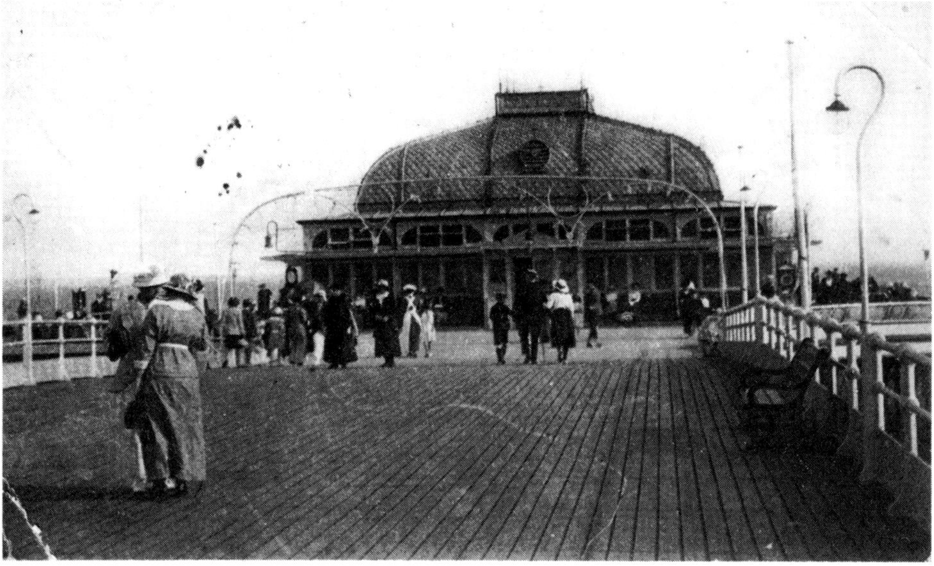

THE ABSENCE OF THE CENTRAL SHELTERS on the pier makes it look very wide in this picture and allows a clear view of the South Pavilion. It must have been very difficult to keep fashionable hats on in a stiff sea breeze.

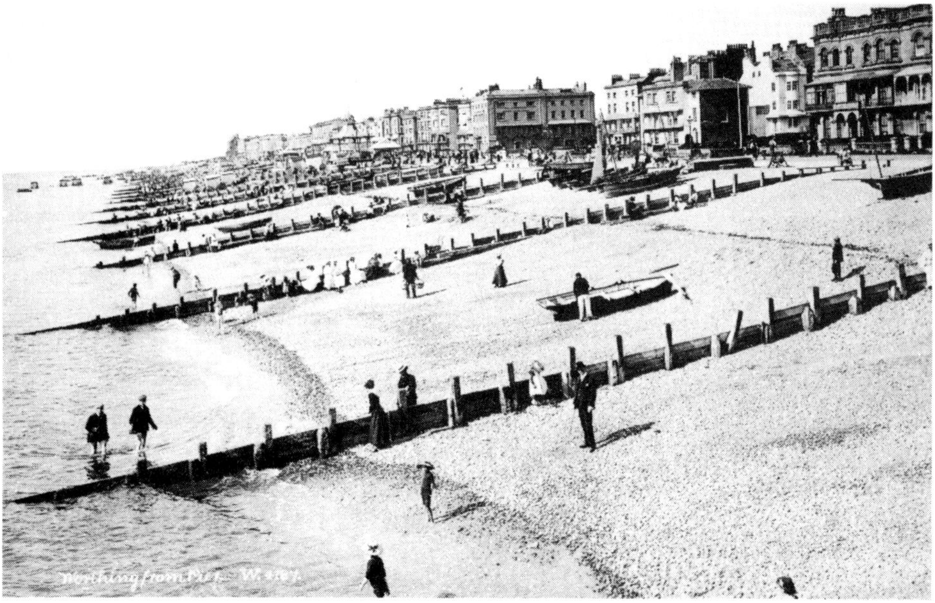

WORTHING SEAFRONT WAS ELEGANT and impressive in its prime. Post-war development has destroyed the continuity and some of the modern infilling has been disastrous. This picture was taken *c.* 1900.

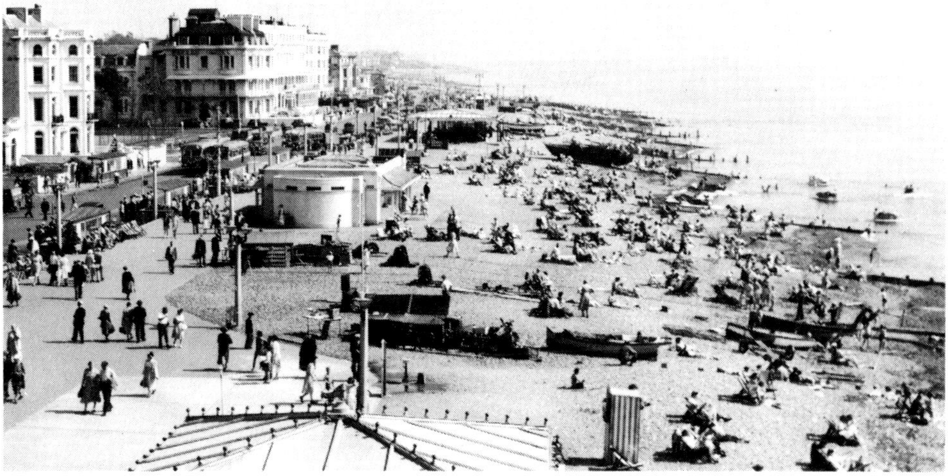

THIS VIEW FROM THE TOP OF THE PIER in the 1950s shows the view along the eastern part of the seafront and includes Warnes Hotel. It also shows the dense seaweed which has periodically cast a blight over a visit to Worthing beach.

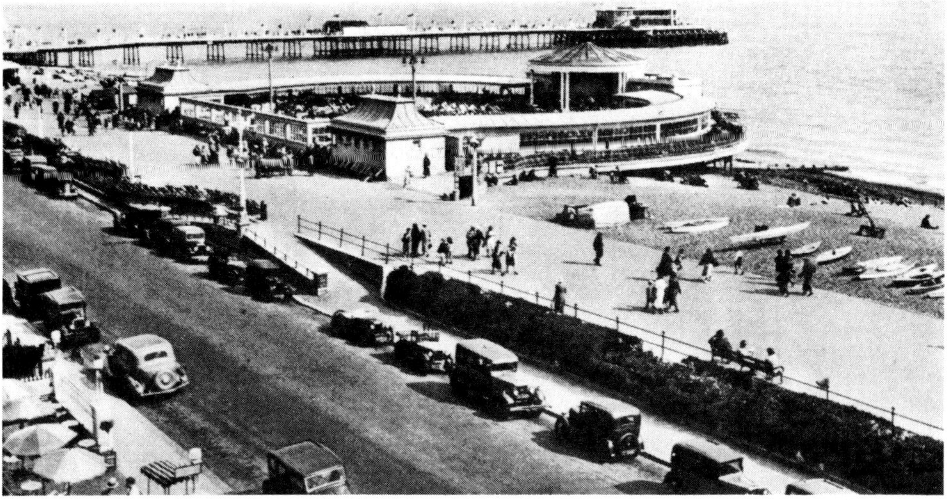

A NEW BAND ENCLOSURE was built on the seafront in 1926 on the site of the old bandstand. Audiences regularly packed the seats to hear bands playing. The stage was covered by an extending canopy which was replaced in 1929 by a domed roof. In 1960 the band enclosure was converted into the Lido swimming pool. It has now been turned into an amusement centre.

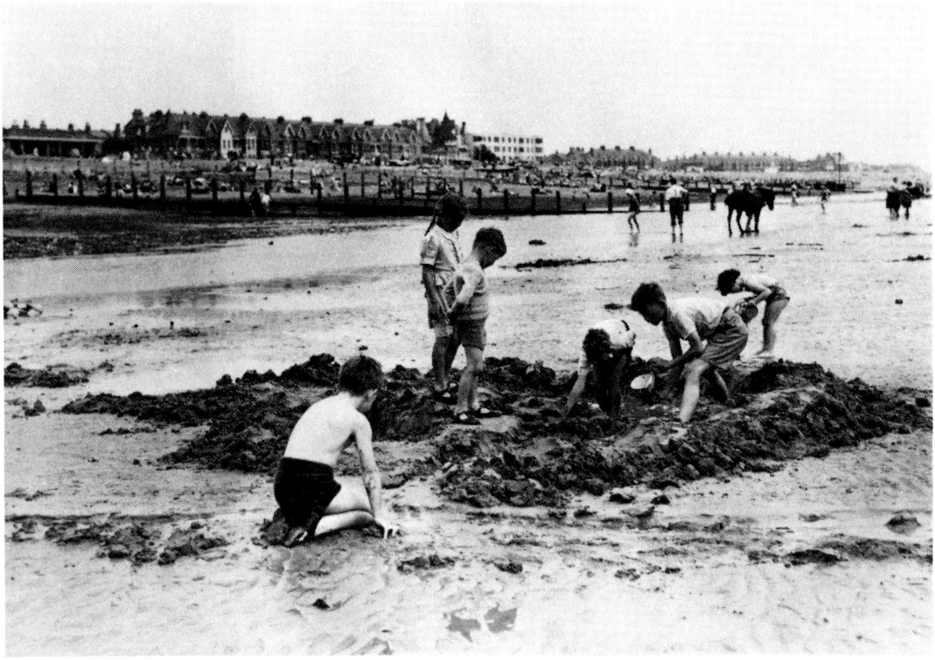

BUILDING SAND CASTLES and digging pools and rivers on the beach has occupied generations of children. This group includes both workers and watchers.

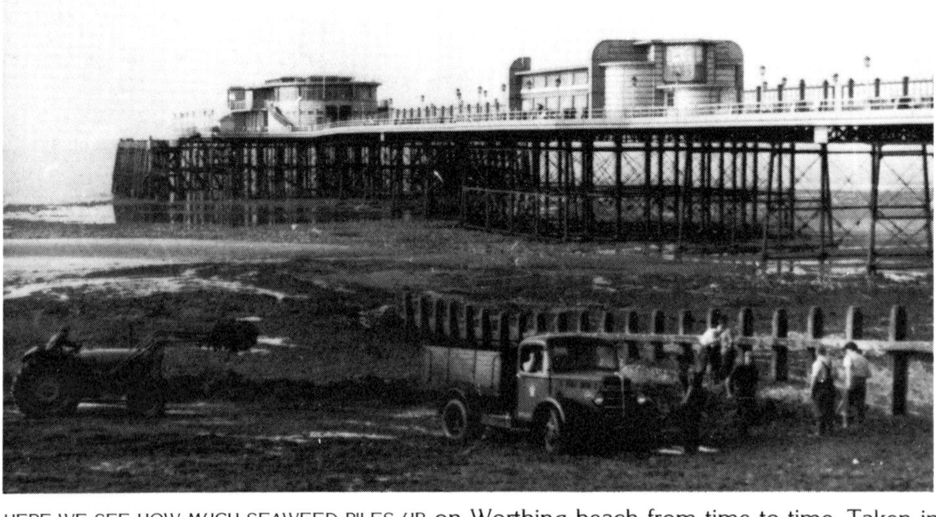

HERE WE SEE HOW MUCH SEAWEED PILES UP on Worthing beach from time to time. Taken in 1956, this photograph shows council workmen filling a lorry with seaweed in an attempt to clear the beach. Many solutions to the 'seaweed problem' have been tried over the years. None has been completely successful so far.

SECTION THREE

# Shops–Commerce Hotels

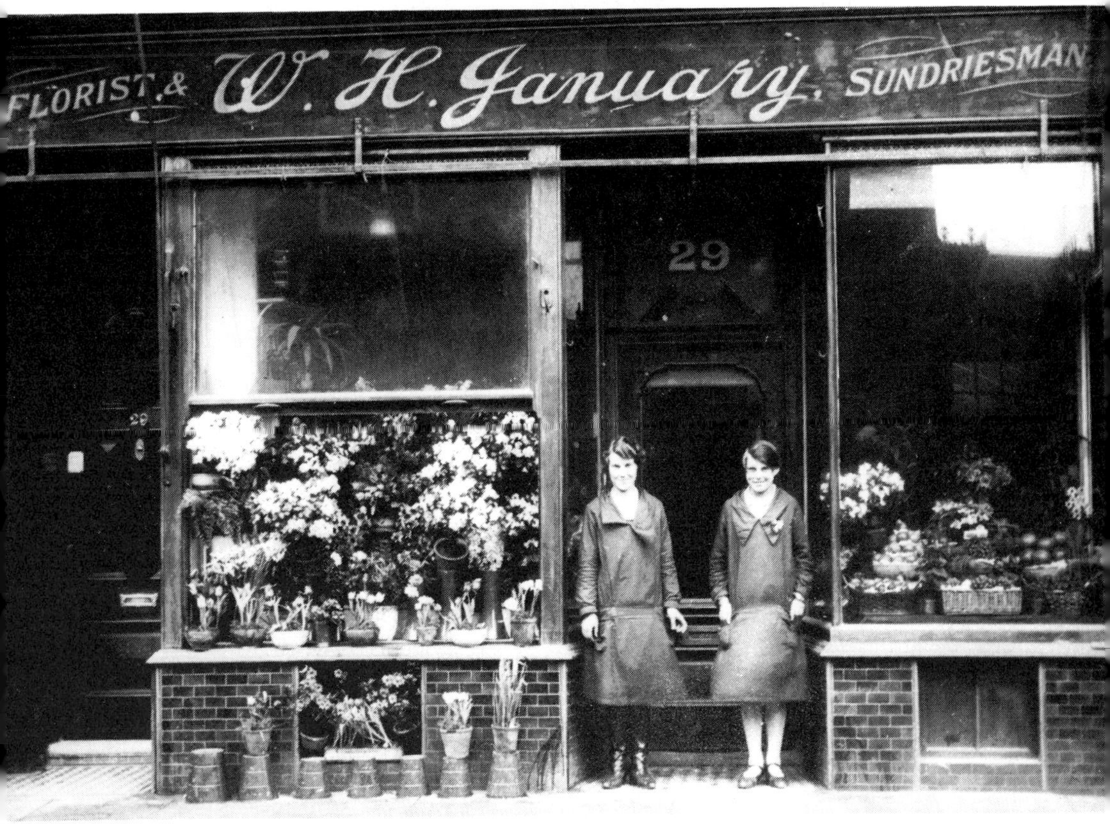


W.H. JANUARY had a florists shop at 29 Warwick Street. This picture, taken in around 1924, shows the two Misses Hearsey standing in the doorway of the shop where they worked. They look awkward and as if they had no time to prepare for the photographer.

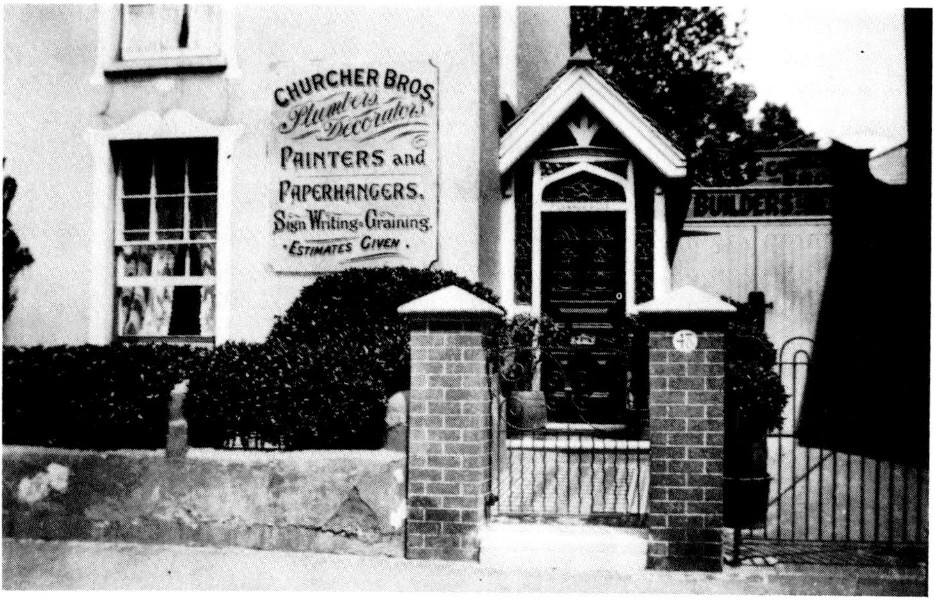


THIE FIRST BUILDERS, PRINTERS AND PAPERHANGERS SHOP owned by Churcher Bros was at 48 Richmond Road. They later moved to No. 44 and that shop, run by the founder's granddaughter, Mrs Barlow, and her husband closed in 1988. Before the Second World War the cheapest wallpaper they sold cost $2\frac{1}{2}$d ($1\frac{1}{2}$p) a roll. After the war it had risen to 1s 9d (9p).

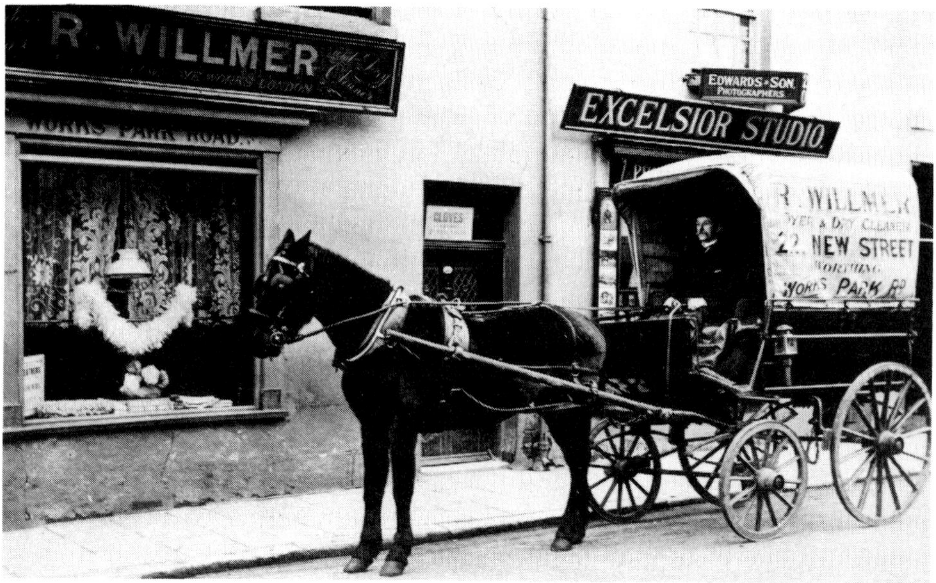


R. WILLMER had a dyers and cleaners shop at 22 New Street and his works were in Park Road. His buggy is shown here outside the shop *c.* 1910.

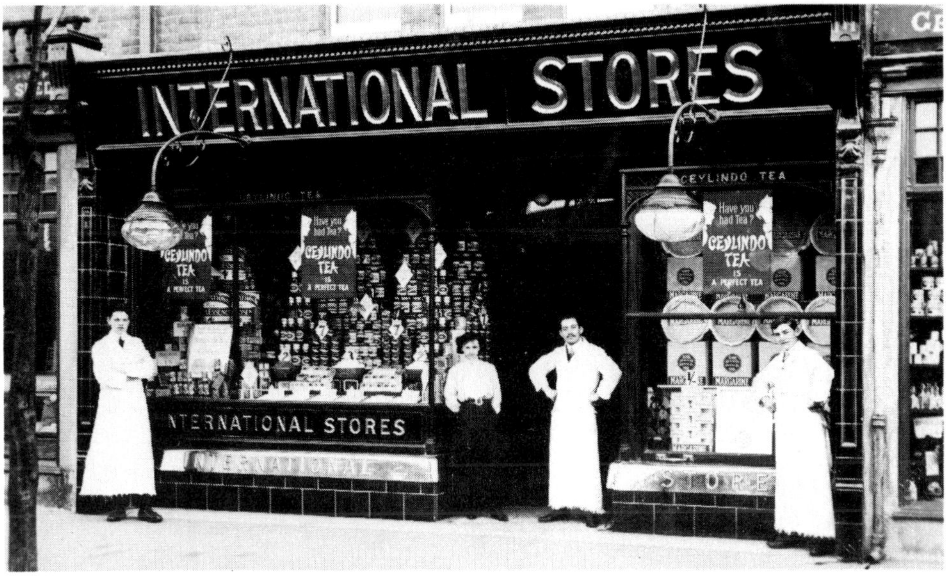


THIS INTERNATIONAL STORES was in Tarring Broadway. Tiled fronts like this were popular in shops early in the twentieth century. Old shop displays are always interesting. This one features Ceylindo Tea, a brand which has since disappeared. Note the rather arrogant attitude of the male assistants who stand outside the shop, arms akimbo.

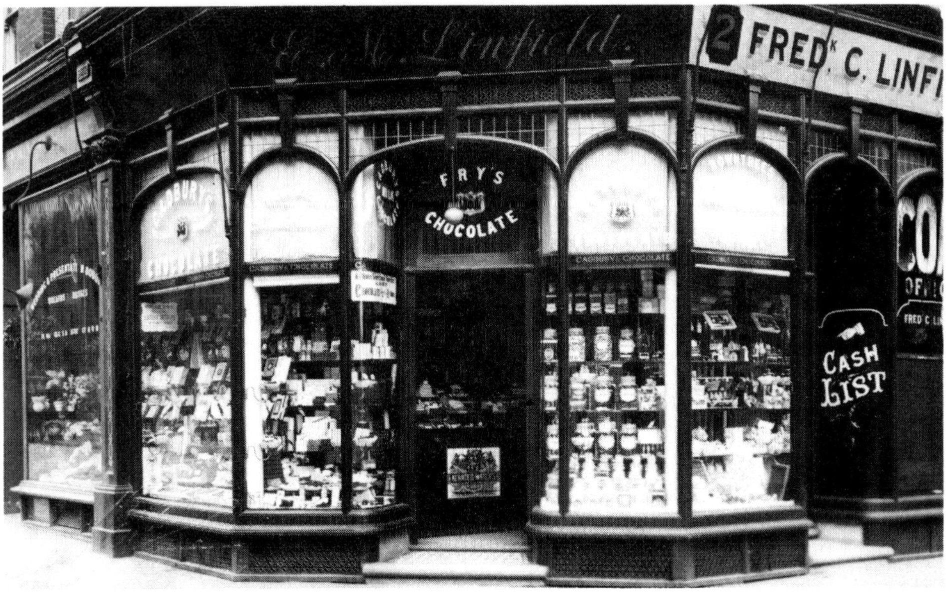


FRED LINFIELD HAD A CONFECTIONERY SHOP at 2 Chapel Road, on the corner with Ann Street. Showing no favouritism, the window displays advertised Cadbury's, Fry's, Pascall's and Rowntree's sweets. This photograph was taken before 1914. The shop finally closed in 1966.

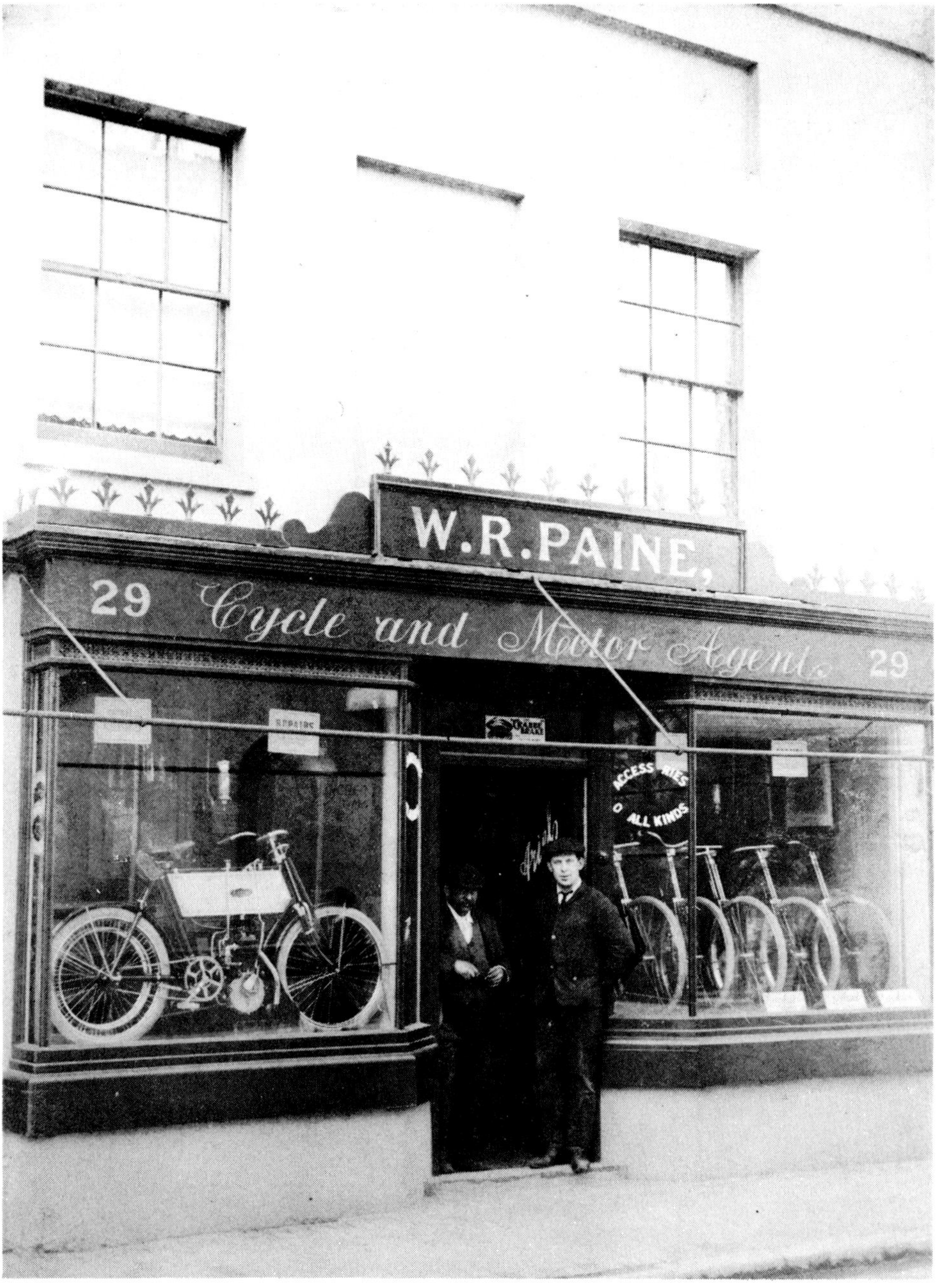


W.R. PAINE was a noted local sportsman and champion cyclist. He is the figure on the right of this picture of his cycle shop, *c.* 1900.

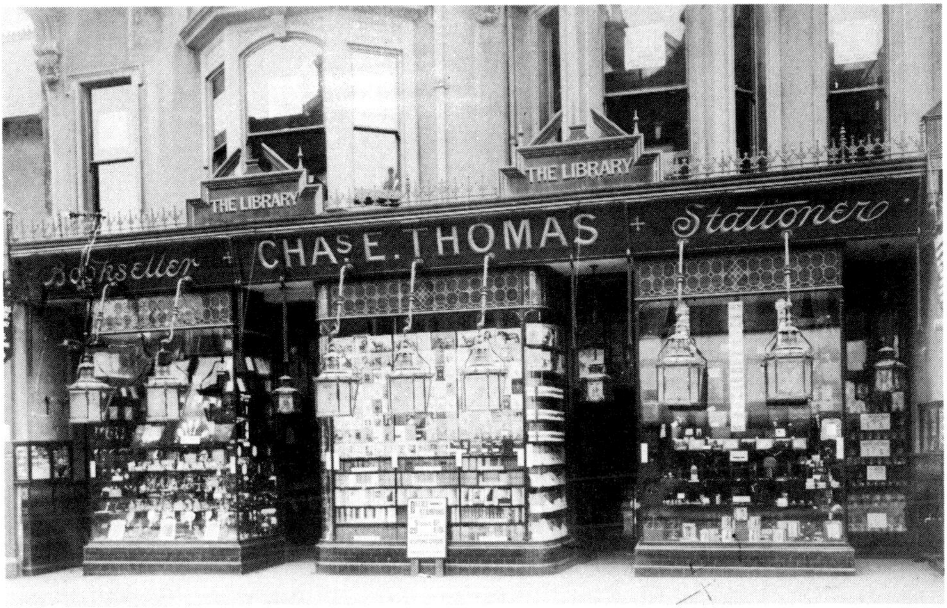


CHARLES THOMAS ran a thriving book and stationery shop in Chapel Road during the early part of the twentieth century. It was later taken over by Ramsdens. The site is now part of Sainsburys and quite unrecognizable.

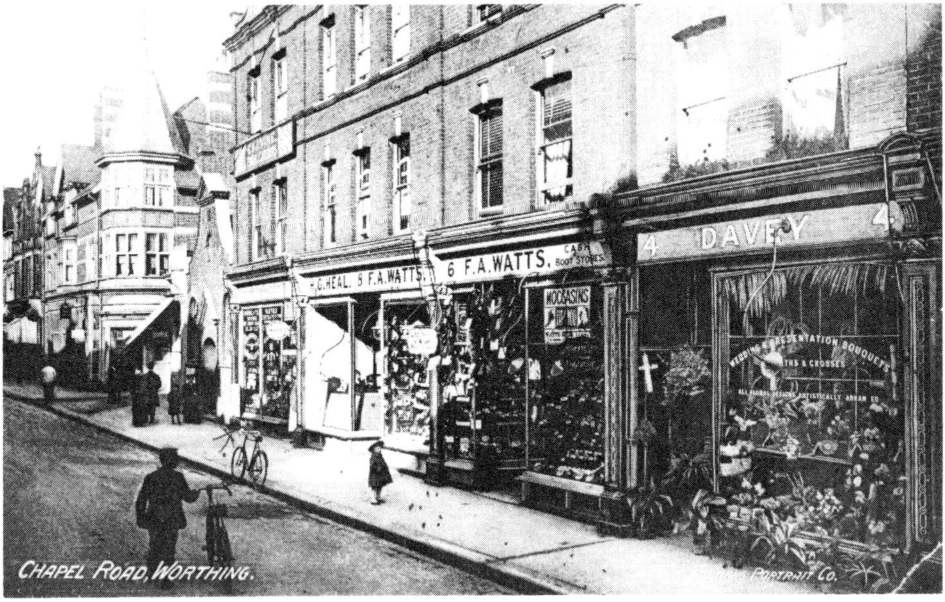


WATTS' SHOE SHOP is still in Chapel Road, opposite Sainsburys, but the neighbouring shops have changed hands. This photograph was taken by the Worthing Portrait Company, c. 1920. The little girl looks rather wistful and seems to have lost her family.

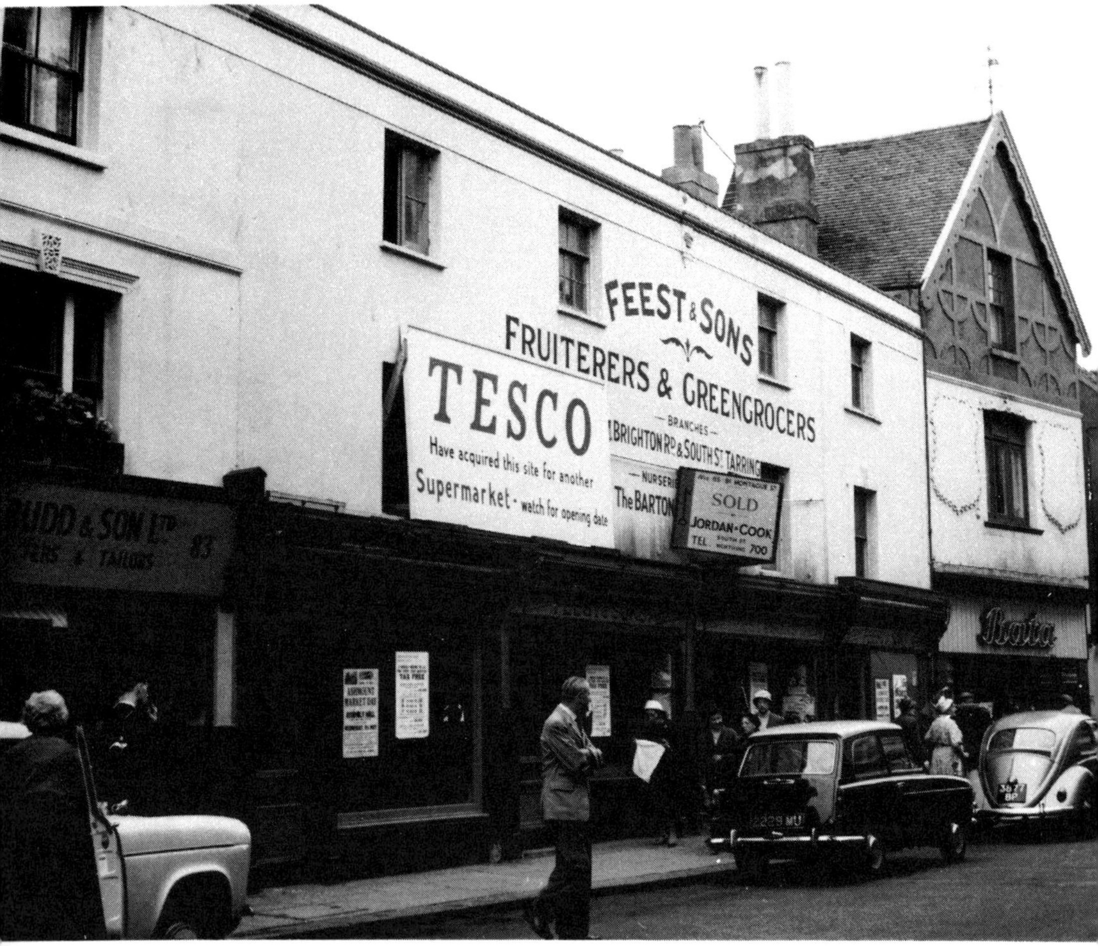


THIS SECTION OF MONTAGUE STREET, shown here in the 1960s, is almost unrecognizable today. Feest and Sons had a shop at 65–7 for many years. Tesco has been replaced by John Farmer and Miss Selfridge and Montague Street is now a pedestrian precinct.

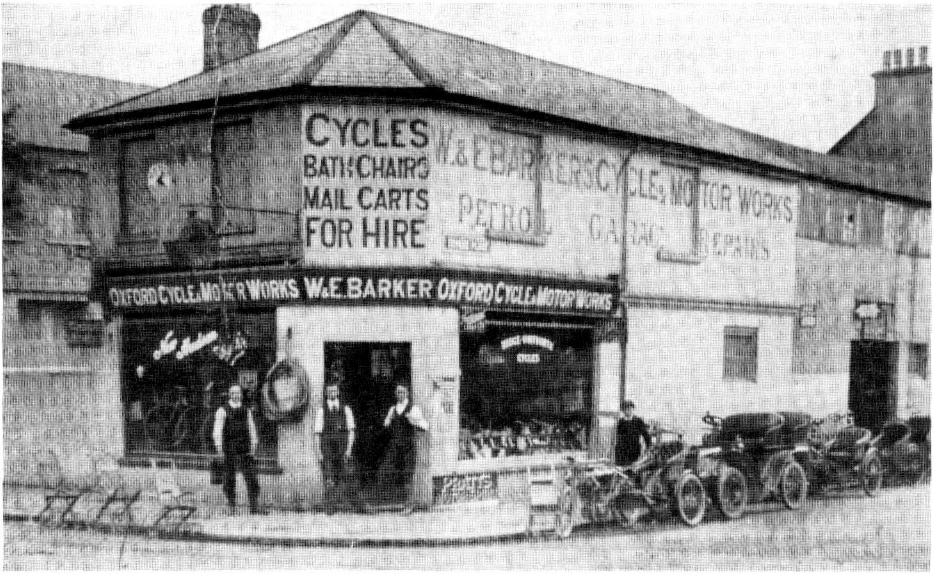


BARKER'S OXFORD CYCLE AND MOTOR WORKS was well known in Worthing. This photograph, taken in 1907, shows that they were quick to turn to motorbikes and cars as well as bicycles. There is still a Barker's shop in Oxford Road, but it now sells videos and televisions rather than bicycles.

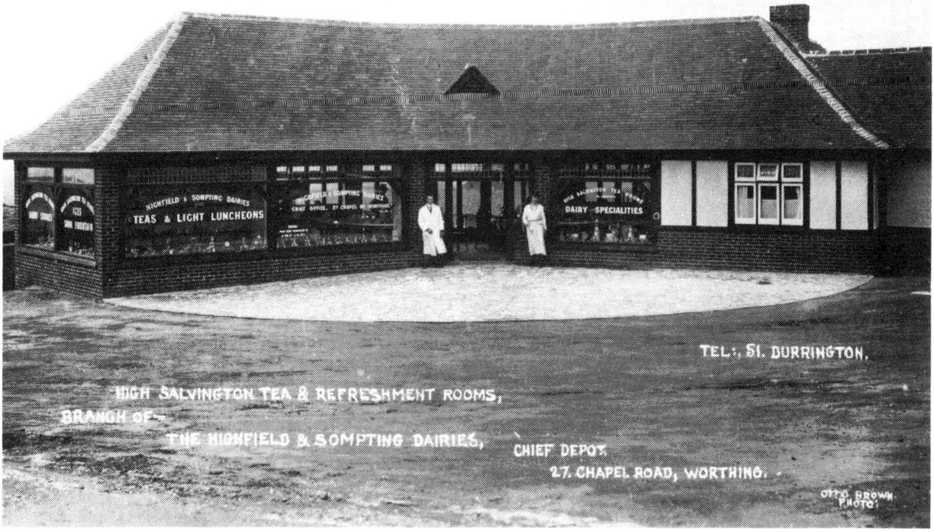


HIGH SALVINGTON TEA AND REFRESHMENT ROOMS, run by the Highfield and Sompting Dairies, on Salvington Hill in the 1920s. The building is still there, but it is now used as a supermarket.

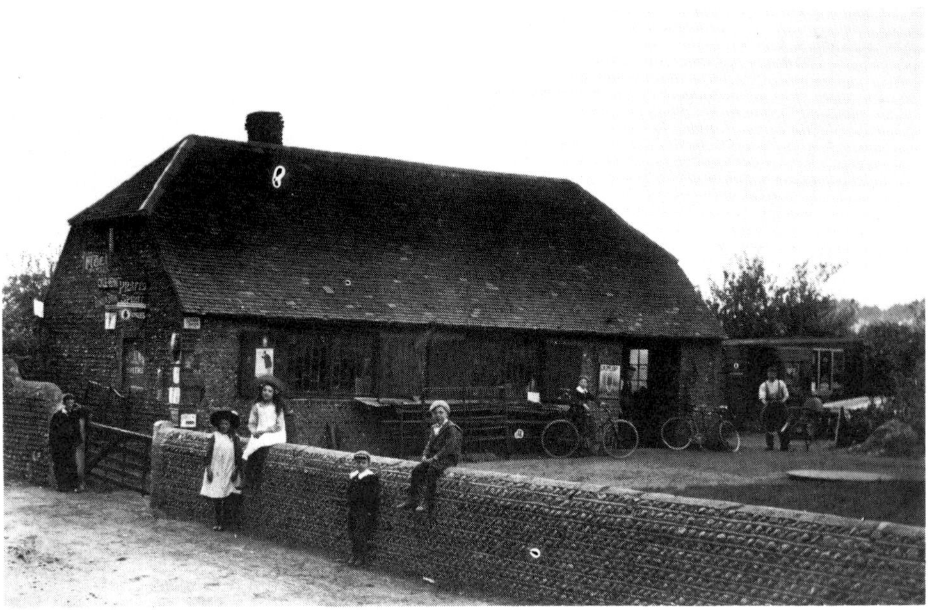

THE HAFFENDEN FAMILY were important members of the Goring community. Early this century Sam Haffenden ran the family blacksmith's business and Miss E.F. Haffenden was a busy dressmaker. The old forge is shown here, c. 1910. In 1966 it was demolished to make way for Steele's garage.

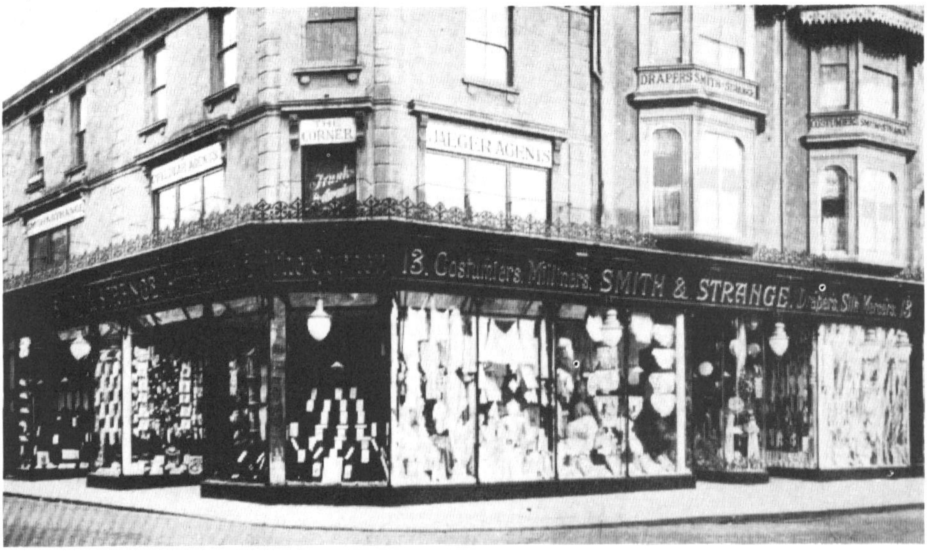


SMITH AND STRANGE'S SHOP, c. 1912. The shop was founded by J.H. Smith and in 1906 G.N. Strange became a partner in the firm. They moved the business to the corner of Montague Street and South Street, shown here, where W.H. Smith is today. The shop was taken over by other proprietors, but the name continued until 1972.

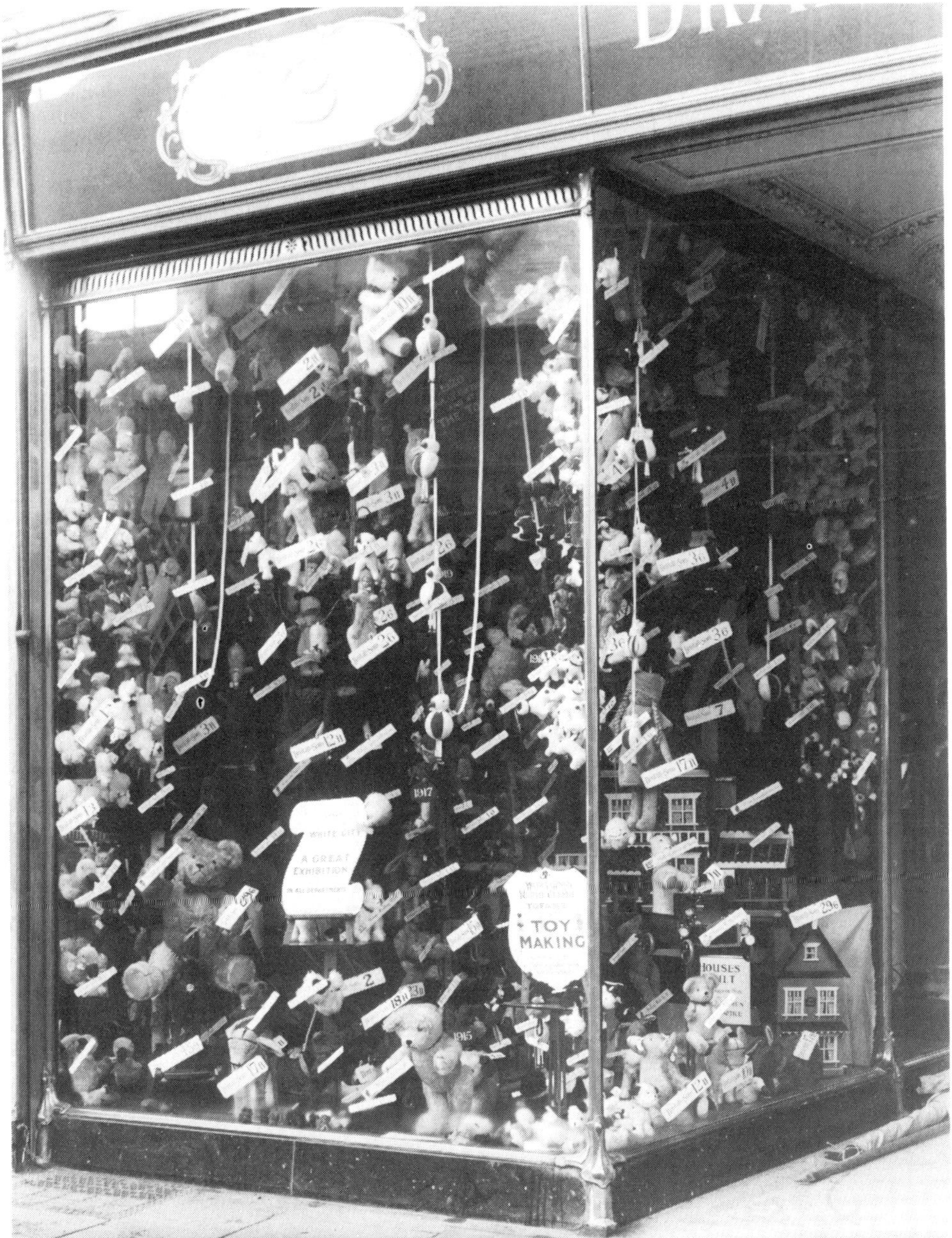


THIS WINDOW IN BENTALLS SHOP, in South Street, was dressed by S. Saywell in 1920. It features products from the Worthing Toy Factory, run by Florence Luke. Though small and little remembered, this local firm was very successful from 1905 to the 1920s, producing over two hundred types of soft toy including Peter Rabbit and teddy bears. In 1924 it was taken over by Ramsden Brothers. Its workers were nicknamed 'Worthings's dolly stuffers'.

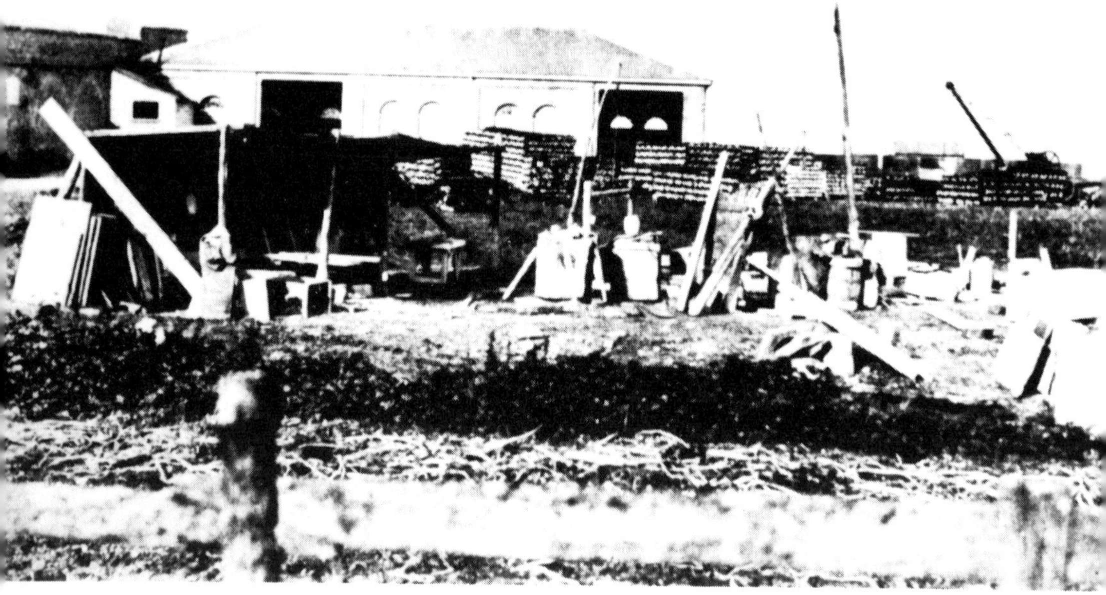

WORTHING GOODS YARD is recorded in this very early photograph of the 1850s.

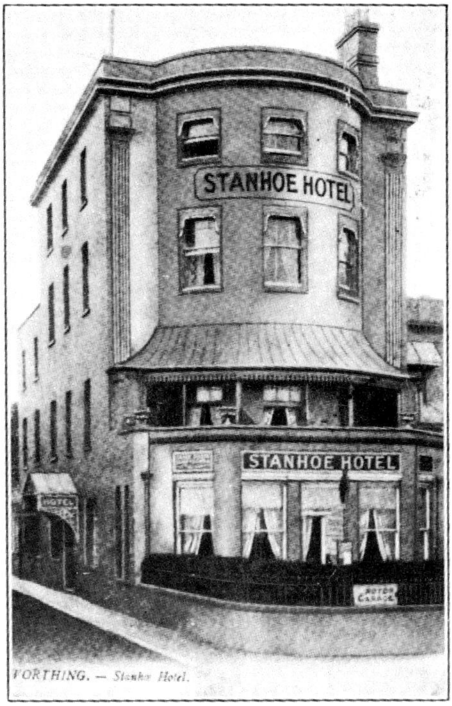


THE STANHOE HOTEL stood on the corner of Marine Parade and Augusta Place. It was originally called Augusta House. It was demolished in 1948, and the site is now part of the Grafton car park complex.

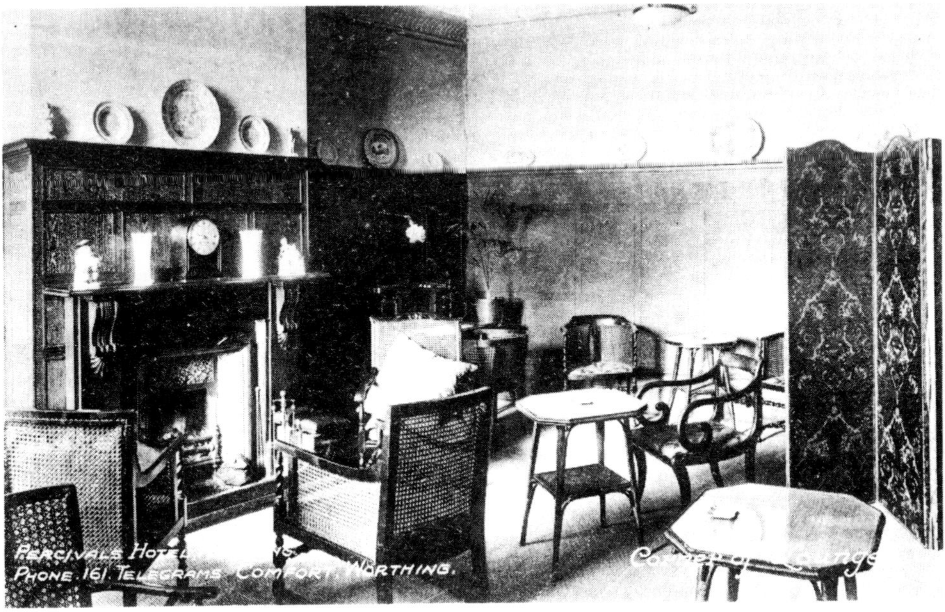


THE LOUNGE IN PERCIVAL'S HOTEL in Heene Terrace in 1922. The caption says that telegrams for the hotel should be addressed to 'Comfort, Worthing'.

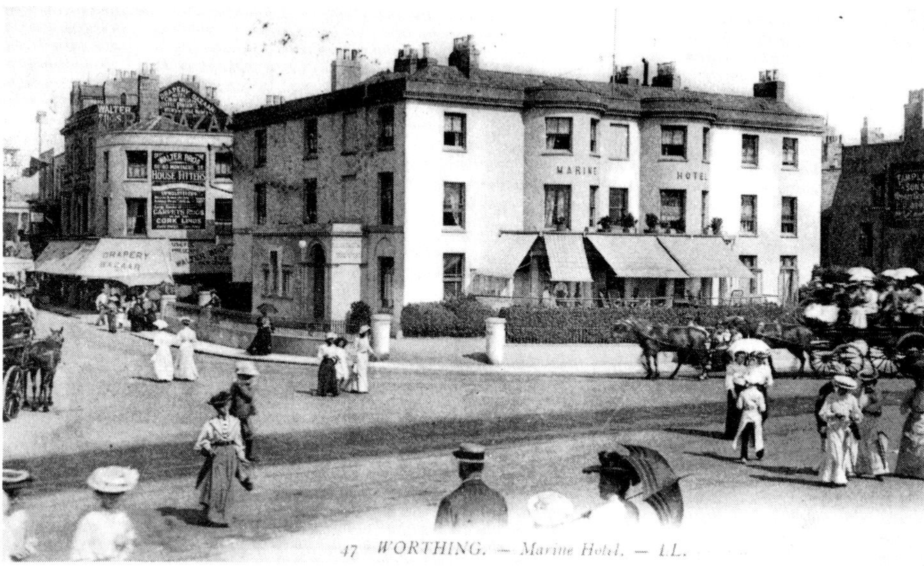


THE MARINE HOTEL started life in the late eighteenth century as the New Inn and at that time it was run by a Mr Bacon. A neighbouring hotel was run by Mr Hogsflesh. In 1826 it was renamed the Marine Hotel. It stood on the eastern corner of South Street and Marine Parade and was visited, briefly, by Queen Victoria in 1842 and 1845, when she was passing through Worthing. The hotel was demolished in 1965.

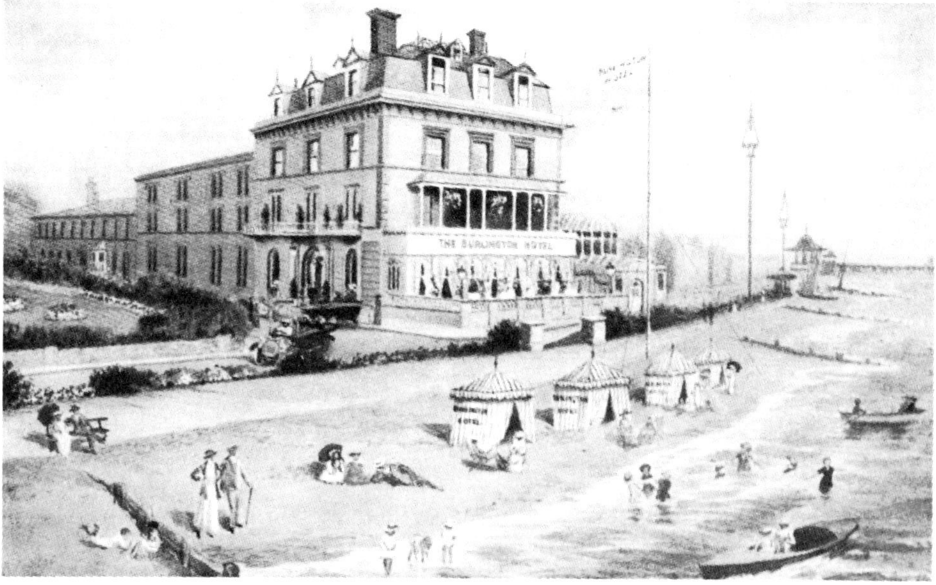


THE BURLINGTON HOTEL is on Marine Parade at the eastern end of Heene Terrace. It was originally called the West Worthing Hotel. It opened in 1864 and claims to be the oldest purpose-built hotel in Worthing.

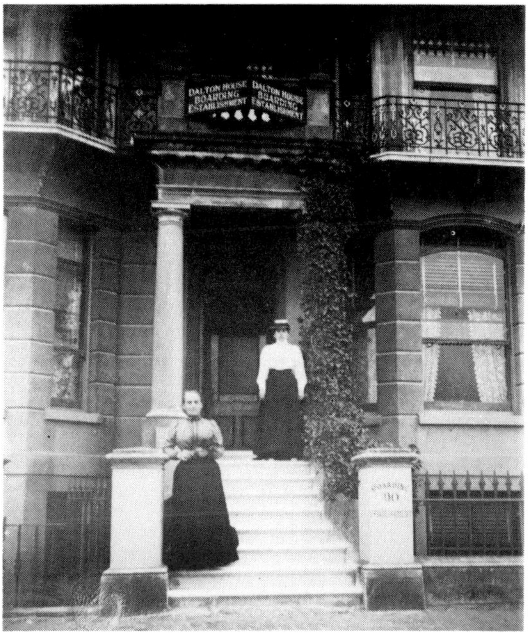

DALTON HOUSE was a boarding house at 90 Marine Parade. It is now part of the Beach Hotel. In 1901 it was called Walton House, but by 1902 the name had changed. It was run by the Misses Johnson who may be the two ladies seen here on the steps.

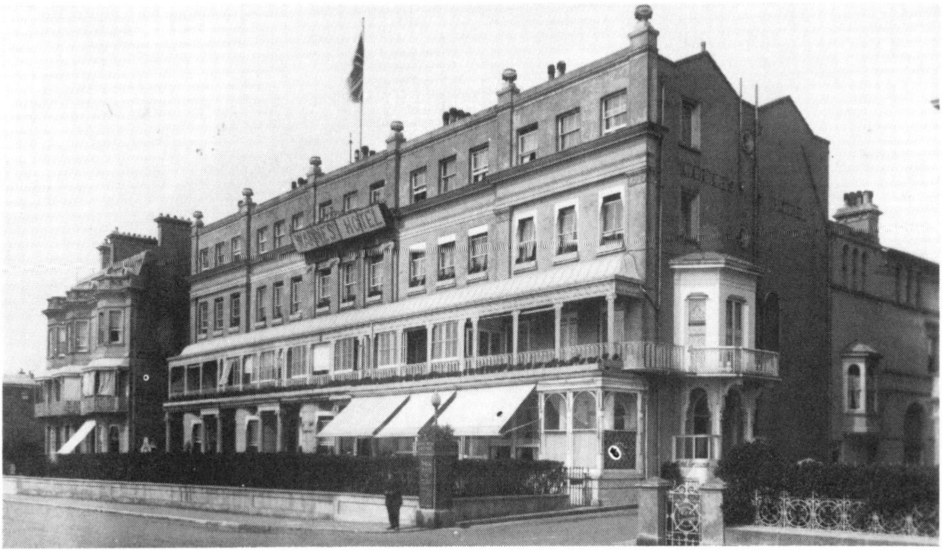

WARNES HOTEL was built as five houses, known as York Terrace, in *c.* 1820. It was converted into a hotel by G.H. Warne in 1899. Realizing the growing importance of cars, Warne pioneered the combination of hotel and garage. The hotel became the headquarters of the Automobile Club of Great Britain and Ireland, the predecessor of the RAC. Visited by Edward VII and George V, Warnes Hotel was the wartime home-in-exile of Emperor Haile Selassie of Abyssinia. After years of decline it closed in 1985 and was gutted by fire in 1987. Local conservationists have struggled to preserve at least the façade of the hotel.

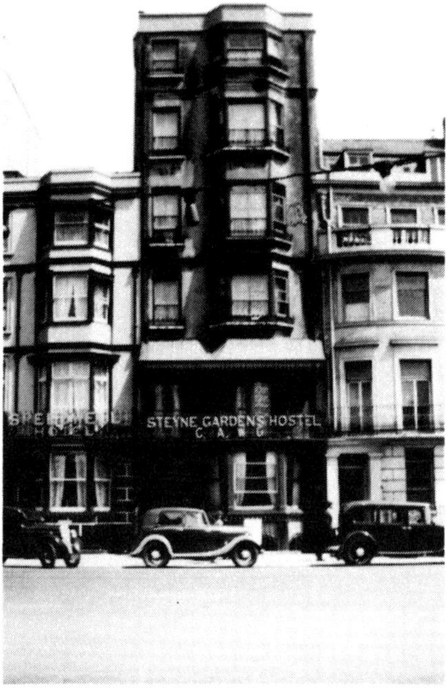


THE SPEEDWELL HOTEL AND STEYNE GARDENS HOSTEL, *c.* 1935. The initials C.A.W.G. on the hostel stand for the Christian Association of Women and Girls.

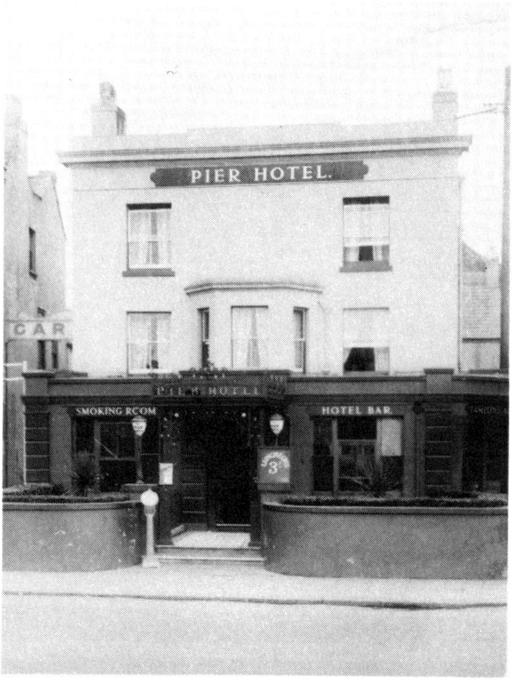


THE PIER HOTEL at the end of Marine Parade, shown here *c.* 1935, originally opened in *c.* 1815 as the Wellington.

SECTION FOUR

# Education and Health

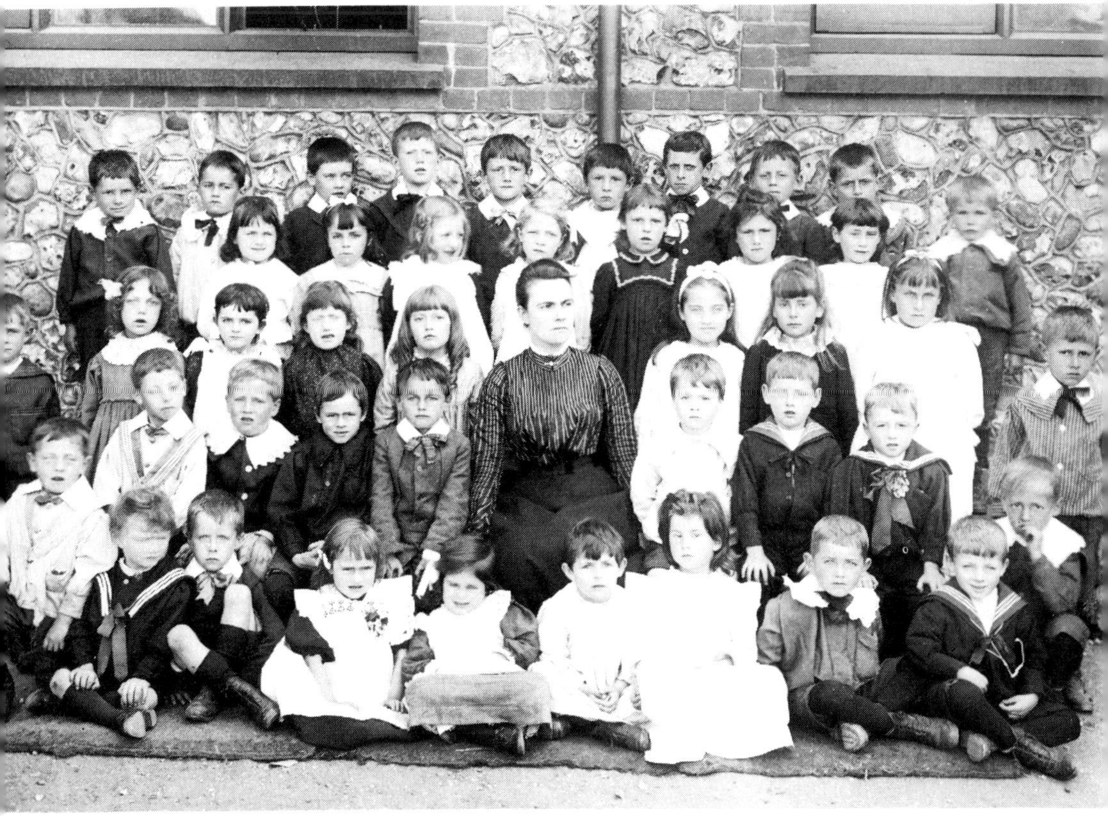

THIS TEACHER, sitting with her class at Broadwater School in *c.* 1905, looks rather fierce. Several of the boys are wearing sailor tops; others have wide lacy collars, some of which are made of pretty broderie anglaise.

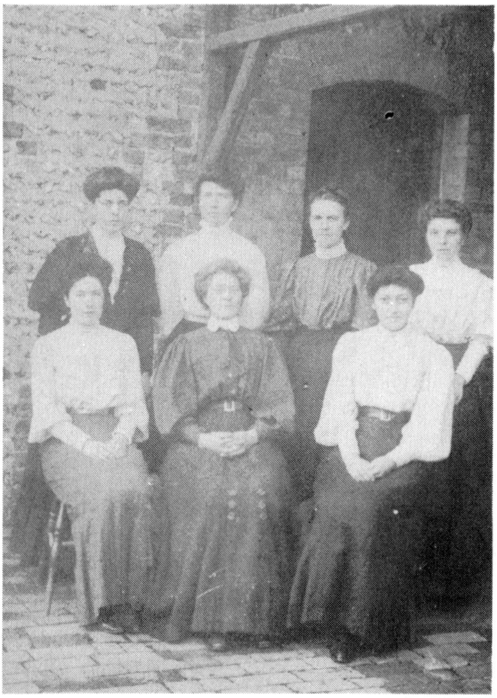

THESE WOMEN WERE ALL TEACHERS at Broadwater School early in the twentieth century. The woman in the centre of the front row was probably the headmistress.

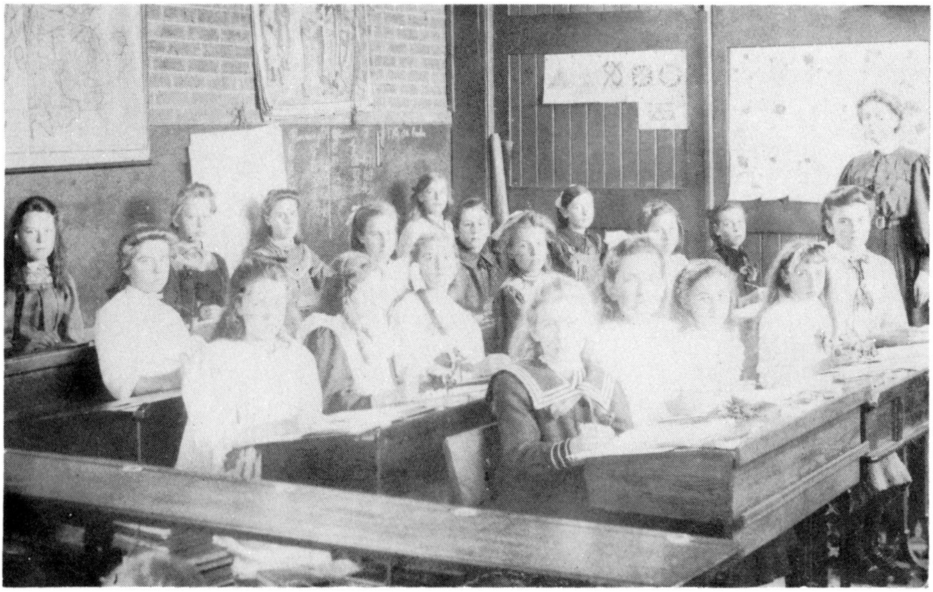

PHOTOGRAPHS OF THE INSIDE OF EDWARDIAN CLASSROOMS are not common. This classroom at Broadwater School has maps and religious pictures on the walls. It looks dull compared with modern classrooms and the children look rather subdued.

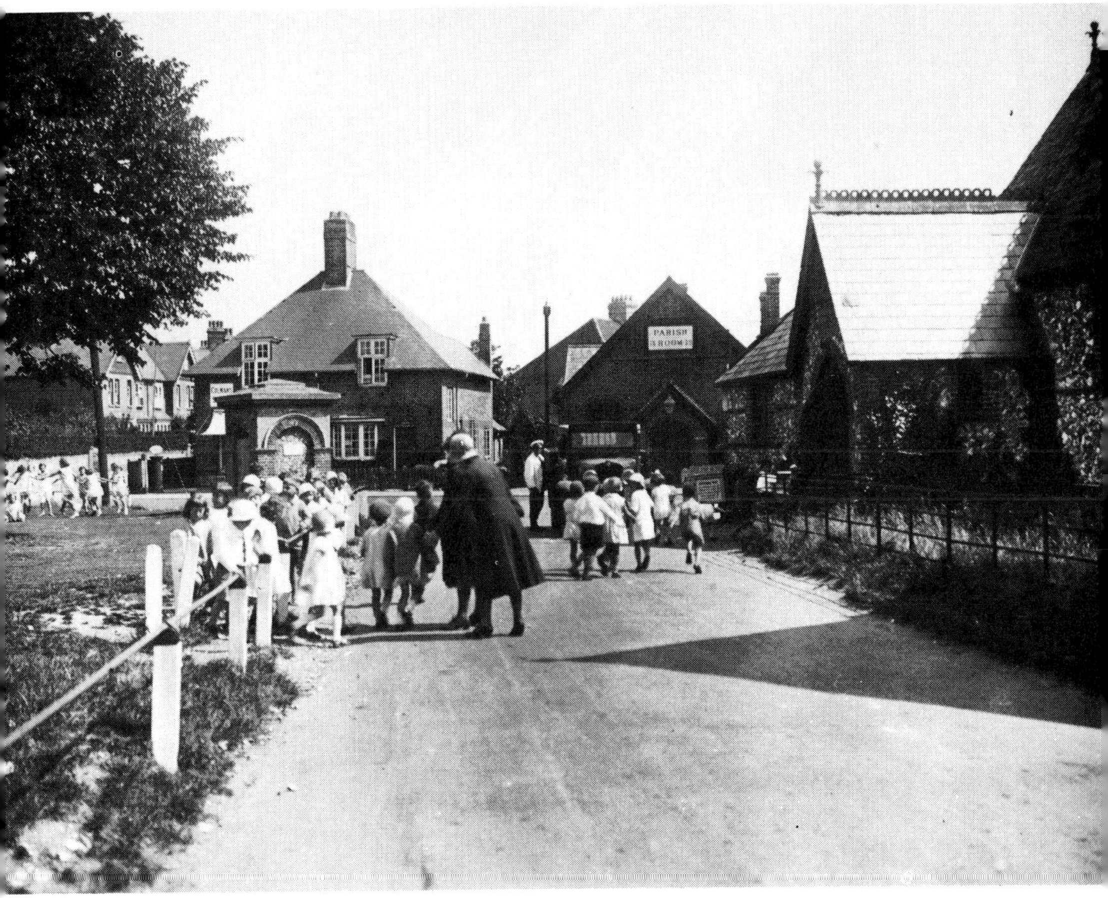


BROADWATER SCHOOL was on a triangle of land at the edge of Broadwater Green, near the Parish Rooms. Opened in 1875, it closed in 1938. As this picture from July 1932 shows, the teachers made use of the green outside the classroom.

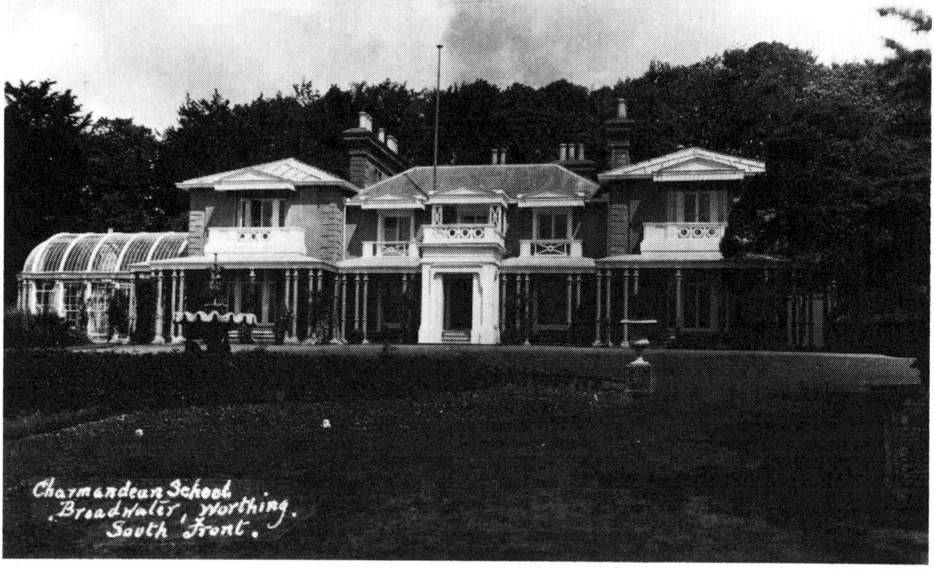


CHARMANDEAN was a house built in Broadwater by John Penfold in the early nineteenth century and later enlarged. In 1926 it was turned into a school and in 1936 became Charmandean School for Girls, owned by Miss C.E. West. After the school moved to Buckinghamshire in 1954, the house was allowed to fall into disrepair. It was demolished in 1963. These views show the south front of the school and one of the dormitories.

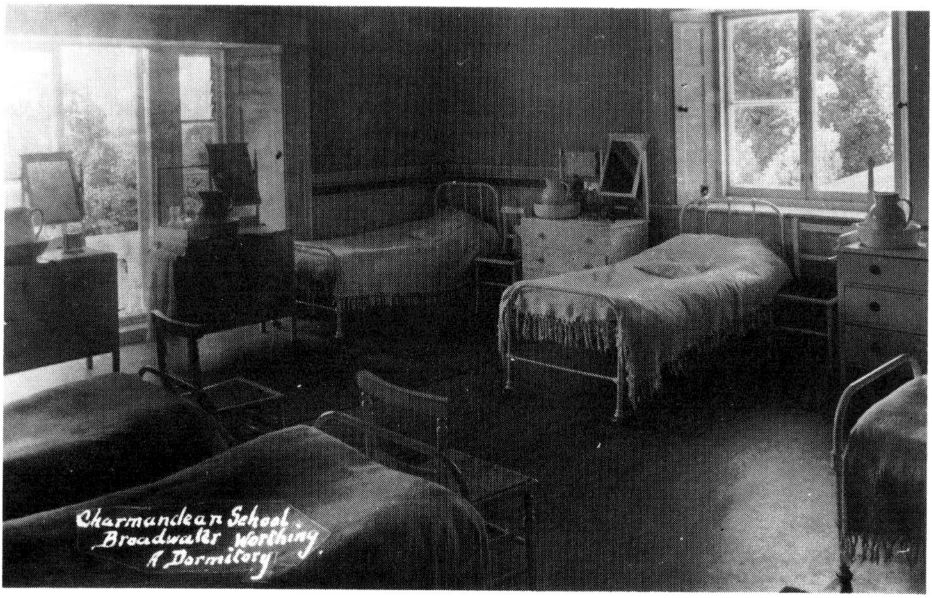

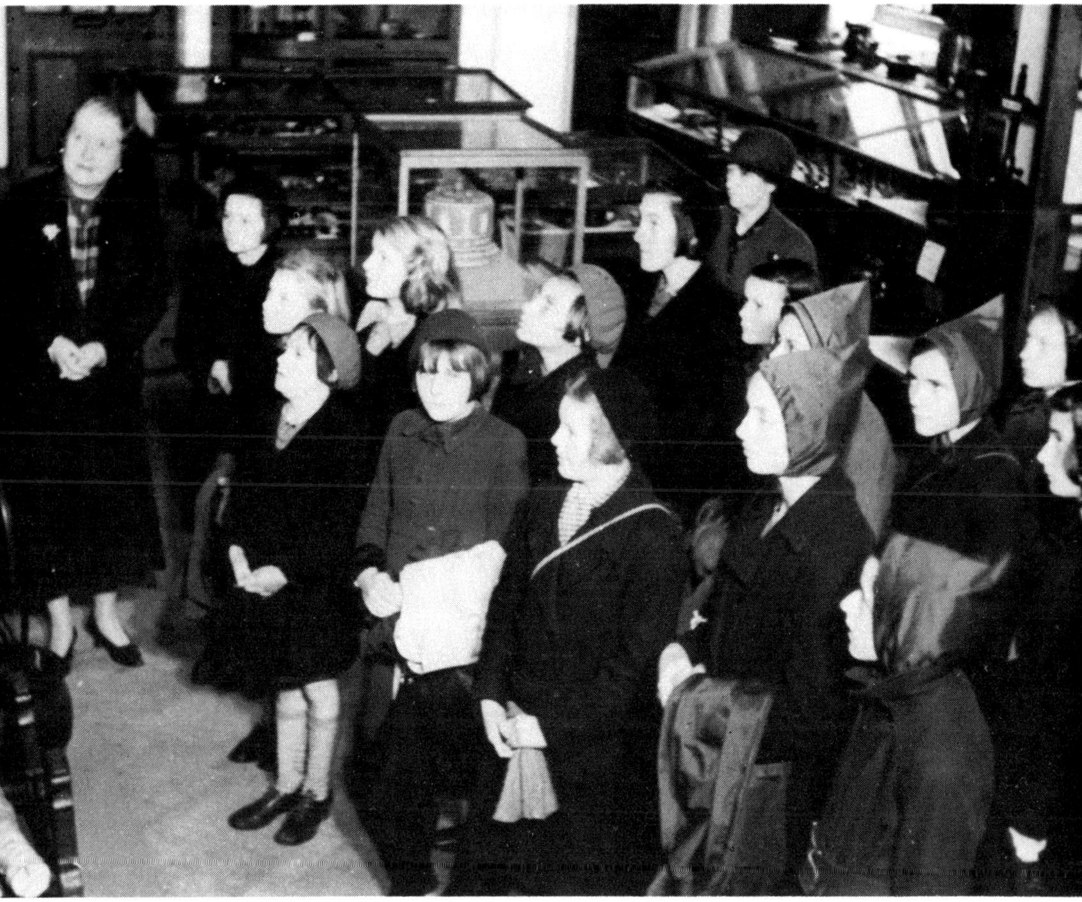

THE STAFF AT THE MUSEUM arranged visits for even more children than usual during the Second World War. In this picture a class is being given a talk in one of the galleries by the curator, Ethel Gerard. The children's pixie hoods help date this picture to *c.* 1940.

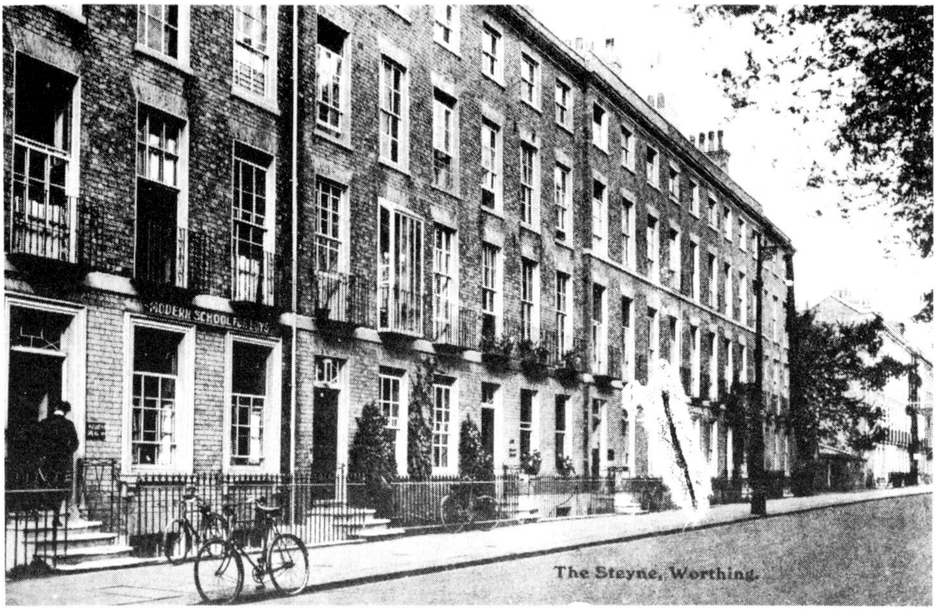


IN THE STEYNE there were a number of schools in the second half of the nineteenth century. This picture shows the Modern School for Boys and the High School for Girls. These buildings now house the Chatsworth Hotel.

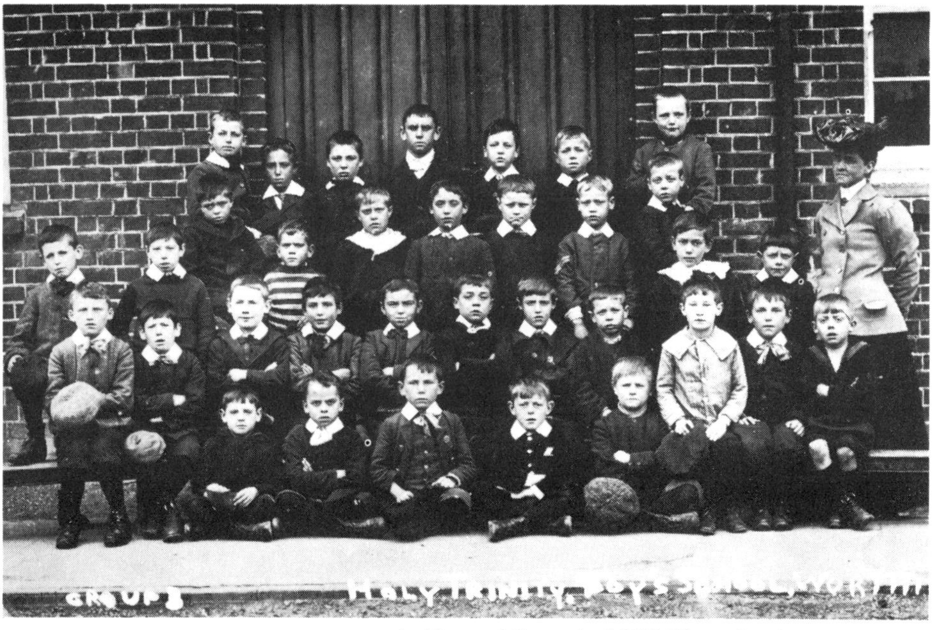

A CLASS FROM HOLY TRINITY BOYS' SCHOOL in Howard Street in 1905. The school was opened in 1891 and provided free education.

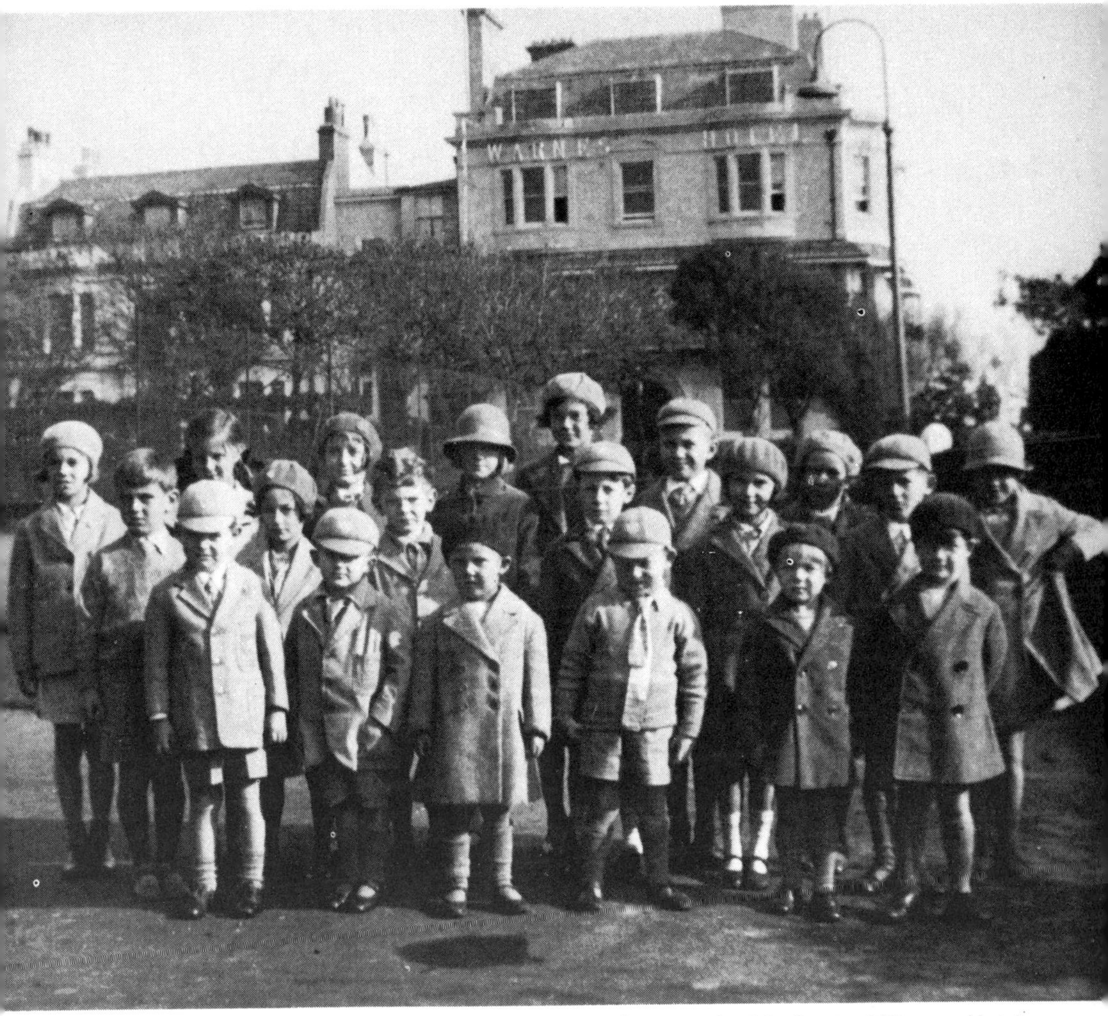

THIS UNIDENTIFIED GROUP OF SCHOOL CHILDREN was photographed in front of Warnes Hotel, *c.* 1935. The clothes of this period allowed the children more freedom of movement than earlier styles, reflecting changing attitudes to children.

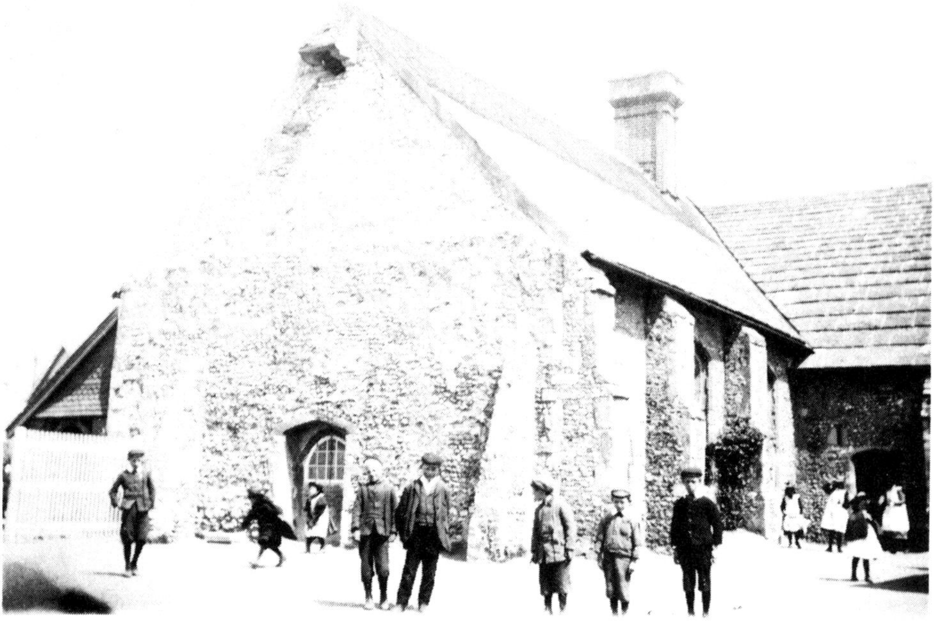

THE ARCHBISHOP'S PALACE in Tarring was built in the early thirteenth century as a place for the archbishops of Canterbury, who owned land in Tarring, to stay when they were on 'progresses' around the country. From 1872 the ecclesiastical commissioners allowed the building to be used as a National School. In 1985 the children were moved to the new Thomas à Becket School in Belleview Road. These pictures of children outside the school were taken between 1900 and 1910.

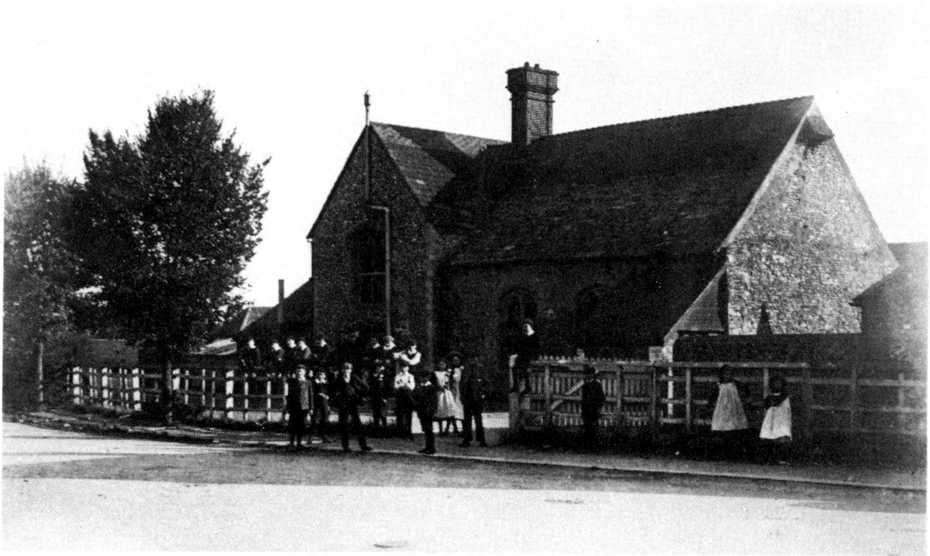

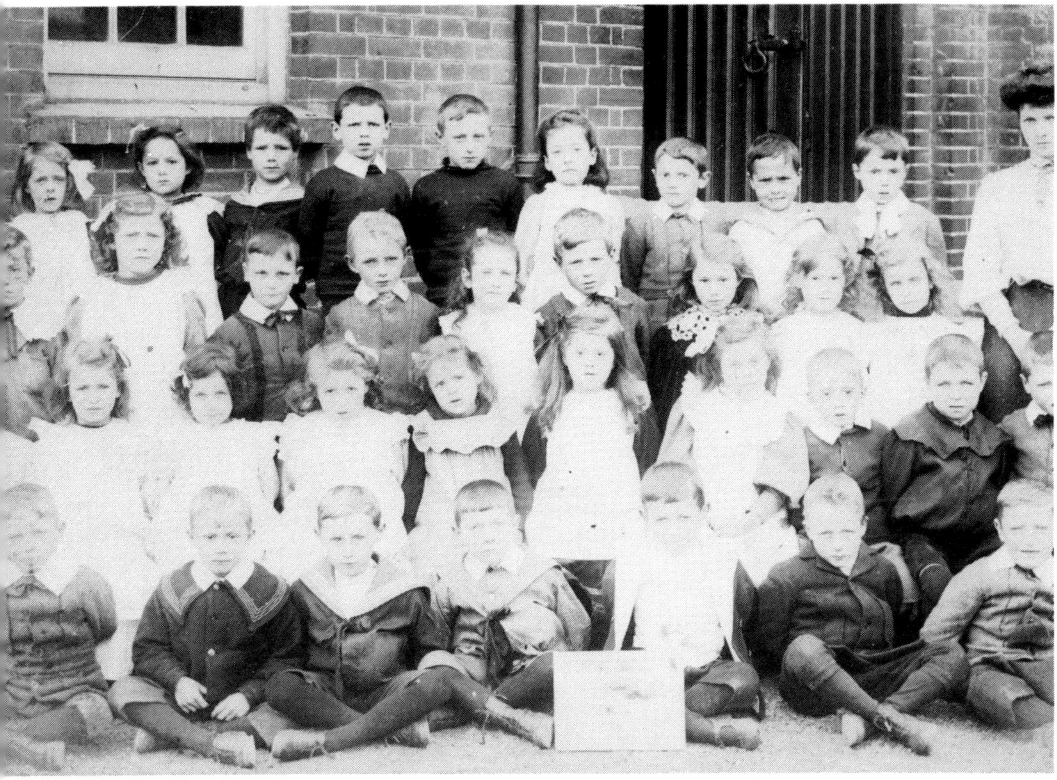

HOLY TRINITY SCHOOL went co-educational after a few years. Each of the girls in this picture is wearing a crisp white apron and the boys are all in suits, some of them with sailor collars.

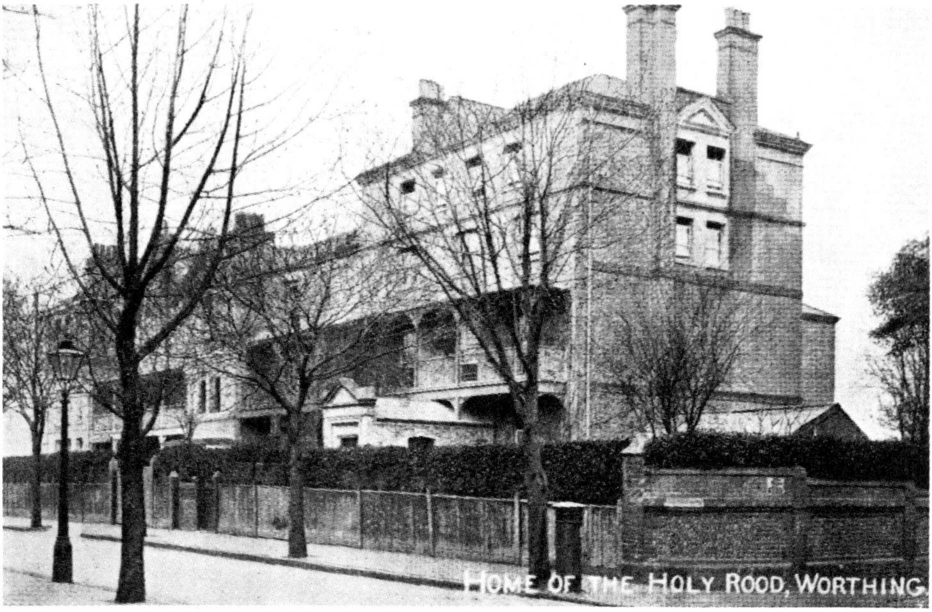


THE HOME OF THE HOLY ROOD was in Worthing House on the corner of Chapel Road and Stoke Abbott Road. It was run by the Anglican Community of the Servants of the Cross in connection with St Andrew's church. It was a home for invalids and incurables. The building was demolished in 1934 to make way for Stoke Abbott Court.

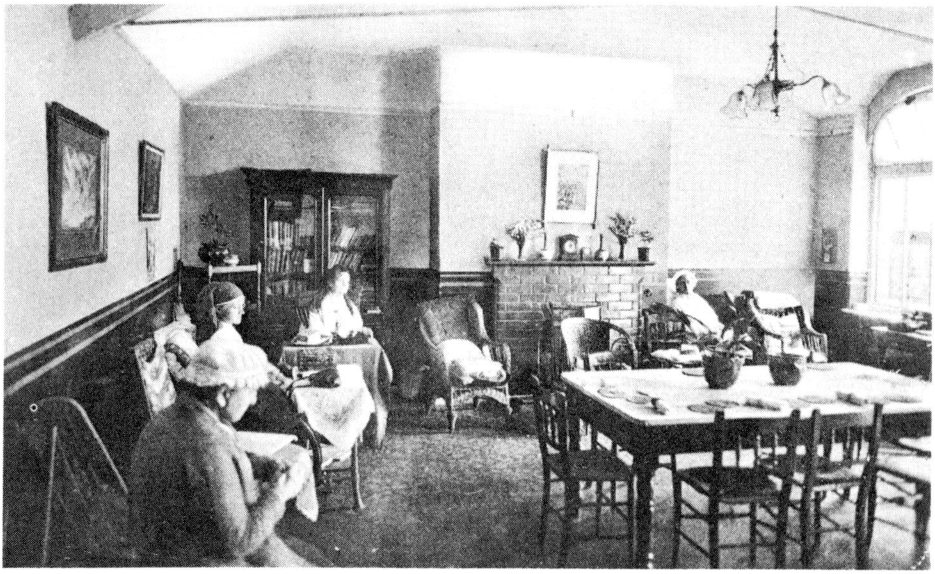

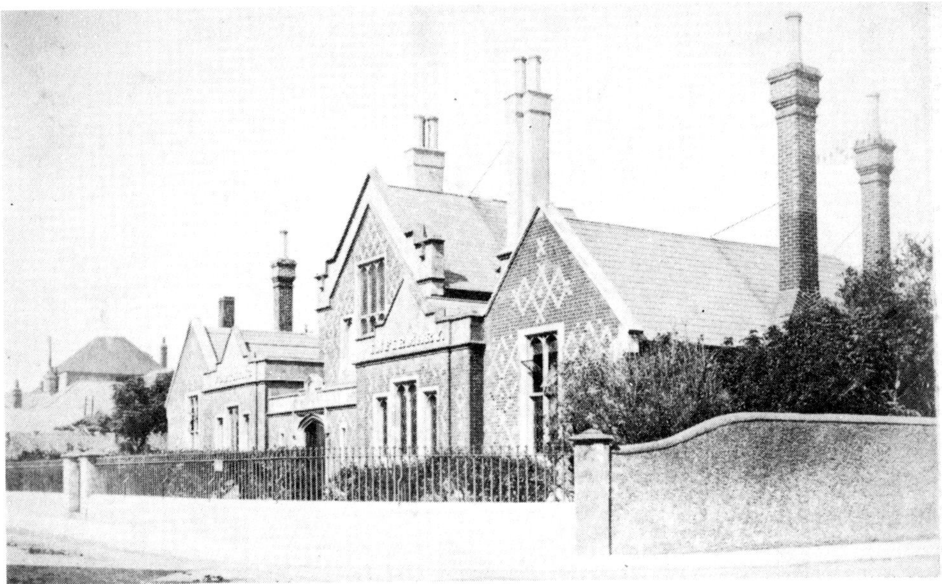

THE WORTHING DISPENSARY was built in Chapel Road in 1845. In 1869 it was enlarged and renamed the New Worthing Infirmary. The building was used until 1881, when the infirmary moved to a new site in Lyndhurst Road.

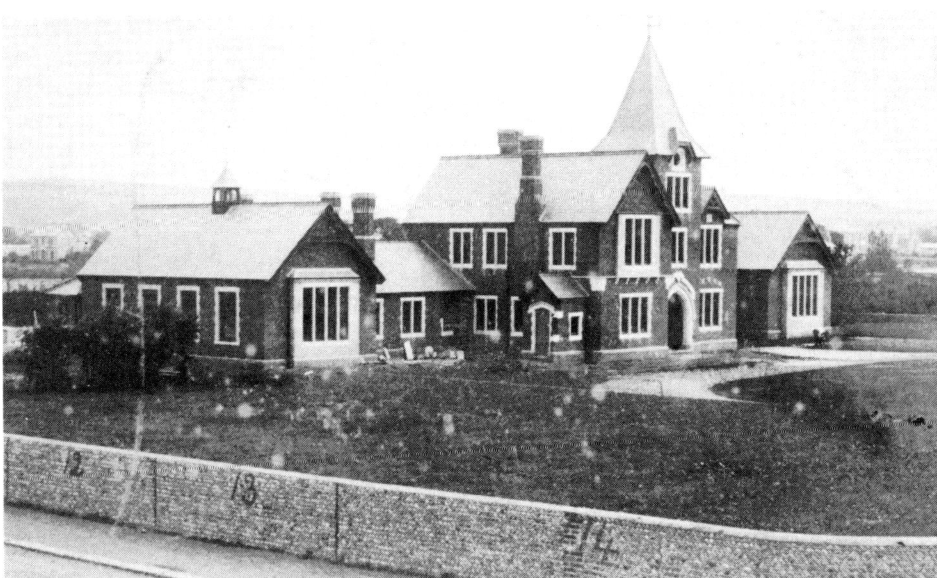

THE NEW INFIRMARY was later renamed Worthing Hospital. The present hospital occupies the same site.

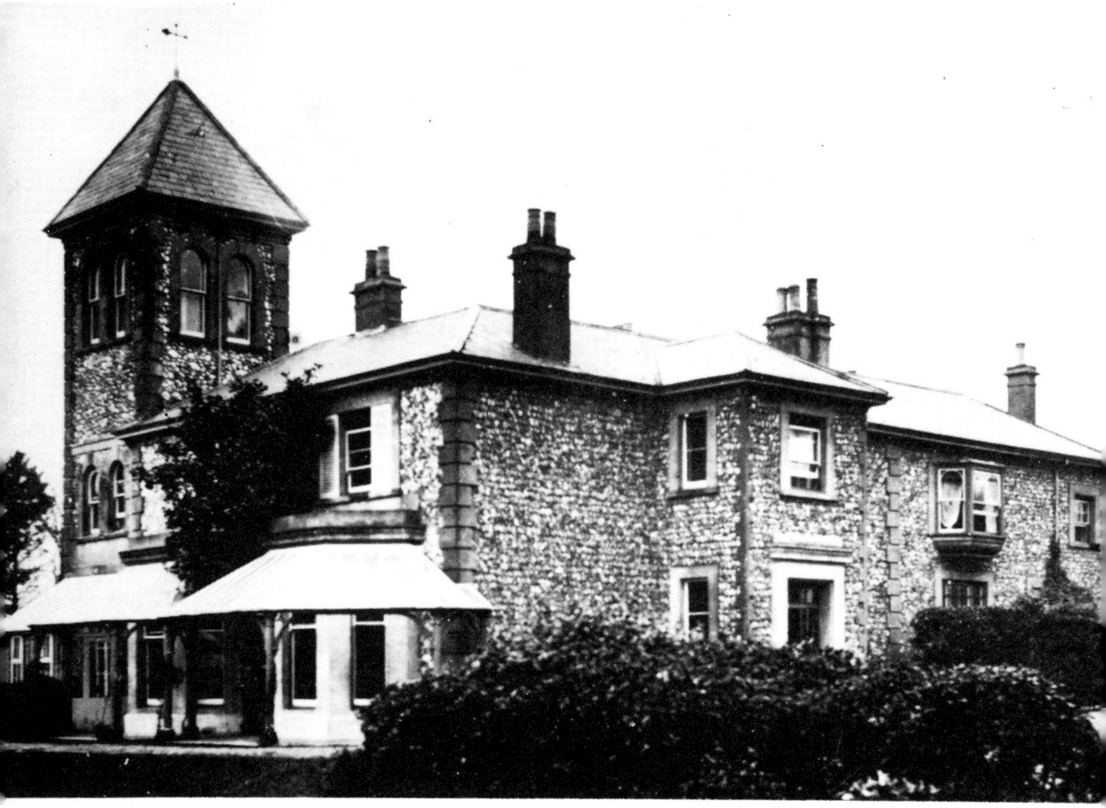

SWANDEAN HOUSE, on the Arundel Road, was first used as a hospital for infectious patients in 1897, but lacked a proper fever nurse until 1905. Until a telephone was installed in 1907, matron could only summon the medical superintendent by cycling to Worthing along wooded and secluded lanes. She always carried a stout stick on her handlebars for protection.

SECTION FIVE

# Entertainment

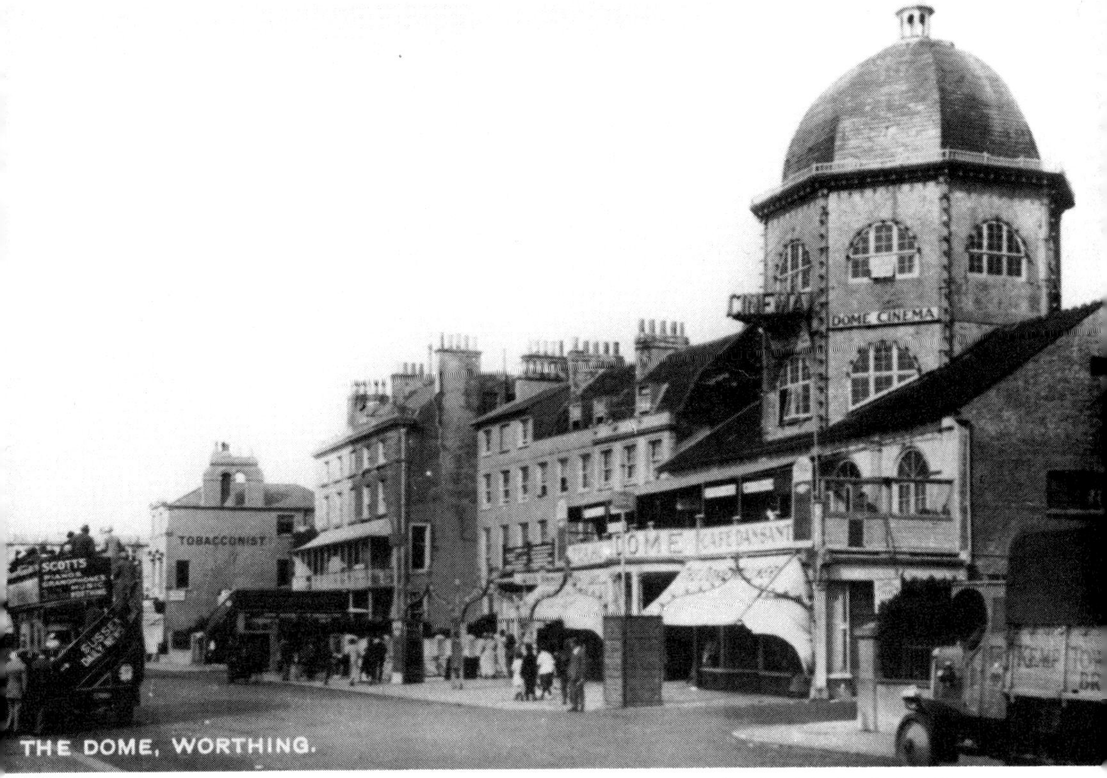


THE DOME WAS BUILT as the Kursaal, c. 1911 and was owned by Carl A. Seebold. There was originally a roller rink on the first floor with a small electric theatre upstairs. In 1921 the rink was turned into a cinema with Billy's Dance Hall above the auditorium.

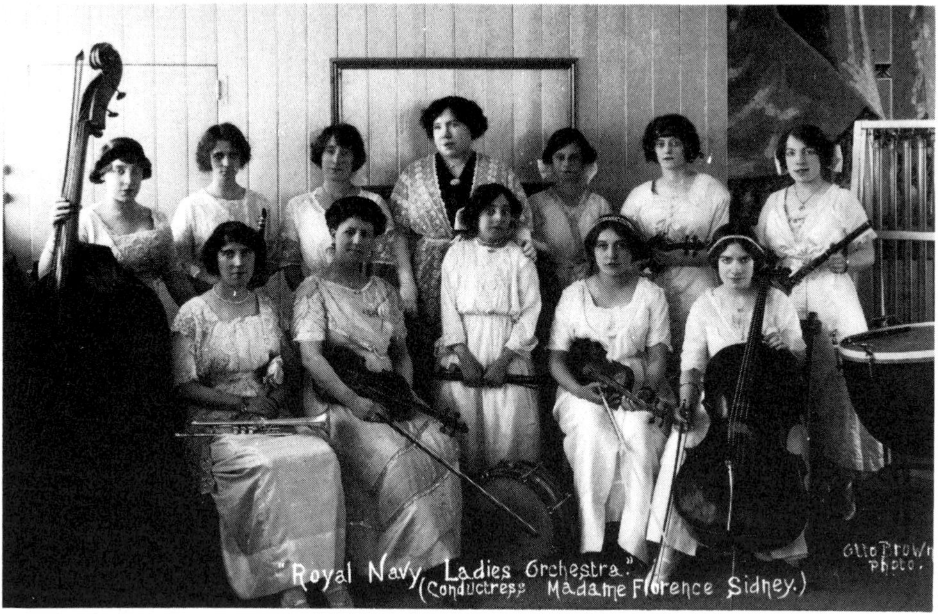


THE NAVAL LADIES ORCHESTRA played annually on the pier for a number of years from 1909. Back row, left to right: Miss Sutton, Miss Curtis, Miss Kent, Madame Sidney, Miss Jones, Miss Hope, Miss V. Haut. Front row: Miss Connolly, Miss Greenhill, Miss Blanche, Miss Bush, Miss J. Haut.

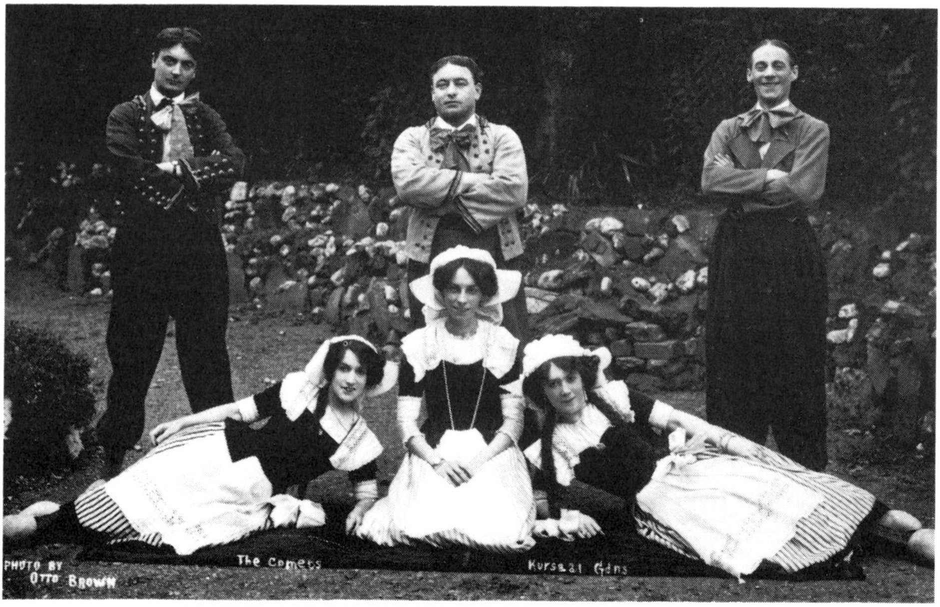


THE COMETS, photographed in the Kursaal Gardens by Otto Brown c. 1925.

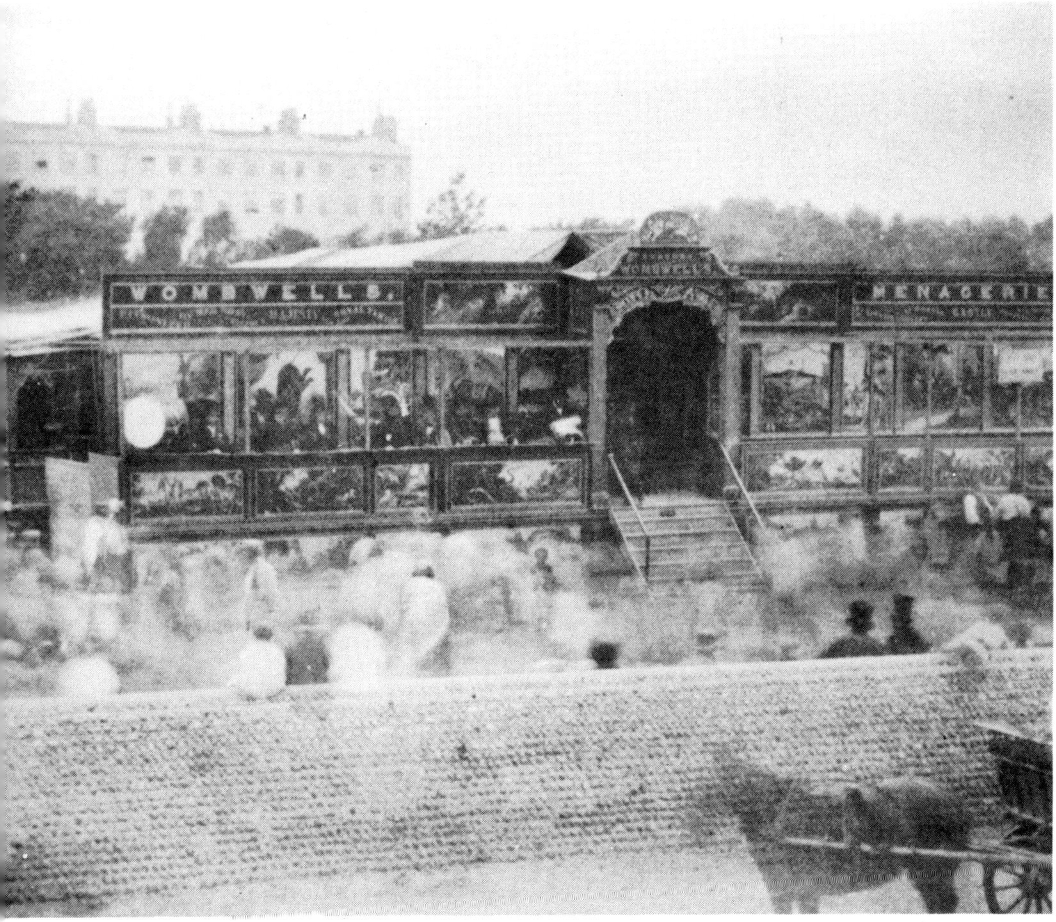


WOMBWELL'S MENAGERIE came to Worthing in September 1853. One of the earliest and largest menageries, it was set up on the pleasure grounds in front of Liverpool Terrace. The show included an elephant, a sloth, a bear, and a monkey or ape which reminded one local writer of 'a human captive pining for liberty'.

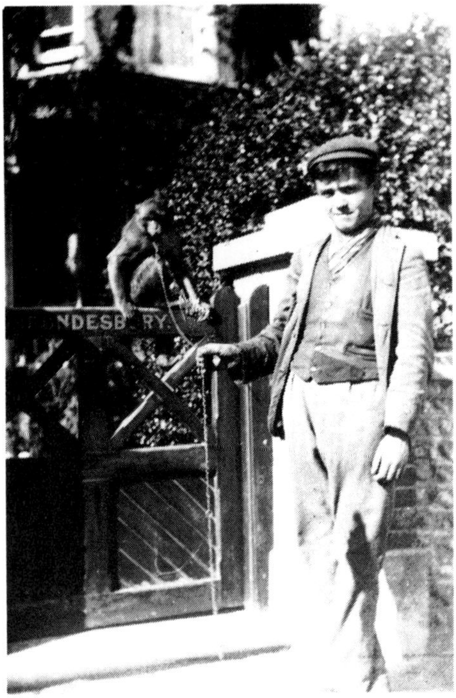

THESE TWO PHOTOGRAPHS SHOW THE SAME LAD with his monkey, *c.* 1901. In the first he is outside Brondesbury, a house in Victoria Road. In the other he is playing his accordion, perhaps with the hope of using the monkey to help him collect money.

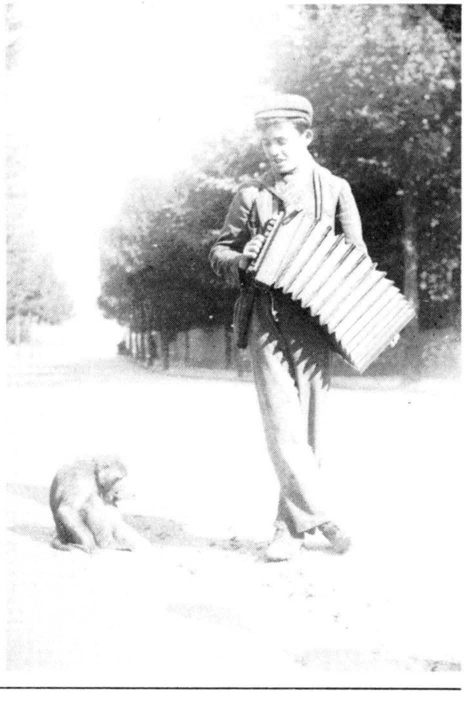

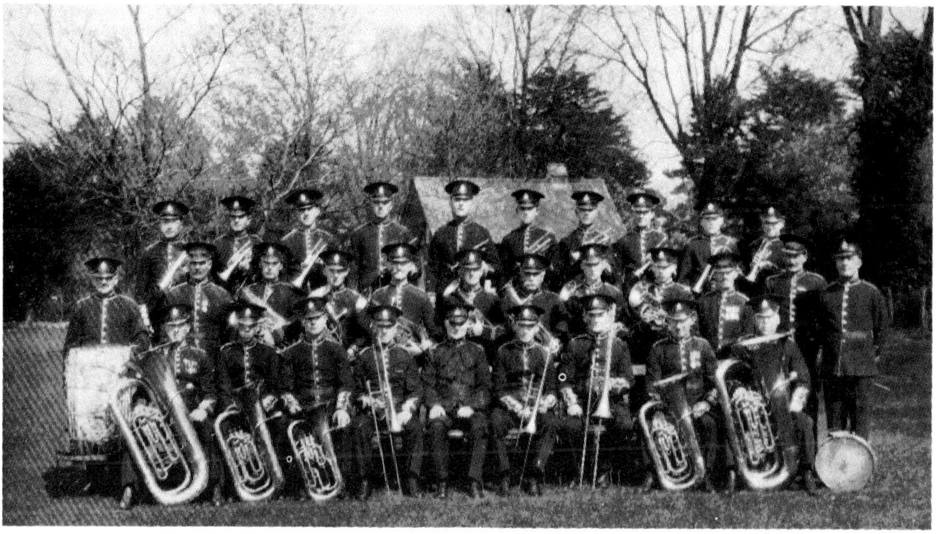

WORTHING BOROUGH BAND in 1926. The borough band and the other bands which played on Worthing seafront during the summer season regularly drew crowds of over two thousand. Clashes between the borough and Salvation Army bands led to a careful agreement about times and places of performance.

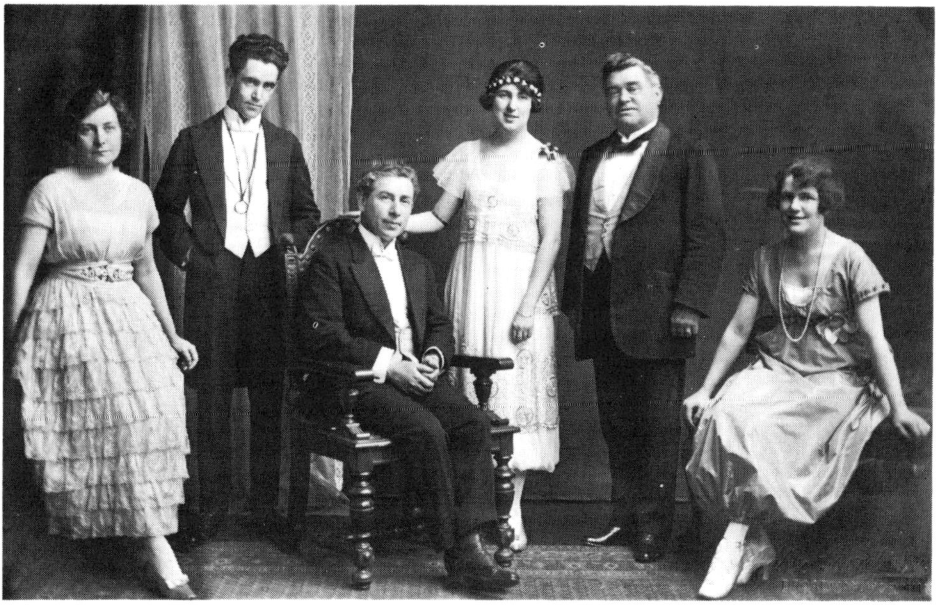

PHILIP RITTE and his Concert Party were regulars at St James' Hall and the Connaught in the 1920s and '30s. Philip Ritte is seated in the middle of this group.

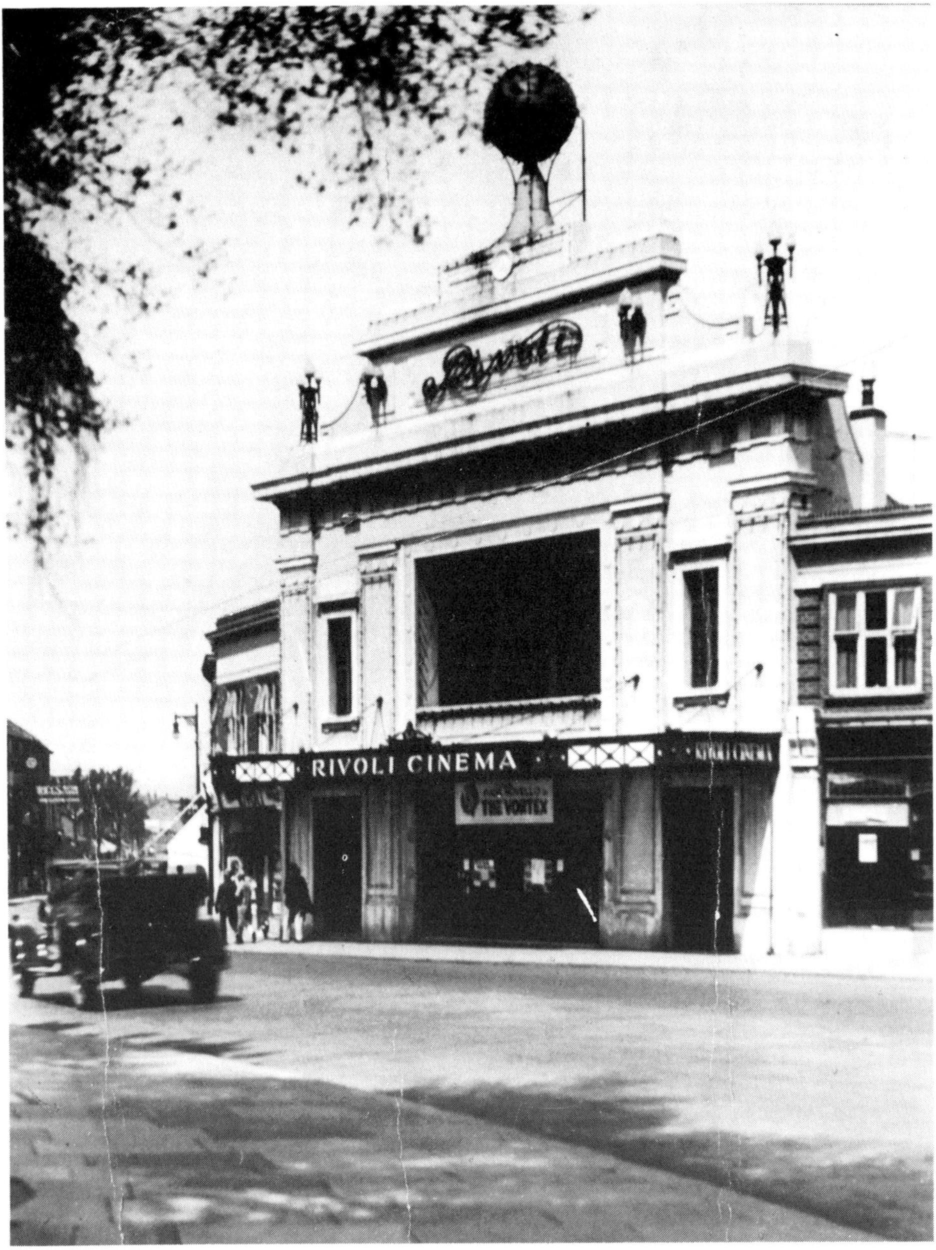


THE RIVOLI CINEMA was built on the corner of Chapel Road and North Street in 1923 and was Worthing's first major cinema. It had a sliding roof and a resident orchestra. The auditorium was destroyed by fire in 1960, but the shell stood until 1984 when it was demolished to make way for a road-widening scheme.

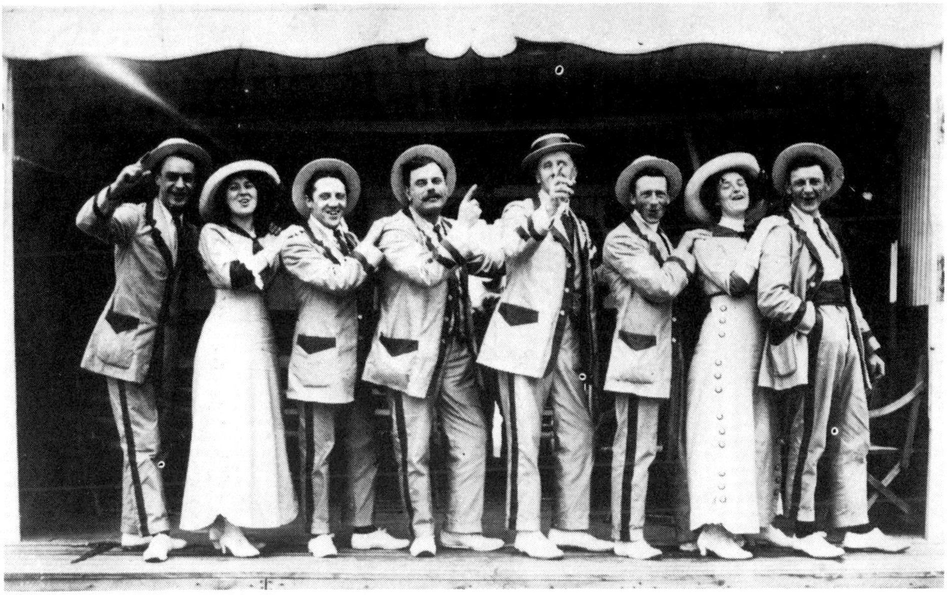

THIS CONCERT PARTY is typical of the many which toured coastal resorts in the 1920s.

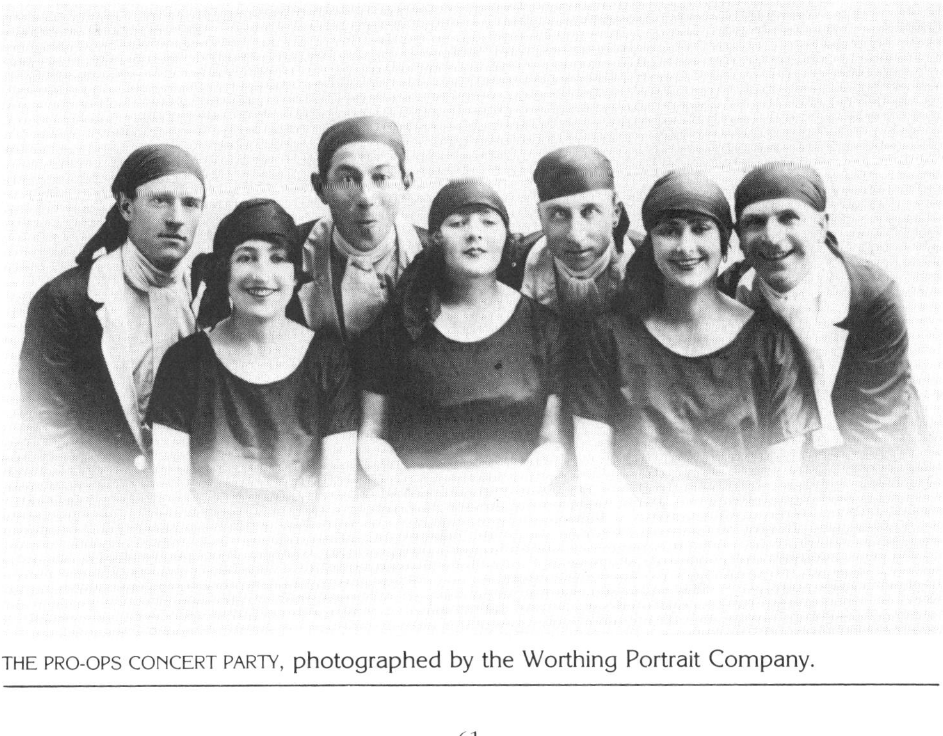

THE PRO-OPS CONCERT PARTY, photographed by the Worthing Portrait Company.

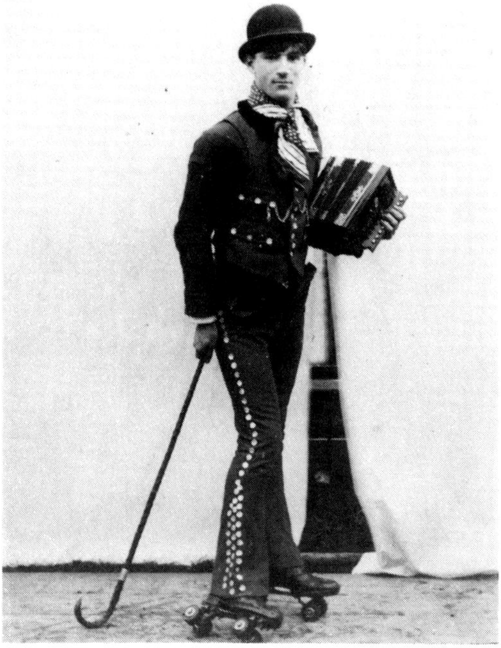

THIS ENTERTAINER, C. 1905, with his pearly buttons, is not only on roller skates but also carries both an accordion and a stick. We do not know who he is or what his act consisted of.

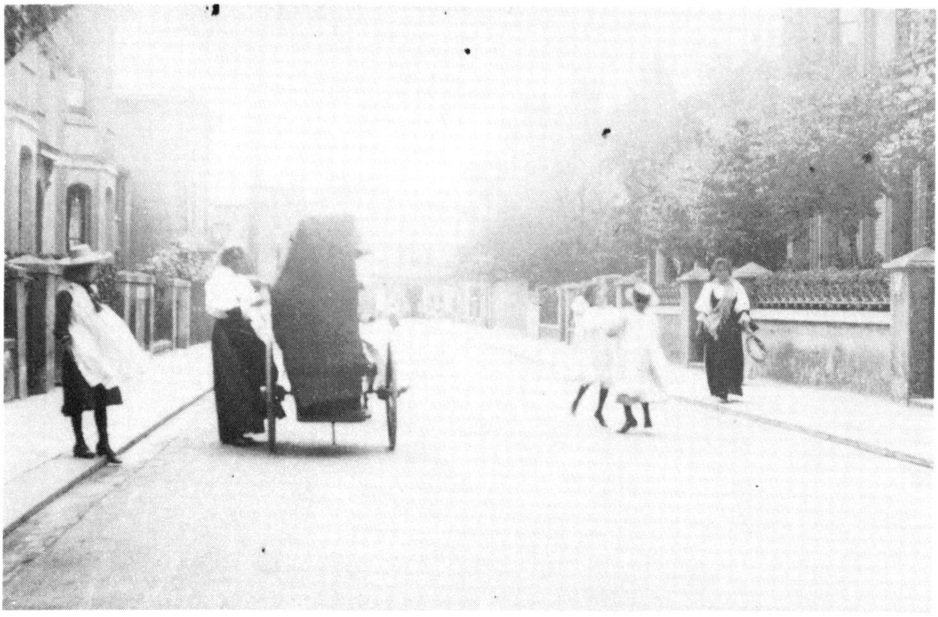

THIS DELIGHTFUL AND UNUSUAL PHOTOGRAPH shows one lady working the barrel organ while another plays a tambourine and the girls dance in the street.

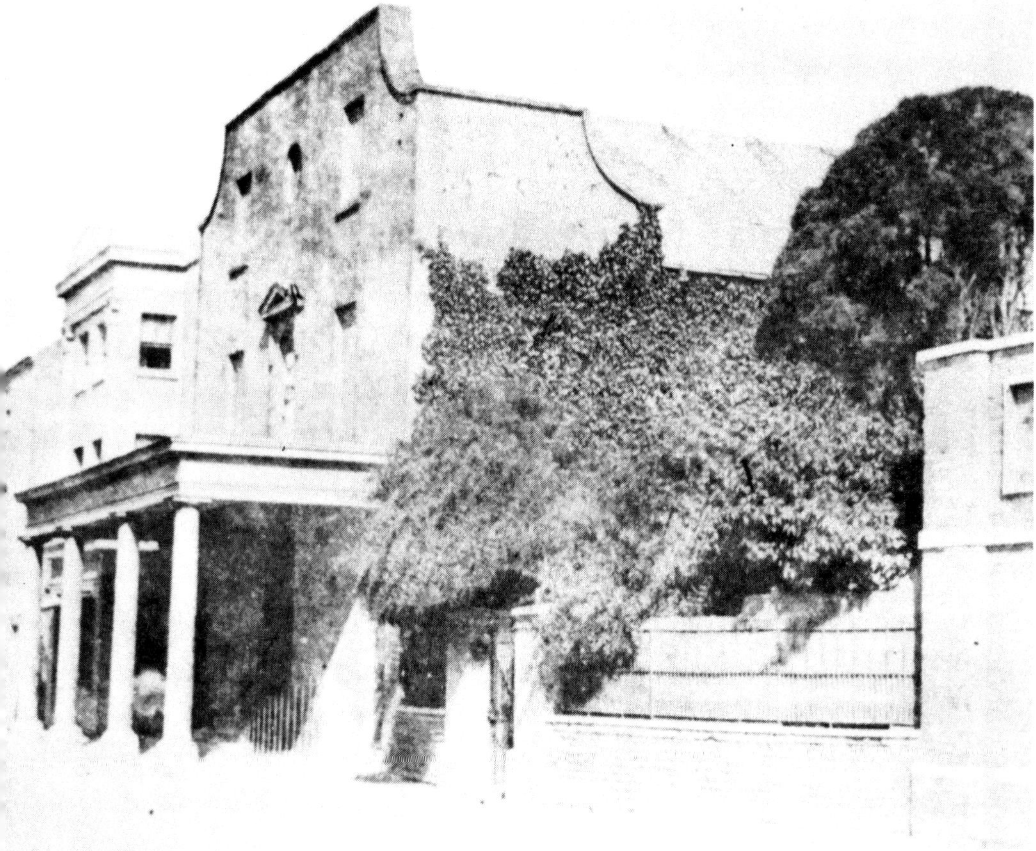

THE THEATRE ROYAL IN ANN STREET opened in 1807 and was owned by Thomas Trotter. It was very successful for some years but closed in 1855, shortly before this photograph was taken. In later years it was used as a warehouse by the grocers Potter and Bailey. It was finally demolished in 1970. Ann Street was named after Thomas Trotter's wife.

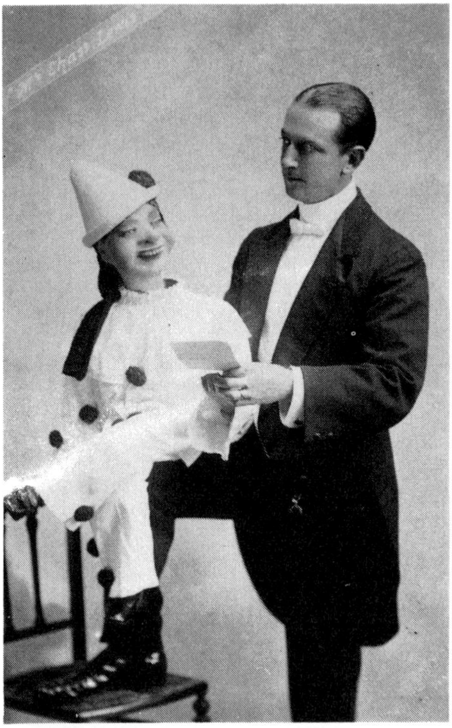

CHARLES LEWIS brought his ventriloquism act to Worthing in the 1920s.

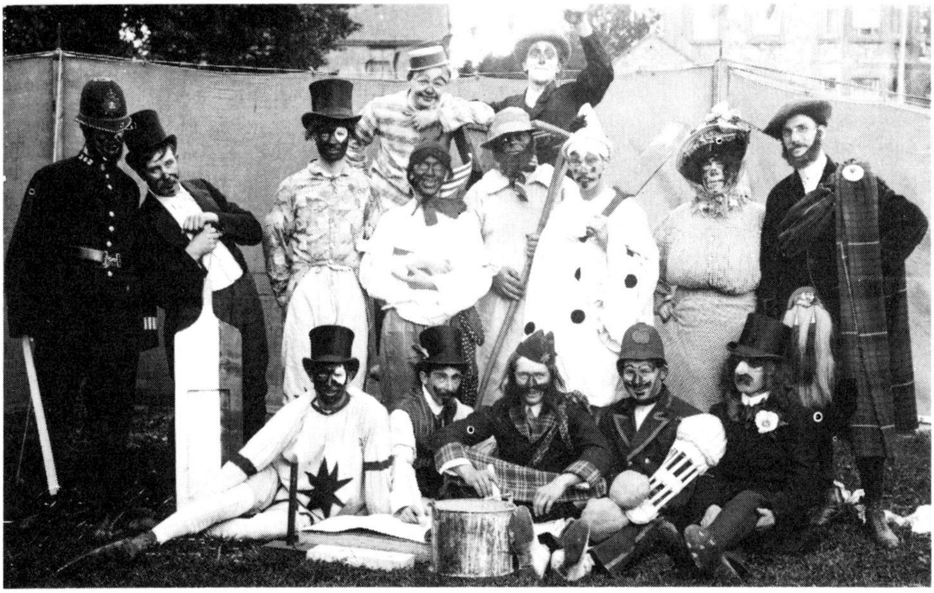

THIS MOTLEY GROUP appear to have been comedians, but their names and that of their show are unknown.

SECTION SIX

# Sports and Pastimes

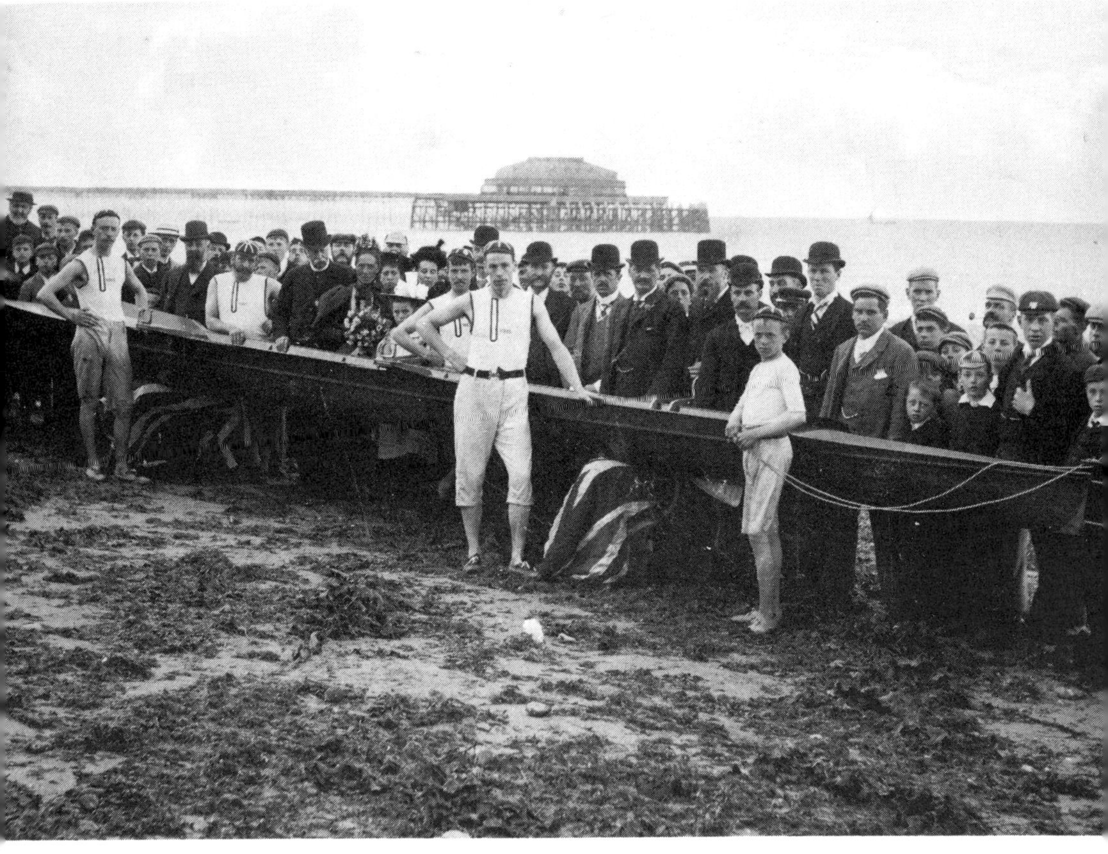

THE MAYORESS CHRISTENED the rowing club's new galley *Worthing* in 1891.

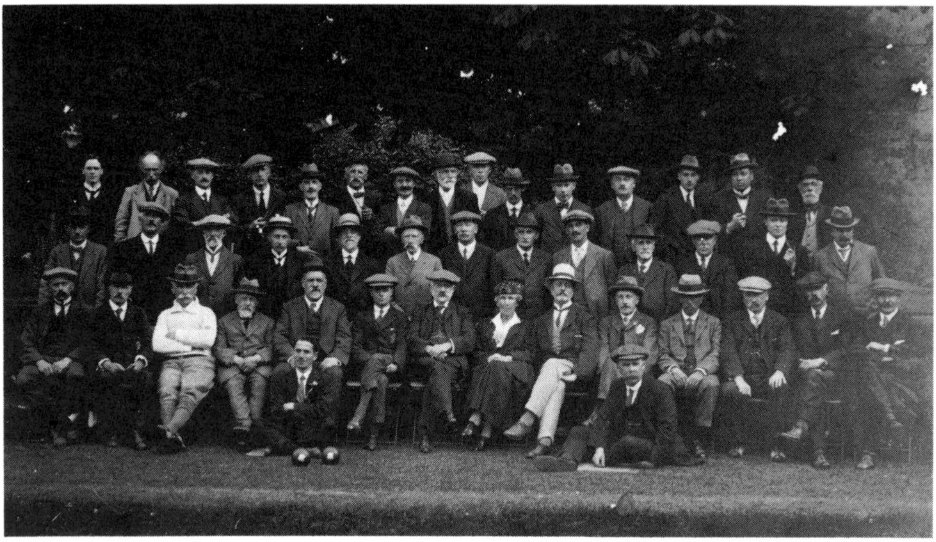

WORTHING BOWLING CLUB was founded in 1909. This group of members was photographed in 1918 and includes S. Saywell, sitting on the ground, capless. He was a prize-winning local window dresser who worked for Bentalls in South Street. The identity of the sole lady is not known.

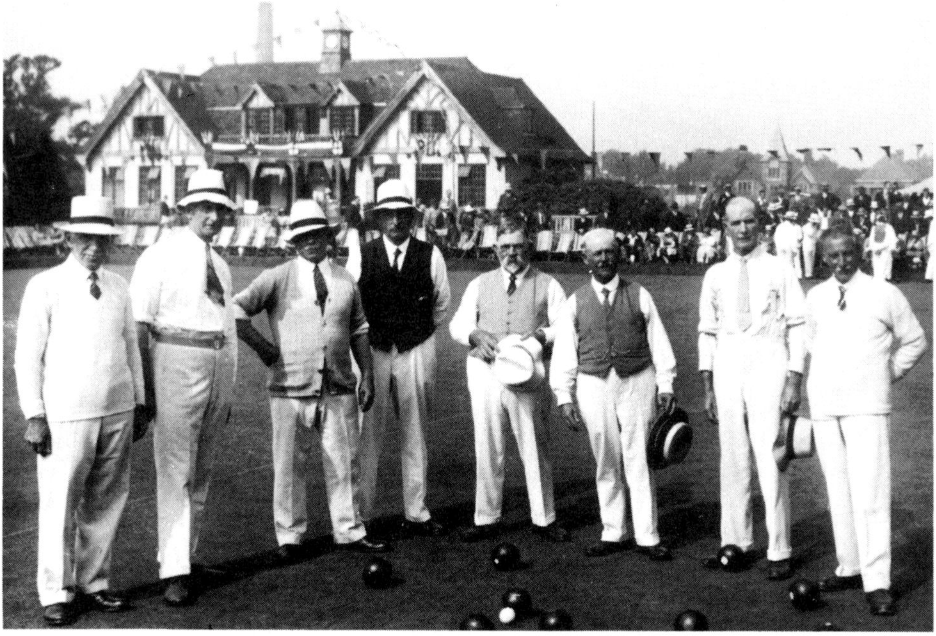

THESE EIGHT MEMBERS OF WORTHING BOWLING CLUB are posing on a green in Beach House Park during a tournament in around 1930.

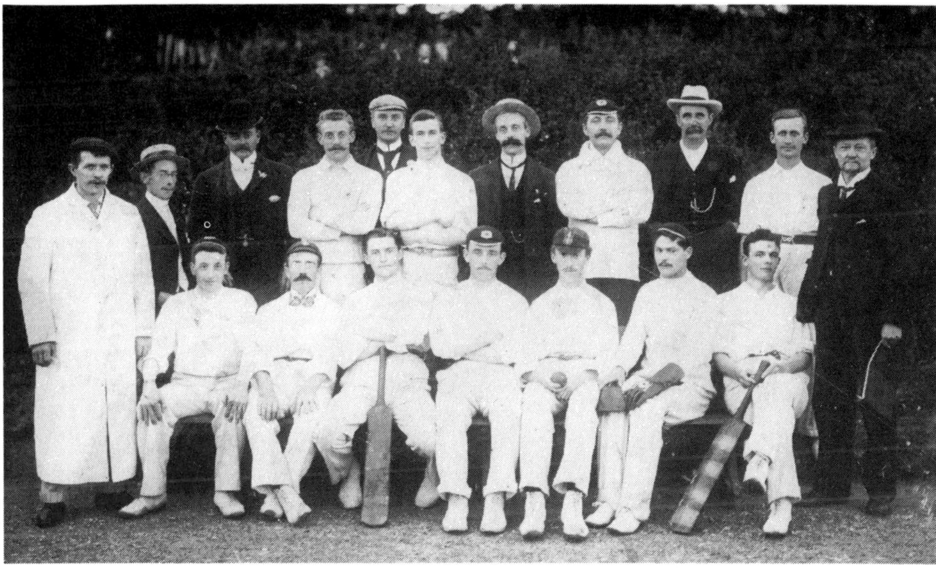

MANY FIRMS HAVE BOASTED THEIR OWN SPORTS TEAMS who competed in local competitions. These gentlemen represented the grocery firm of Potter Bailey and Company, c. 1910. On the whole a serious looking group, there are appealing signs of individuality in their headgear and in the tartan bow-tie sported by the gentleman in the front row.

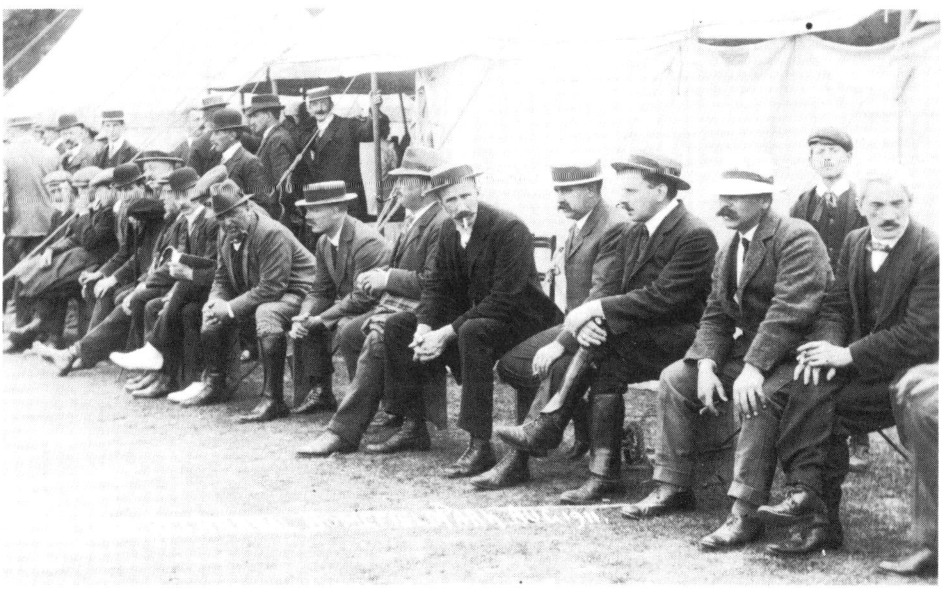

THESE MEN OUTSIDE THE REFRESHMENT TENT at the annual cricket match in Homefield Park look as if they were stern critics of the players. There is only one lad visible and not a woman in sight. Cricket matches appear to have been a firmly male preserve in 1911.

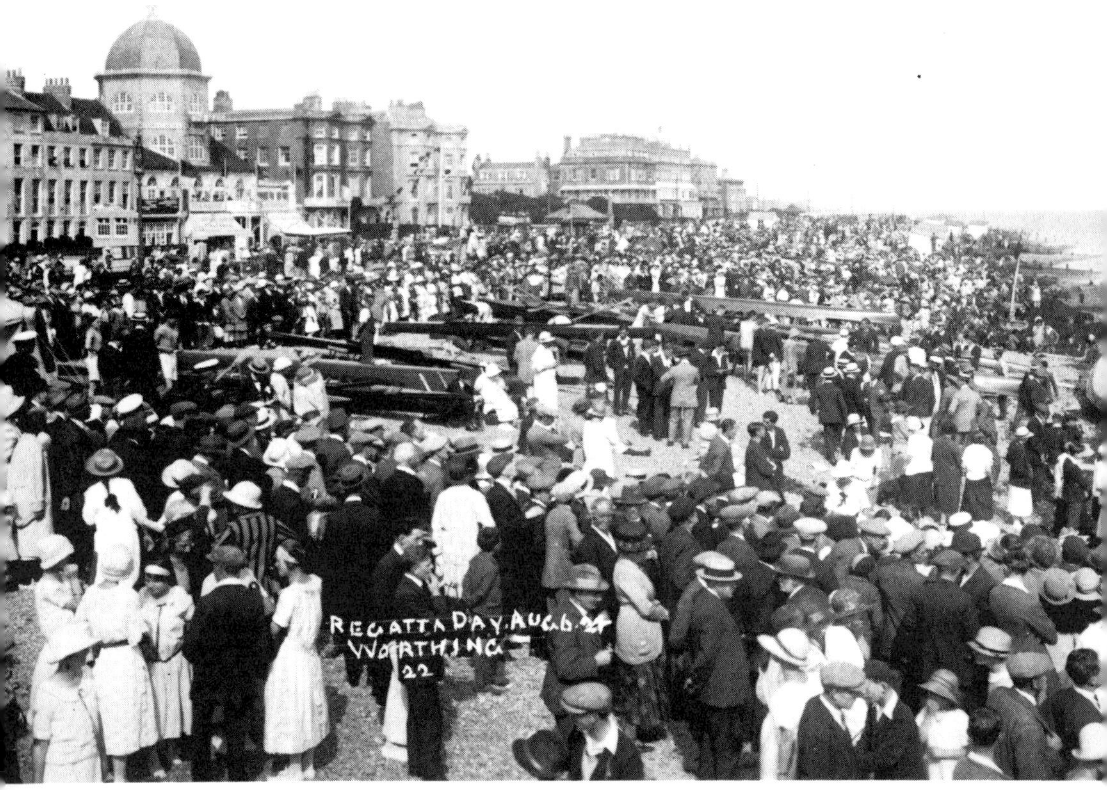


WORTHING REGATTA was a popular annual attraction for a long time and included lifeboat and rowing races, as well as events like climbing the greasy pole. This crowded scene shows just how popular the regatta was in 1924.

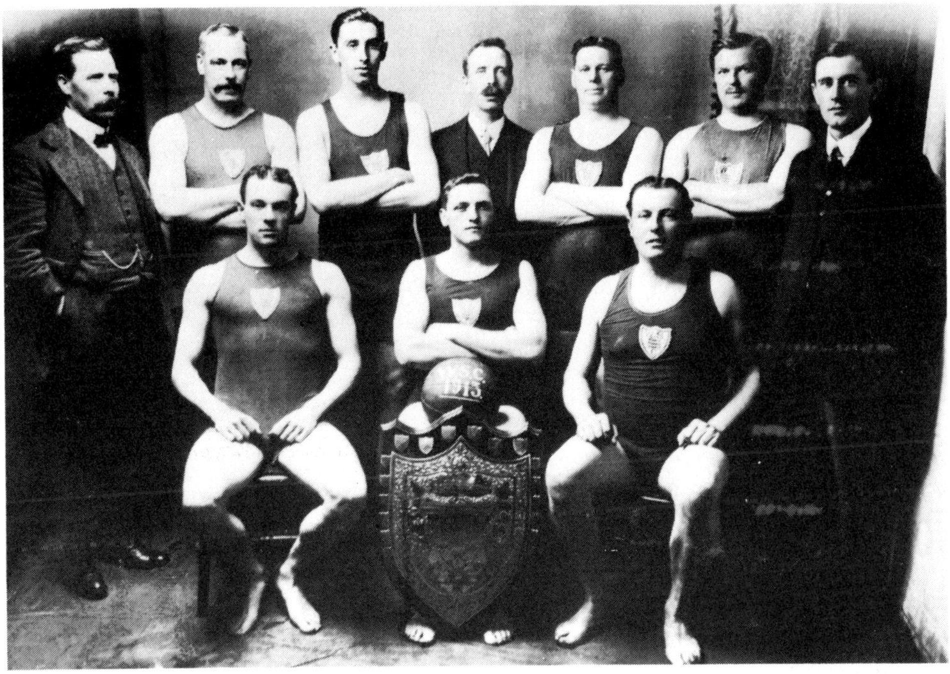


WORTHING SWIMMING TEAMS were very successful in competition in the years leading up to the First World War. This group from Worthing Swimming Club won the Sussex senior water polo championship in 1913.

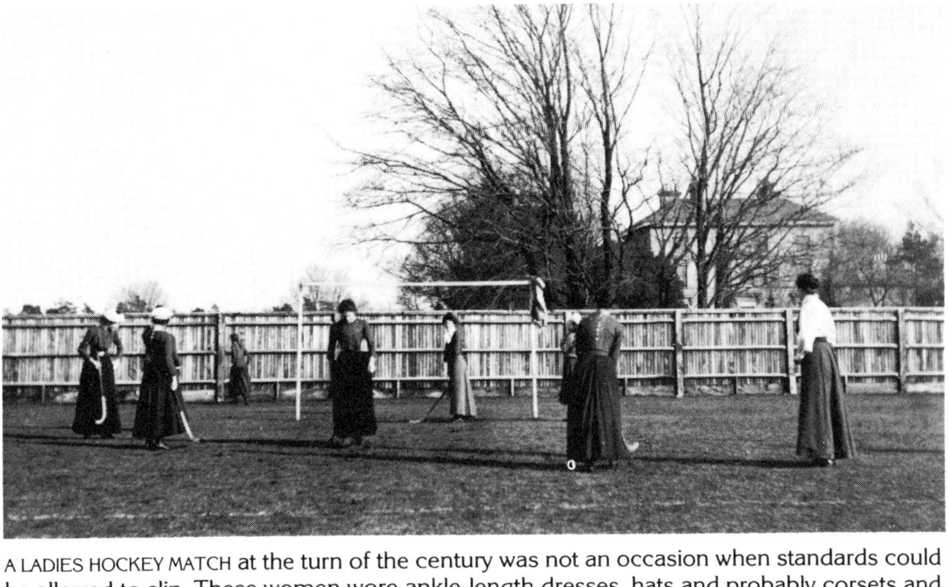

A LADIES HOCKEY MATCH at the turn of the century was not an occasion when standards could be allowed to slip. These women wore ankle-length dresses, hats and probably corsets and gloves as well.

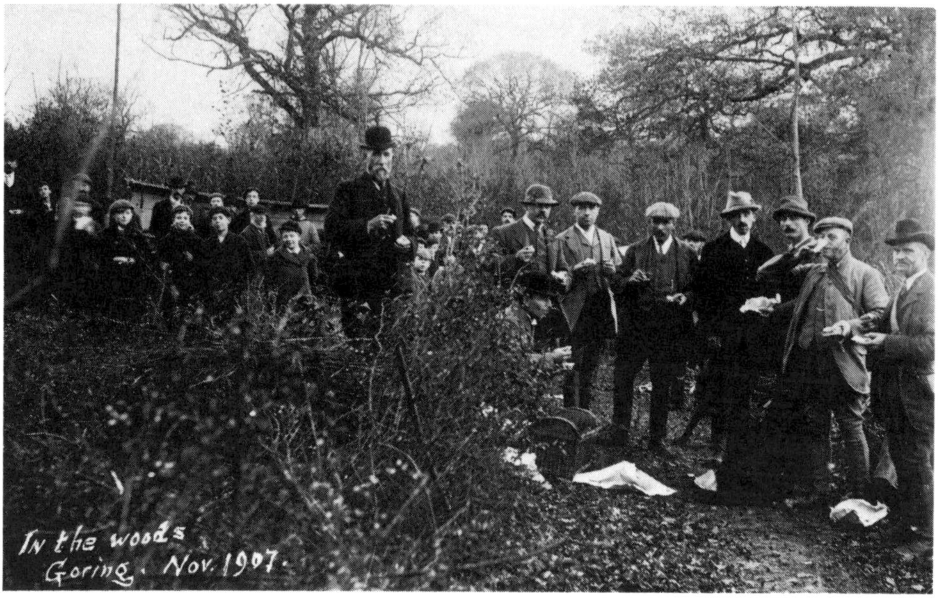


THIS GROUP OF HUNTERS IN GORING WOODS appears to have stopped for refreshments. The children on the left are taking an eager interest in the proceedings and in the camera.

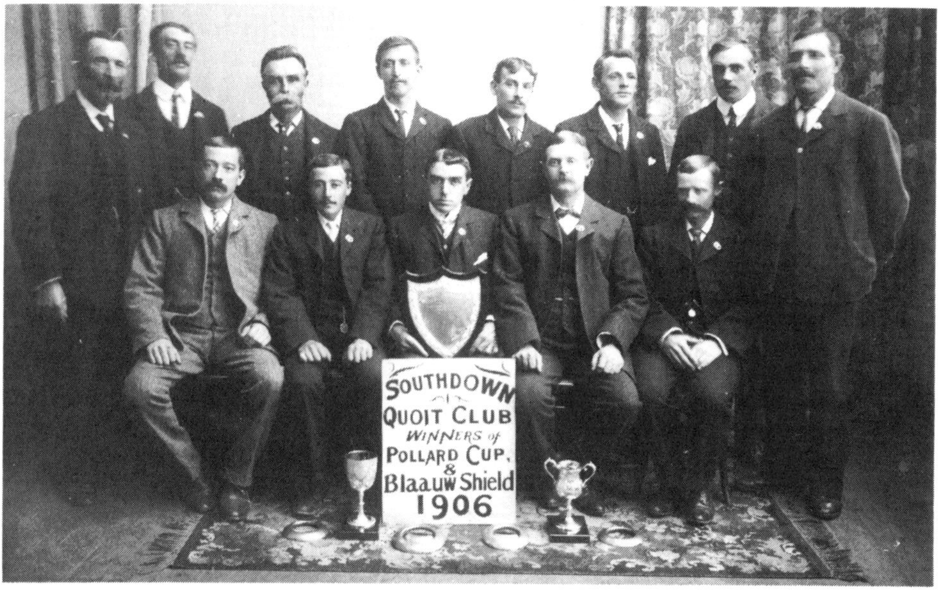


QUOITS IS NOT PLAYED VERY OFTEN NOWADAYS, but early in the twentieth century local competition was fierce. This group from the Southdown Quoit Club were clearly experts at throwing the heavy metal quoits. Back row, left to right: H. Sparks, J. Churcher, F. Wyatt, A. Lish, N. Tutt, C. Grevatt, J. Asser, F. Collins. Front row: L. Phillips, W. Charles, G. Waite, G. Brazier, E. Chilcott.

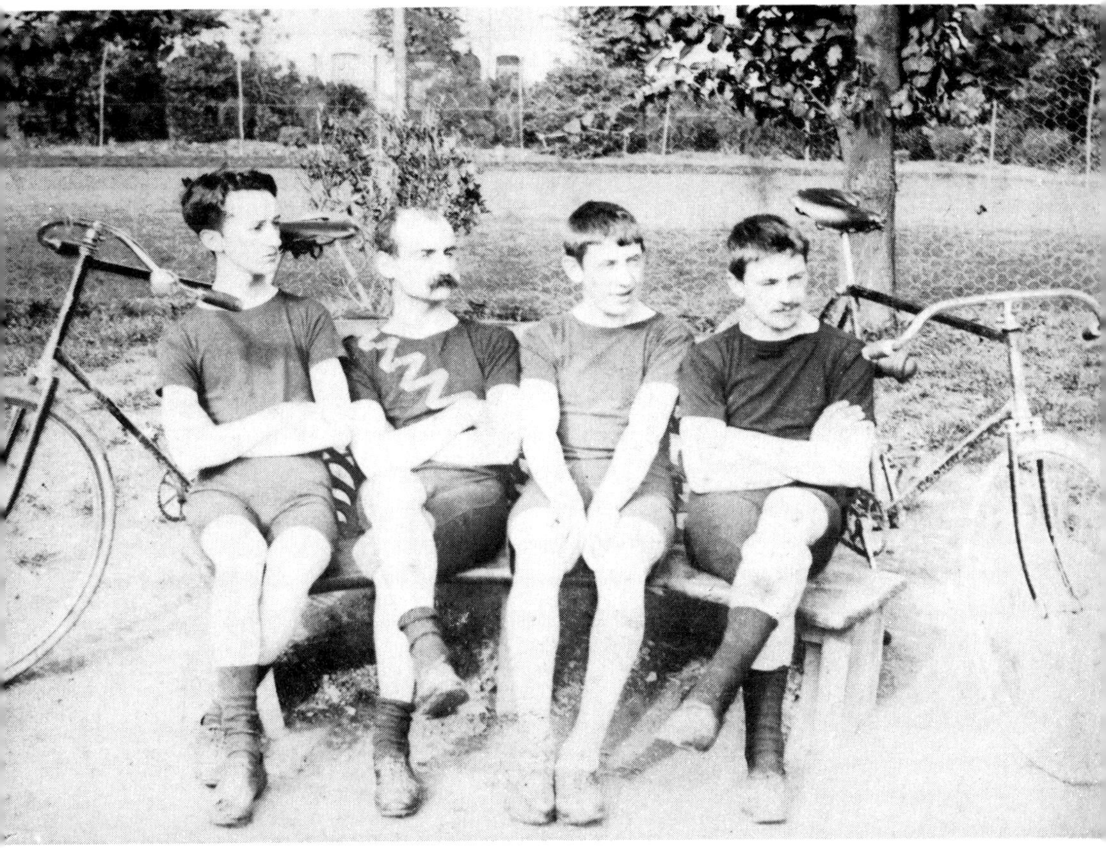

THESE FOUR CYCLISTS are seen in Homefield Park early one morning in 1895. Left to right; Dick Long, N. Fothergill (from Southport), W.R. Paine, Ted Brockley.

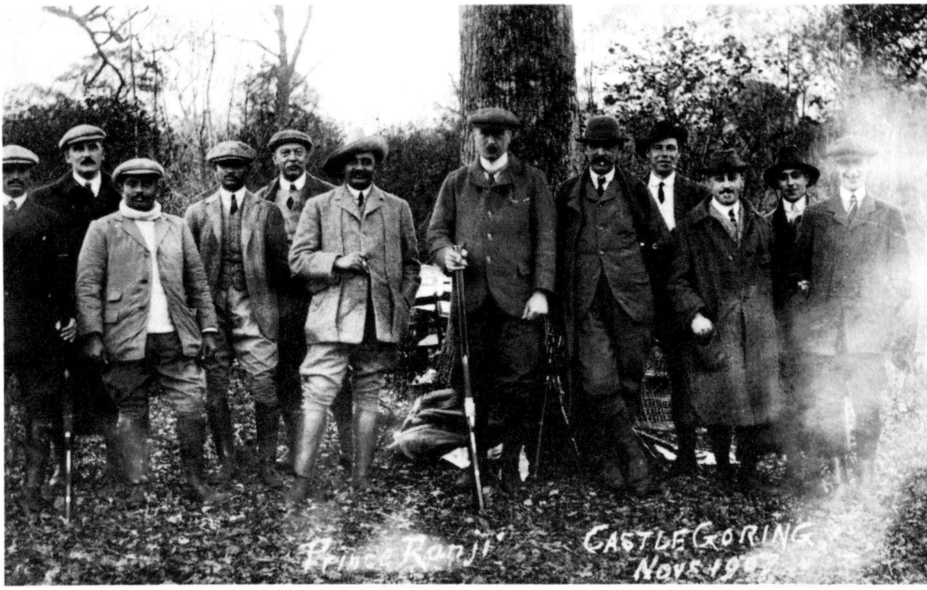


THE FAMOUS CRICKETER PRINCE RANJITSINJI (sixth from the left) visited Castle Goring to go shooting in November 1907. The group also includes his host Arthur F. Somerset of Castle Goring (fifth from the left) and the England cricket captain Archy MacLaren (ninth from the left).

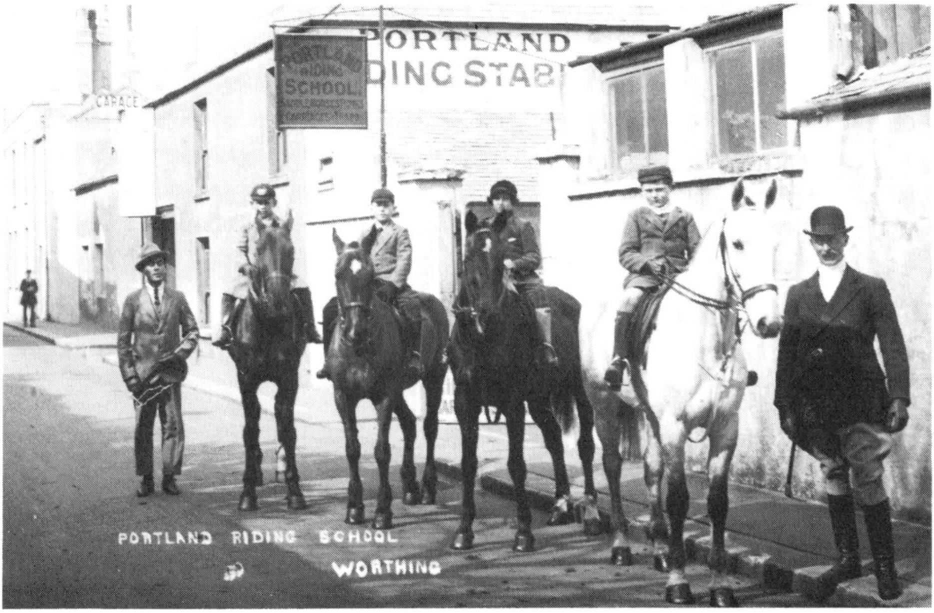


THE PORTLAND RIDING SCHOOL was near the southern end of Portland Road. This photograph was taken not long before it closed in 1936.

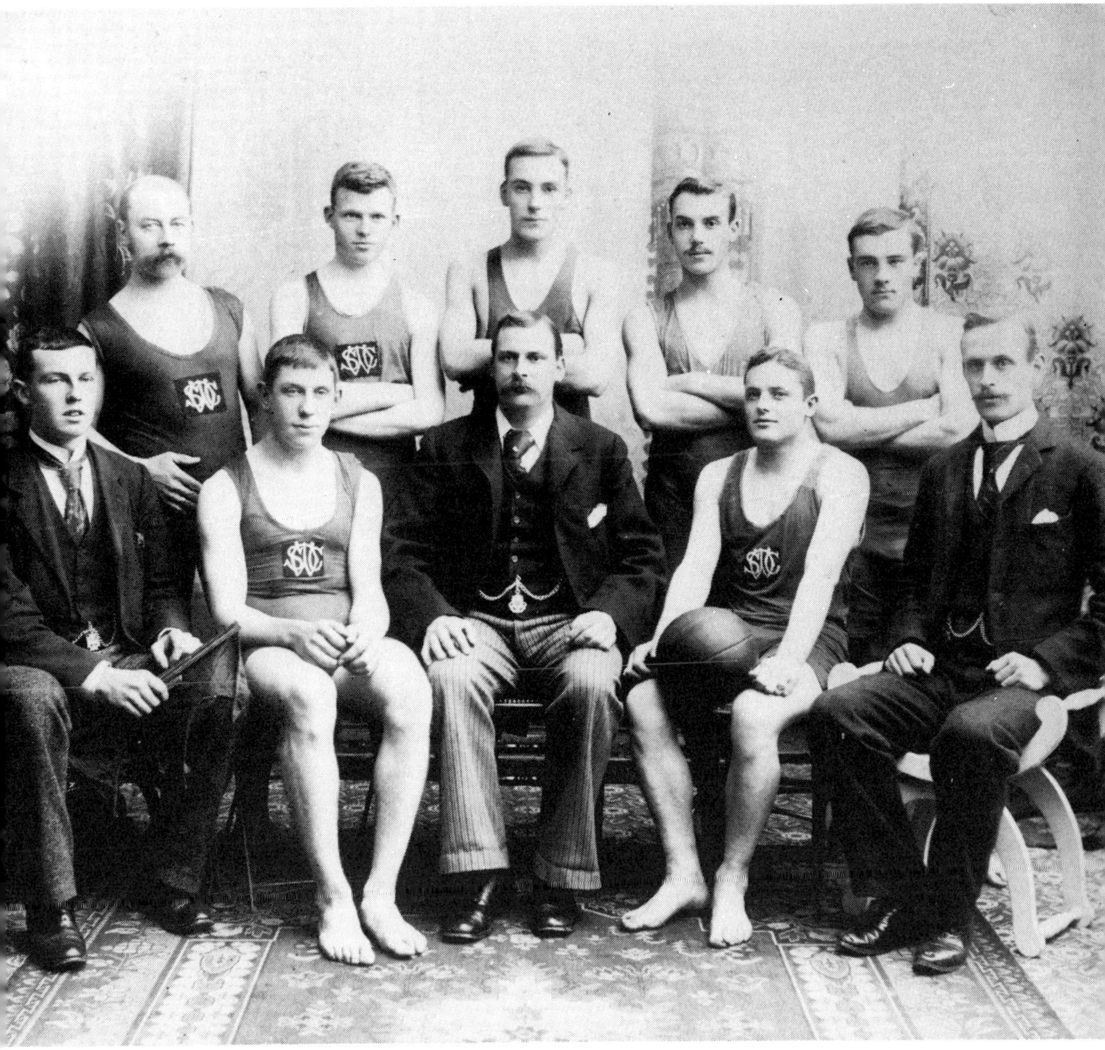

THE WORTHING WATER POLO TEAM were runners up in the Sussex junior championships in 1896. Back row, left to right: F. Urch, R. Isted, R.C. Paine, J.A. Tuff, H.D. Tee. Front row: J. Head, W.R. Paine, T. Greet, B.J. Blaker, W. Dean. W.R. Paine was also a noted local cyclist.

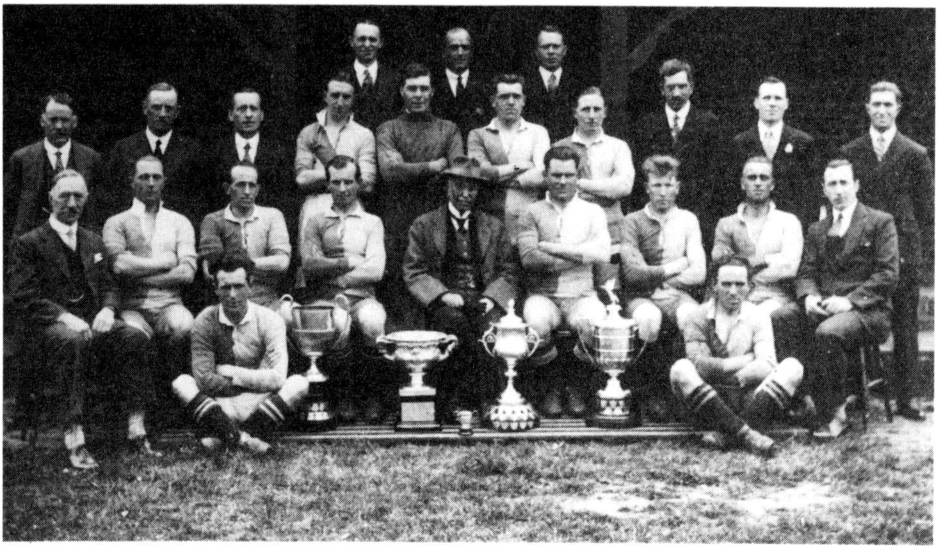

WORTHING FOOTBALL TEAM, after a very successful season in 1926 during which they carried off four trophies. Back row, left to right: J. Roberts, L. Manwaring, G. Wingfield. Second row: J. Patterson, H.E. Scott, H. Madgwick, A.H. Fuller, L. Steel, H. Clarke, J. Hills, E. Mould, J. Punter junior, A. Wady. Third row: R.J. Fry, L. Nairn, A. Norgett, J. Langmaid, T. Hawkins, E. Hanmore. Front row: J. Hide, F. Northcott. The club celebrated its centenary in 1986.

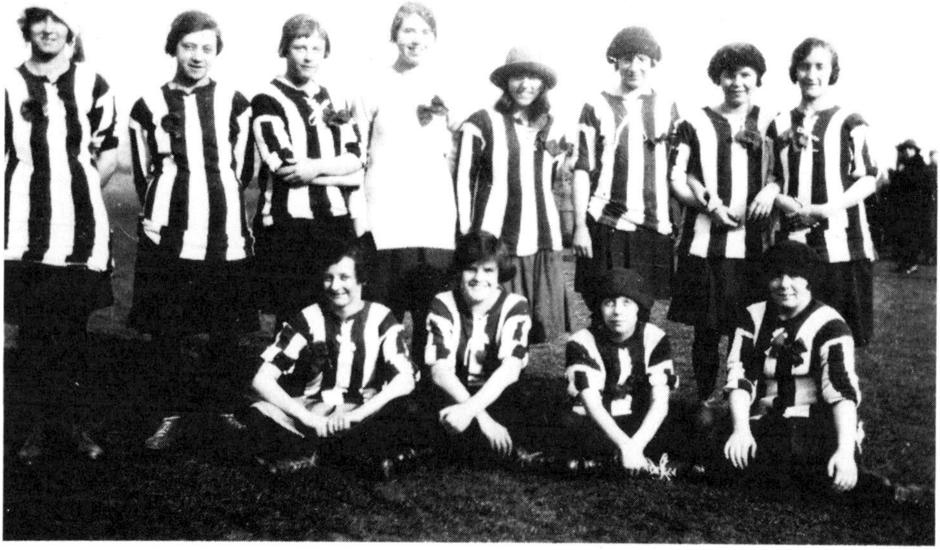

THE WORTHING LADIES FOOTBALL TEAM played a number of successful charity matches during the 1920s. The captain was H.K. Williams and the other players were D. Slaughter, D. Steel, L. Harvey, K. Baker, G. Steele, W. Chipper, R. Peake, E. Neal, G. Lyne and D. Neal.

SECTION SEVEN

# Parks and Gardens

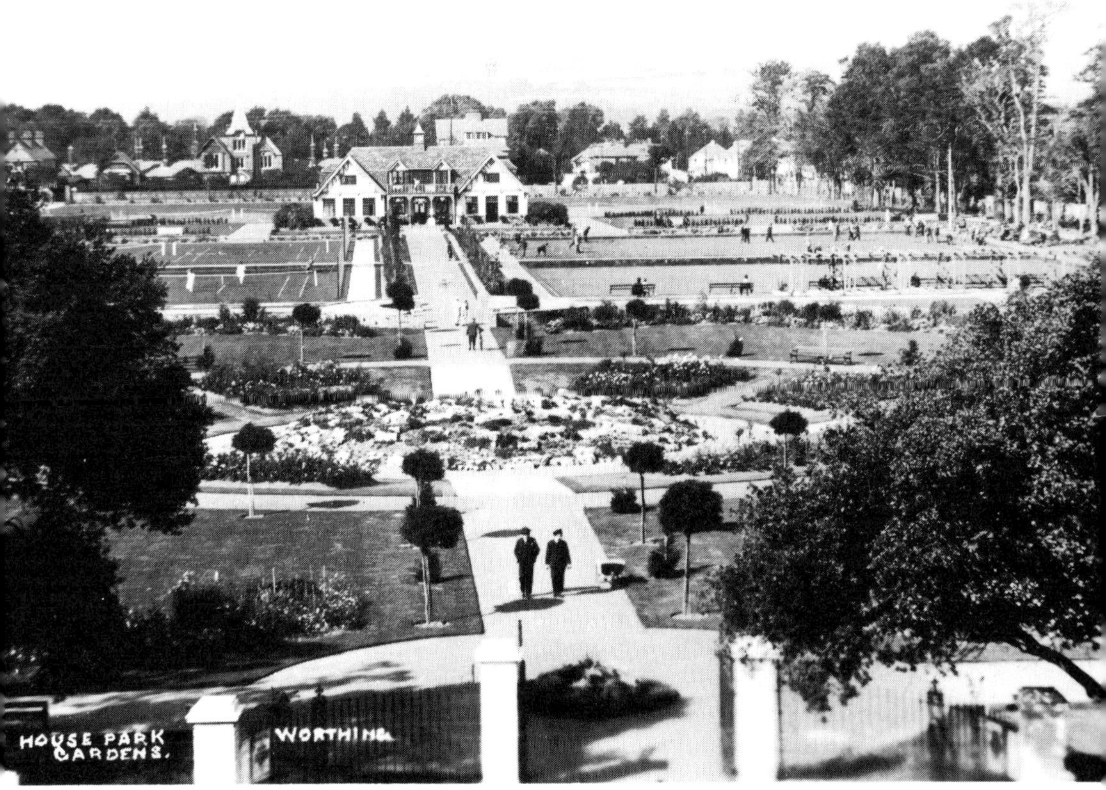


BEACH HOUSE PARK is the site of a very unusual memorial. Actress Nancy Price and the People's Theatre, London erected a memorial and bird bath in the round flower bed which says, 'In memory of warrior birds who gave their lives on active service 1939–45 and for the use and pleasure of living birds'.

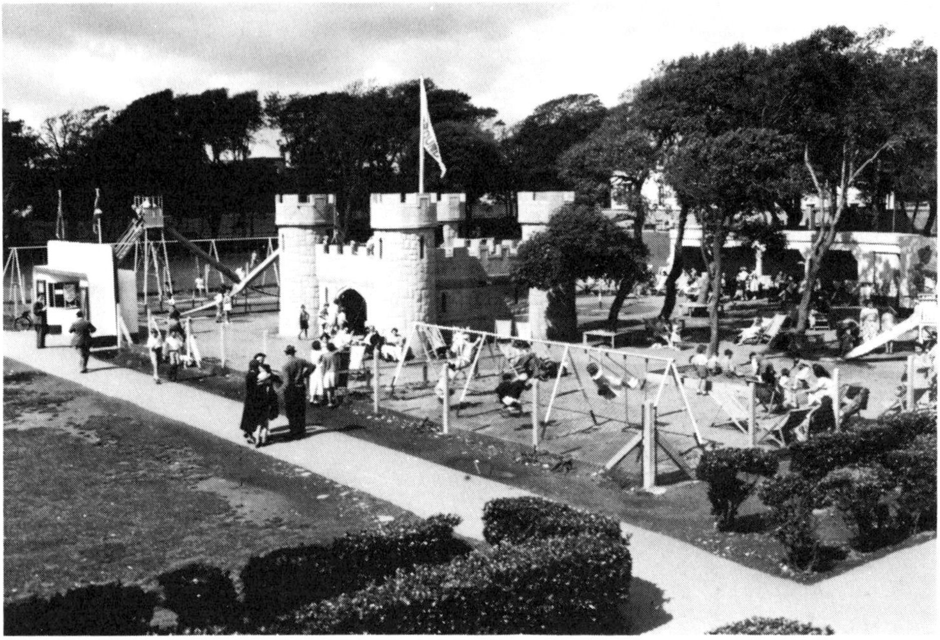

PETER PAN'S PLAYGROUND is just behind the promenade, near the Aquarena. The playground has given delight to thousands of children, like those in this picture from the 1950s. Today it looks sadly run down.

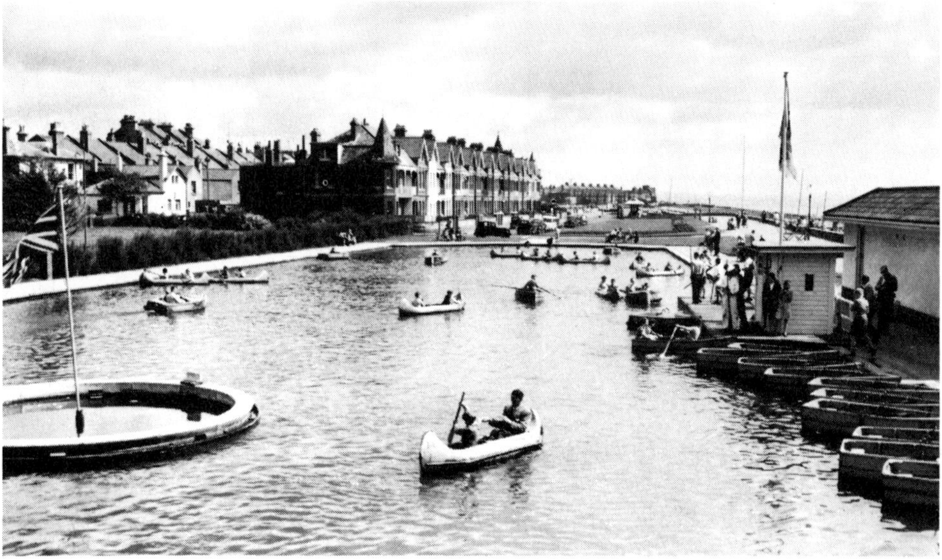

THE BOATING LAKE on the seafront near Peter Pan's Playground, where generations of families have enjoyed themselves in canoes and rowing boats. It is, regrettably, no longer used as a boating lake.

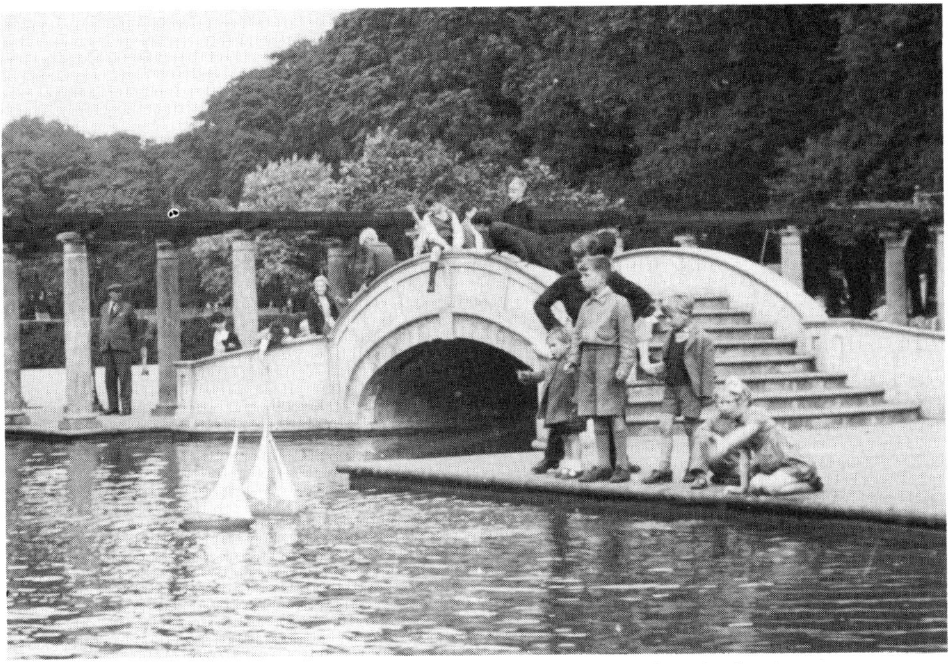

THIS BRIDGE is between the shallow pool and the boating lake beside the Aquarena.

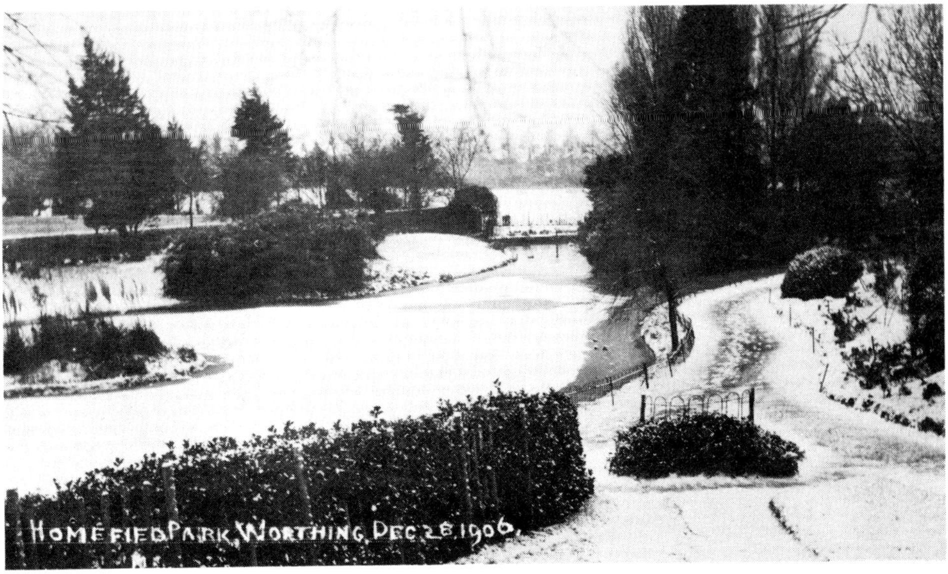


LASTING SNOW is a rarity in Worthing, but even this modest fall on 28 December 1906 added a gentle beauty to Homefield Park.

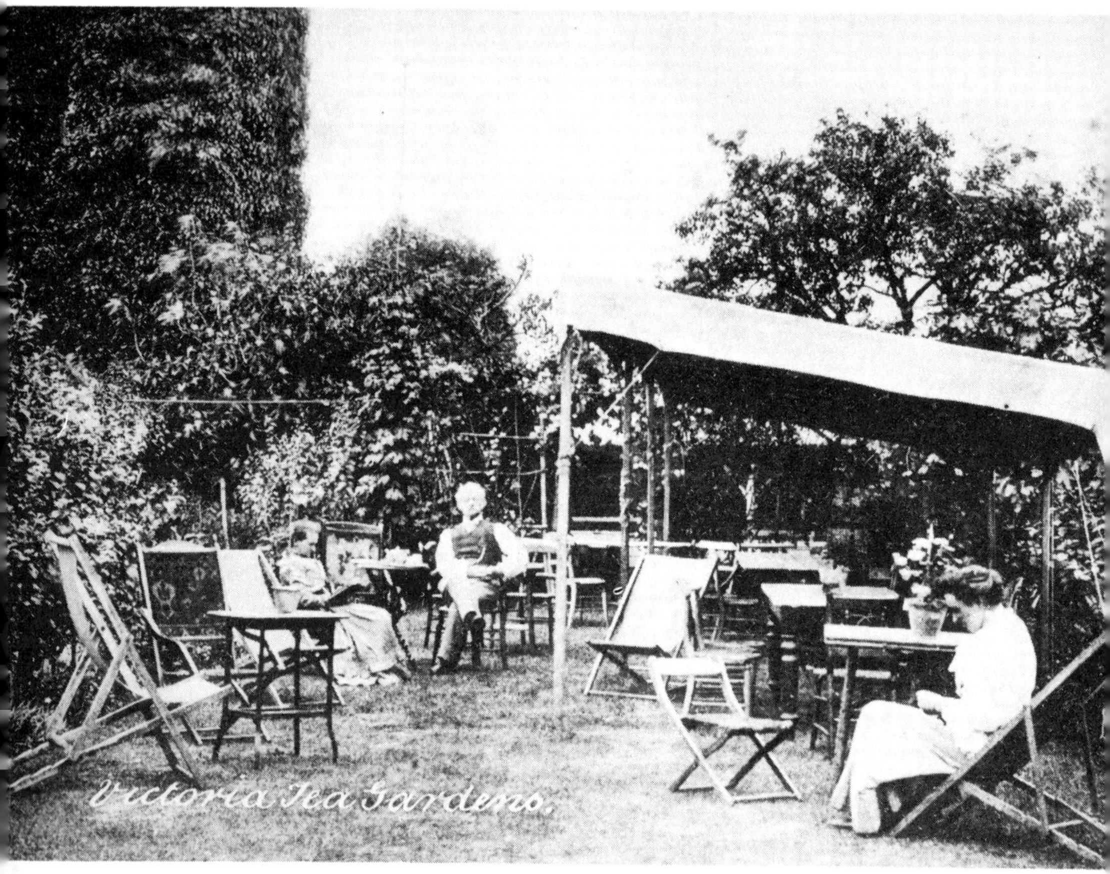


THE VICTORIA TEA GARDENS were in South Street, West Tarring, early in the twentieth century. The owner and caterer was Alfred Carter. It looked more like someone's garden, with a few extra tables and chairs, than a proper café.

SECTION EIGHT

# War and Peace

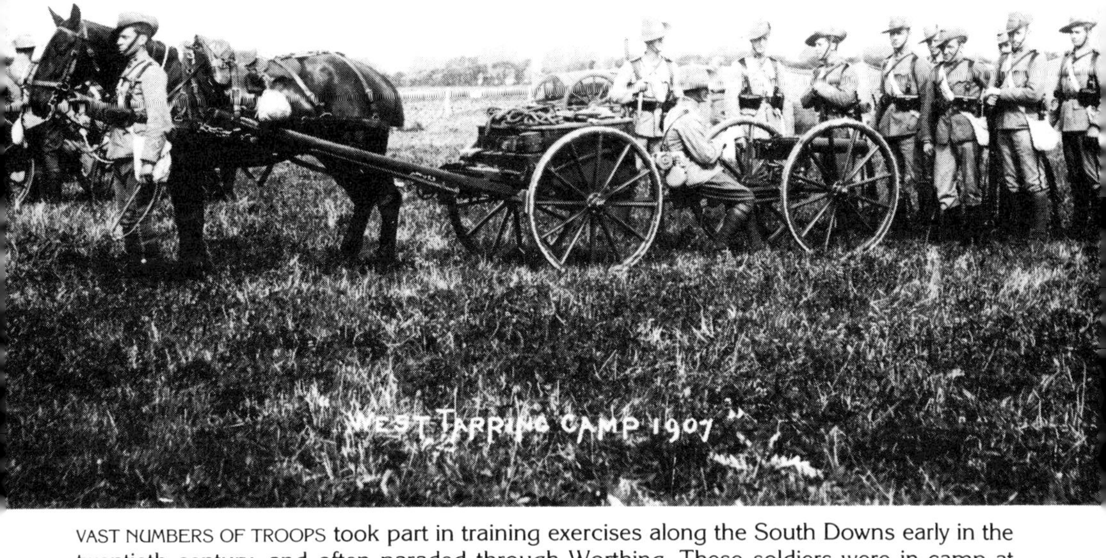


VAST NUMBERS OF TROOPS took part in training exercises along the South Downs early in the twentieth century, and often paraded through Worthing. These soldiers were in camp at Tarring in 1907.

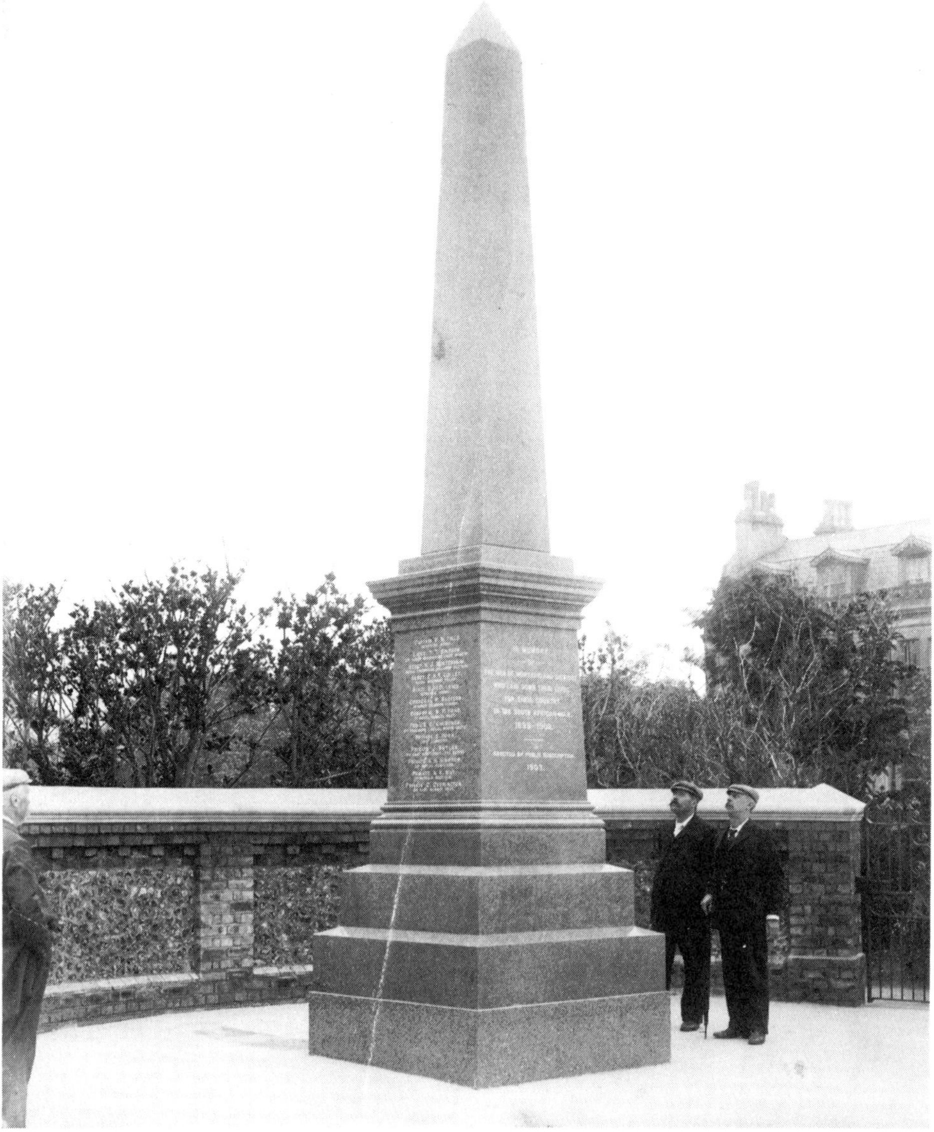

THIS OBELISK was unveiled at the southern end of Steyne Gardens on 8 August 1903. It commemorates the twenty-six local men who died in the South African Wars between 1899 and 1902.

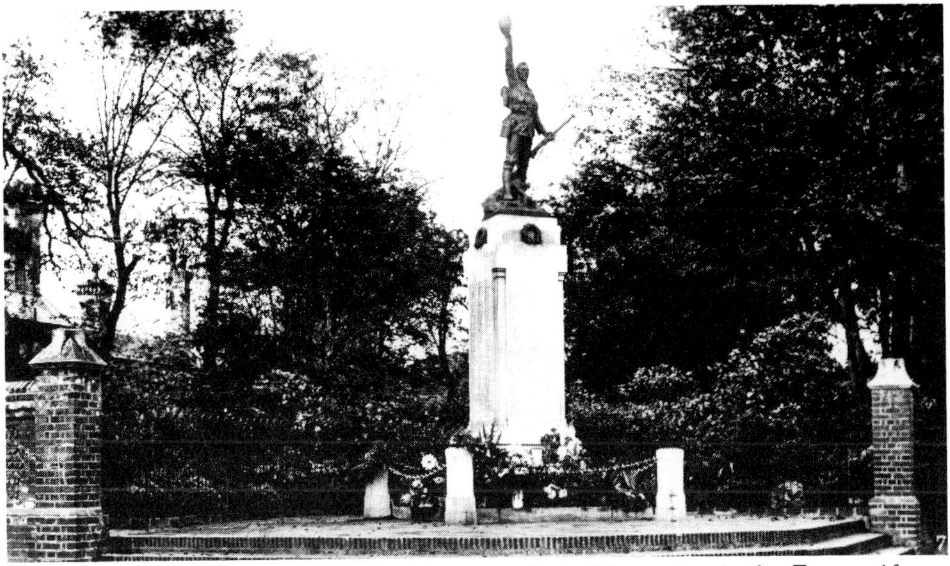

DURING THE FIRST WORLD WAR 660 Worthing men died while serving in the Forces. After a number of abortive plans, this memorial was erected to their memory. On the corner of Stoke Abbot Road and Chapel Road, it is over eighteen feet high and consists of a Portland stone column topped by a bronze statue of a soldier. The names of the 342 local men who died in the Forces during the Second World War were later added to the memorial.

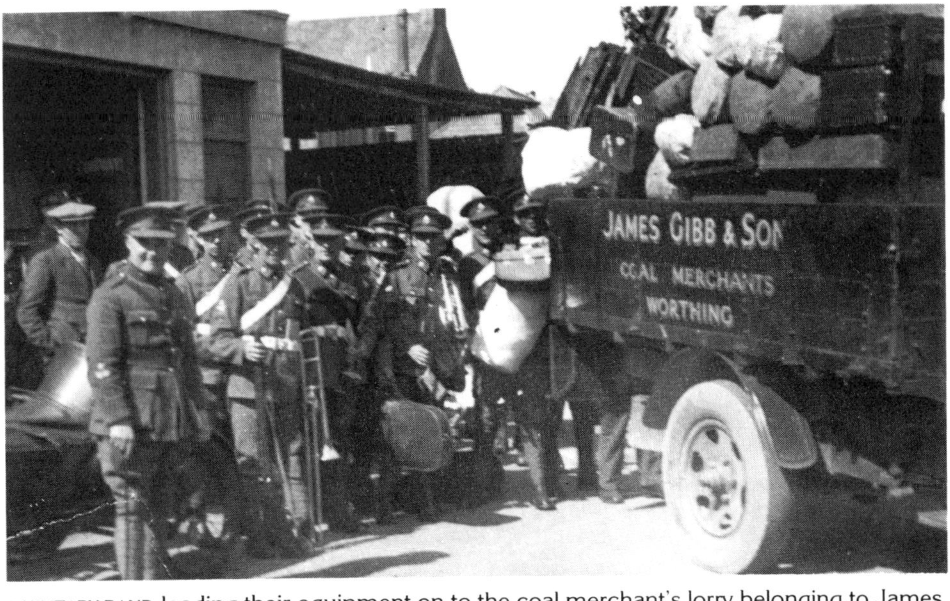


A MILITARY BAND loading their equipment on to the coal merchant's lorry belonging to James Gibb in Little High Street.

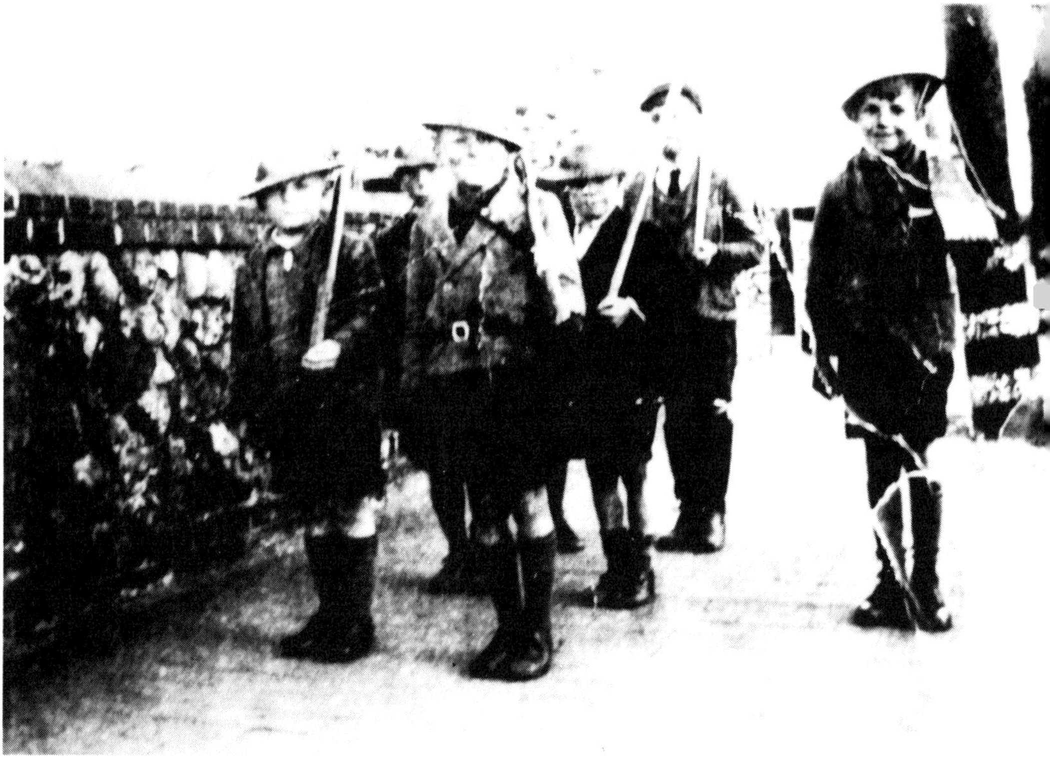

THESE LADS WERE SNAPPED IN SOUTH FARM ROAD while pretending to be members of the Home Guard. Their 'guns' may have been sticks, but most of them had managed to get hold of a tin hat to add a touch of authenticity to the game.

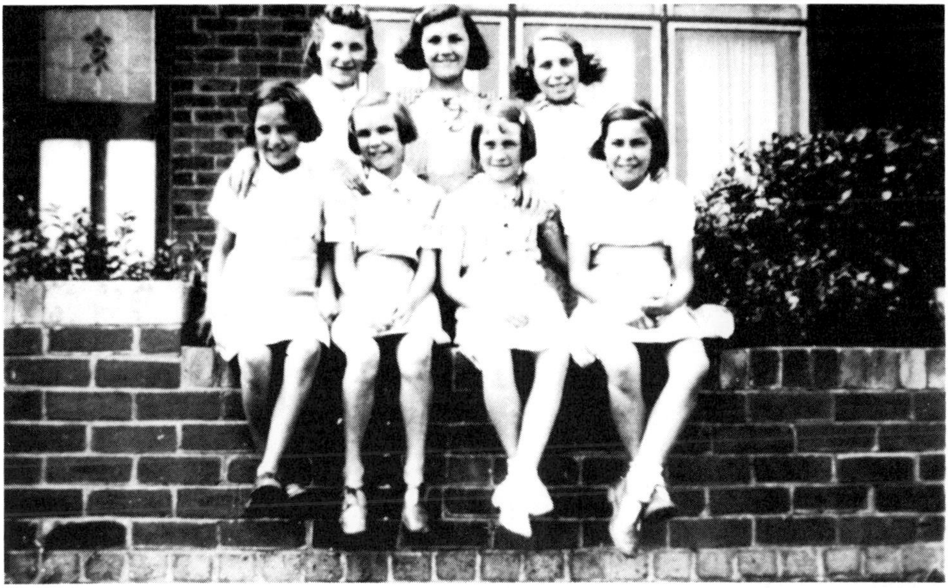

A GERMAN INVASION was considered a real possibility in 1941 and thousands of local children were evacuated to Nottinghamshire and Leicestershire. These seven friends from Holy Trinity School in Howard Street went to Mansfield in Nottinghamshire. Back row, left to right: Joan Simmonds, Jean Saunders, Trixie Gratwicke. Front row: Marie Gladwell, Pamela Saunders, Connie Simmonds, Phyllis Gladwell.

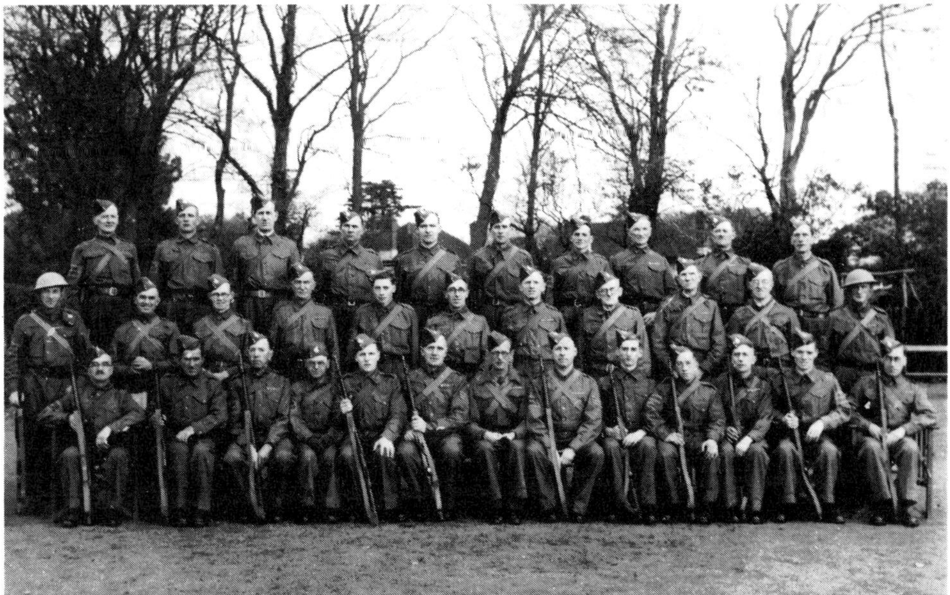

A GROUP PHOTOGRAPH OF D COMPANY of the Worthing Home Guard, pictured in Broadwater.

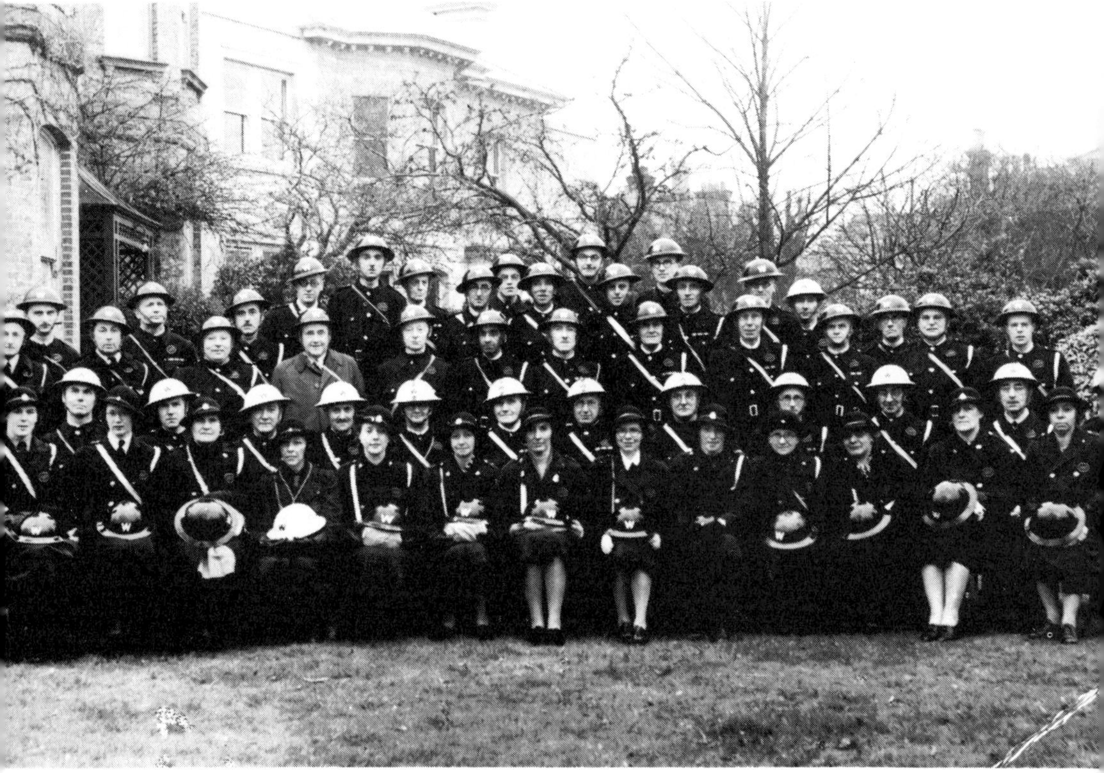

WORTHING GROUP 3 CENTRAL AIR RAID WARDENS in the grounds of a house in Liverpool Gardens. Their group headquarters was nearby. Captain Wilson, head warden of the group, is in the centre of the second row. Like all head wardens, he is wearing a white helmet.

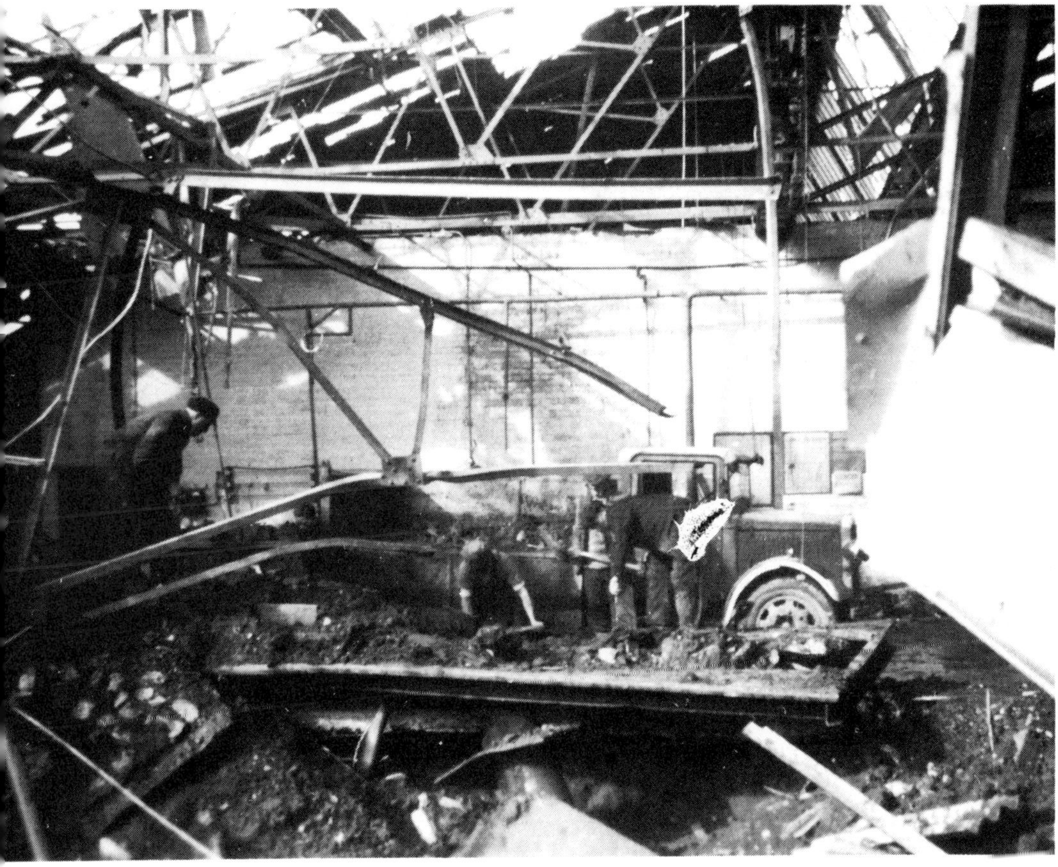

THESE MEN ARE WORKING in the ruins of Hall and Company's Park Road depot after it was bombed in March 1940.

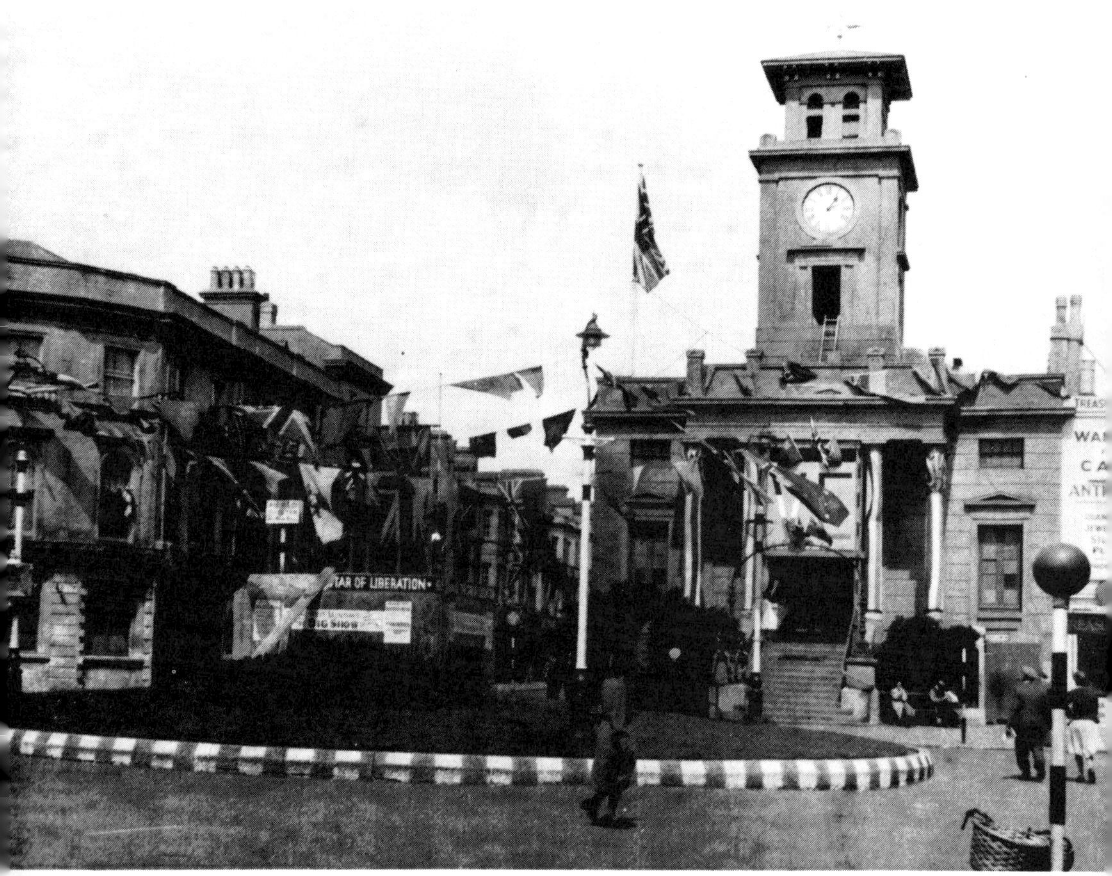


VICTORY IN EUROPE (VE) DAY on 8 May 1945. The roundabout and old town hall are decked with flags and bunting. In the centre of the roundabout is the concrete pillbox which was nicknamed 'Hyam Already'. It is decorated with posters. The pillbox was so strong that workmen had great difficulty demolishing it after the war.

SECTION NINE

# Religious Life

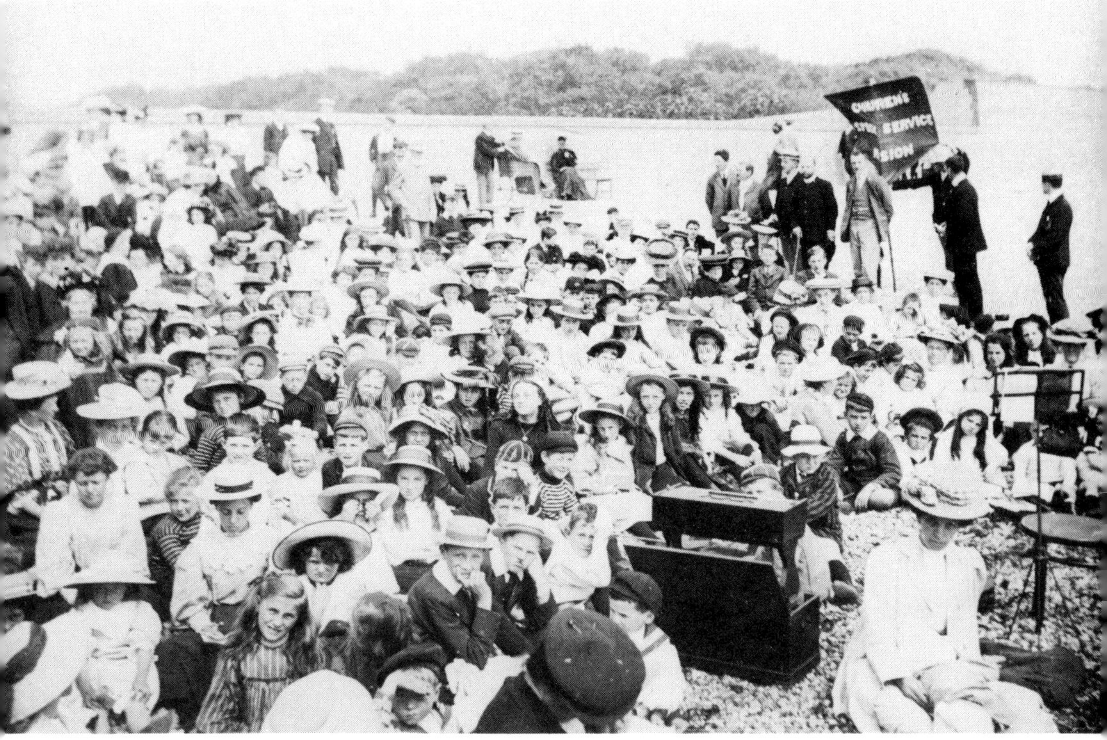

THIS GROUP ATTENDED A MEETING OF THE CHILDREN'S SPECIAL SERVICE MISSION on the beach at Splash Point in September 1907. The music stand and harmonium are ready for use, but everyone is looking at the camera. Most of the children are wearing hats and a number have striped jerseys.

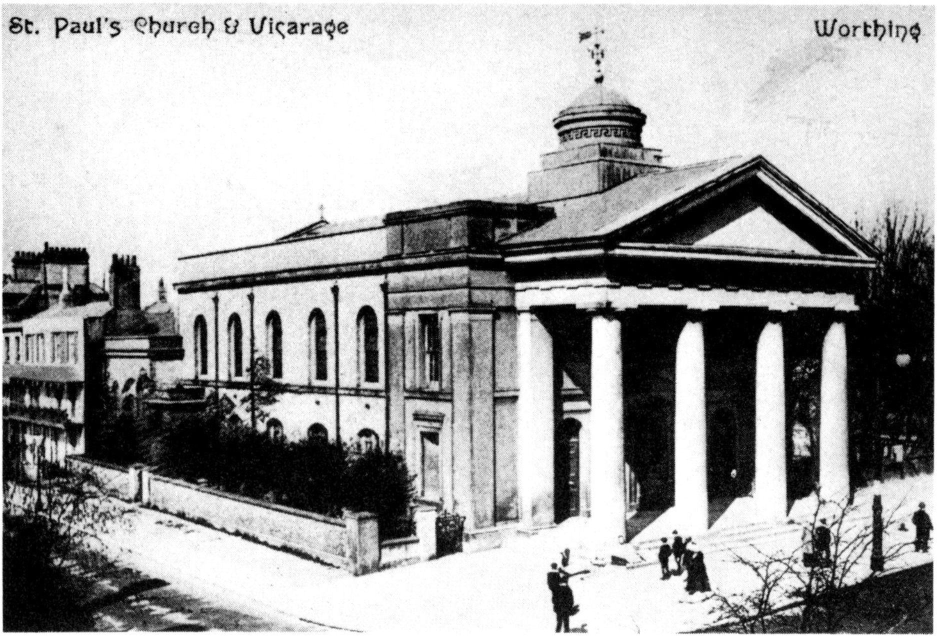


THERE WAS NO CHURCH IN WORTHING until the early nineteenth century. In 1812 the chapel of ease, linked to Broadwater church, was opened on the corner of Chapel Road and Ambrose Place. It was designed by John B. Rebecca. Later renamed St Paul's, it had pews which were bought, sold or leased to help finance the running of the church.

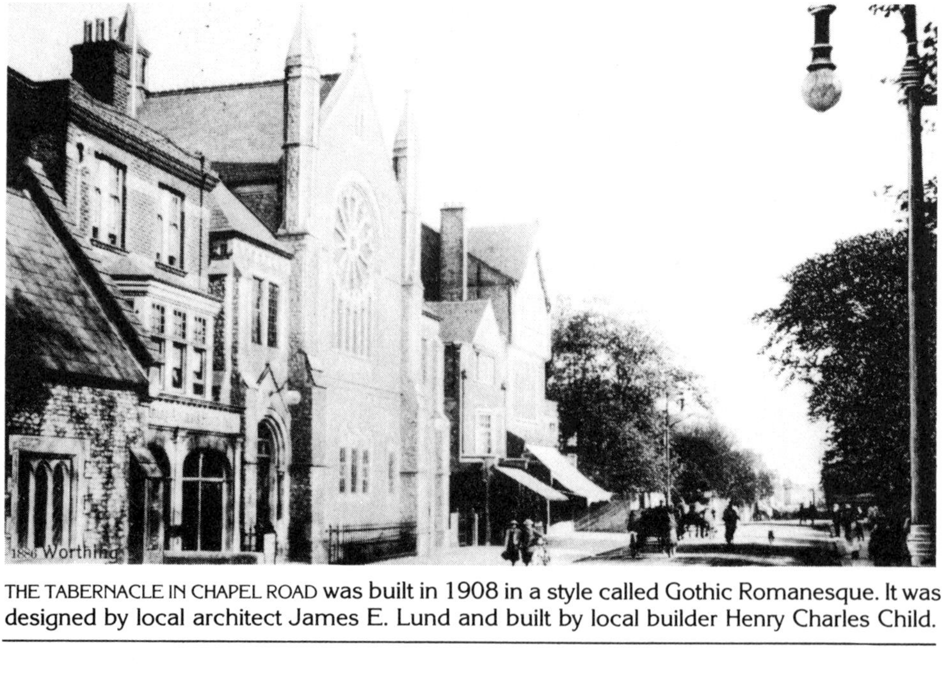


THE TABERNACLE IN CHAPEL ROAD was built in 1908 in a style called Gothic Romanesque. It was designed by local architect James E. Lund and built by local builder Henry Charles Child.

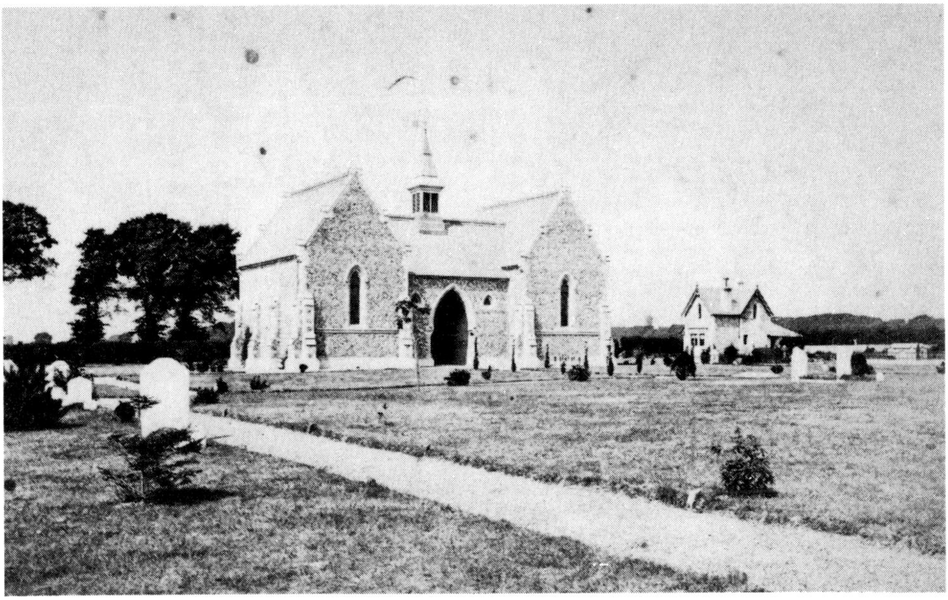

THE TWIN CHAPELS IN BROADWATER CEMETERY were designed by Charles Hyde and opened in 1852. This picture was taken *c.* 1860 and shows how few people had then been buried there. The cemetery is now crowded and neglected. People buried there include the first mayor of Worthing, Alfred Cortis, and two naturalists, Richard Jefferies and William Henry Hudson.

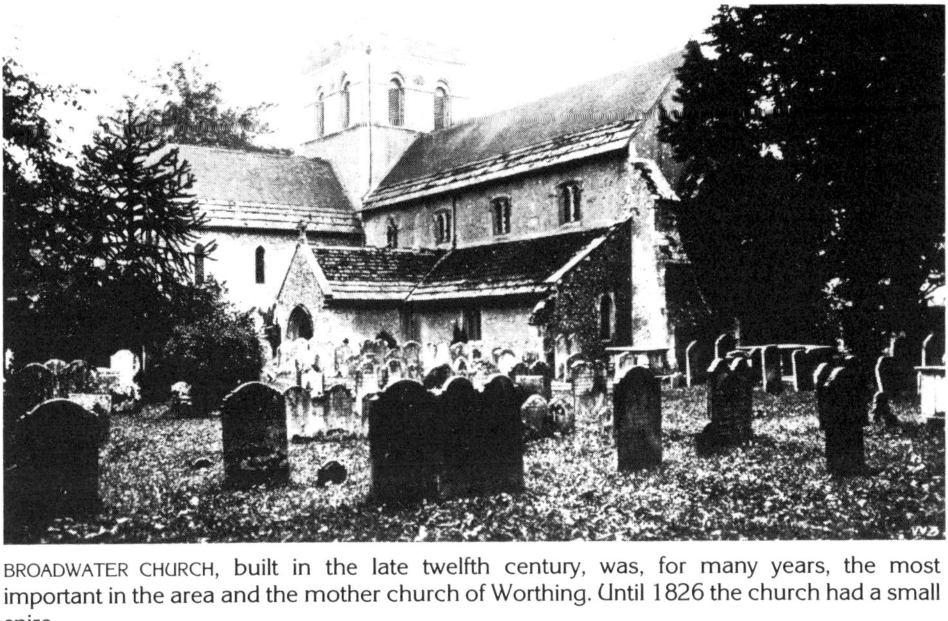

BROADWATER CHURCH, built in the late twelfth century, was, for many years, the most important in the area and the mother church of Worthing. Until 1826 the church had a small spire.

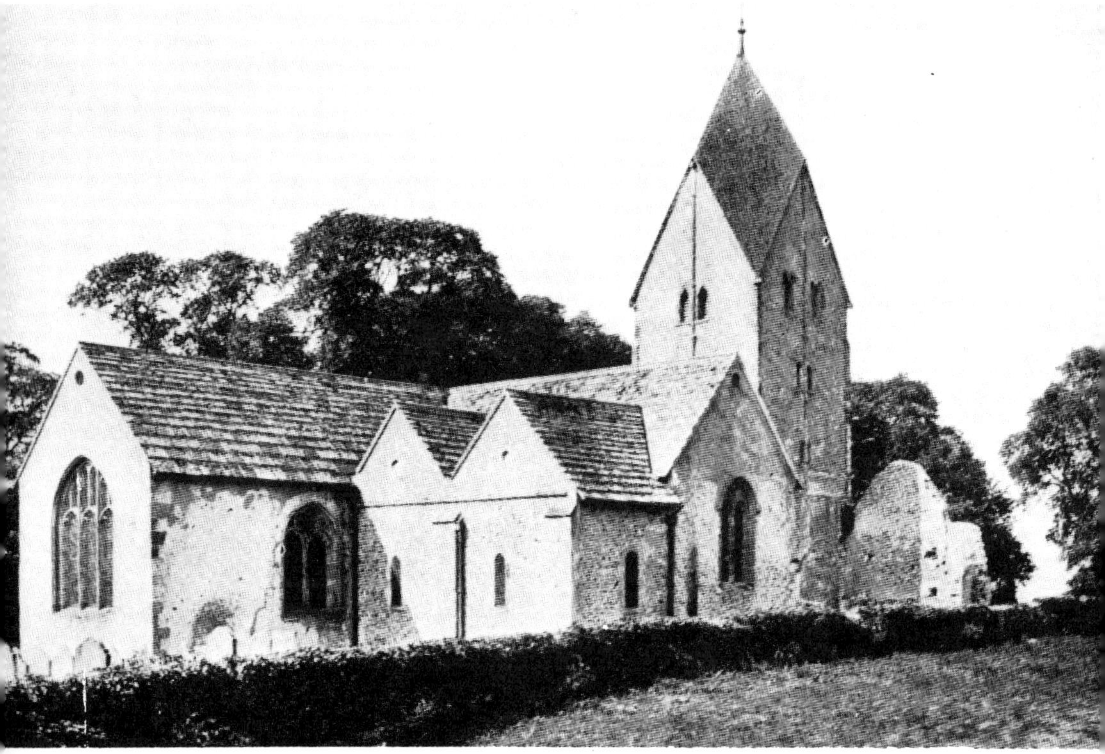

THE UNUSUAL RHENISH HELM TOWER on Sompting church has made it a landmark since it was built about nine hundred years ago. The church contains several pieces of interesting Anglo-Saxon sculpture. Built on the lower slope of the Downs, the church has been separated from Sompting village by the main A27 road.

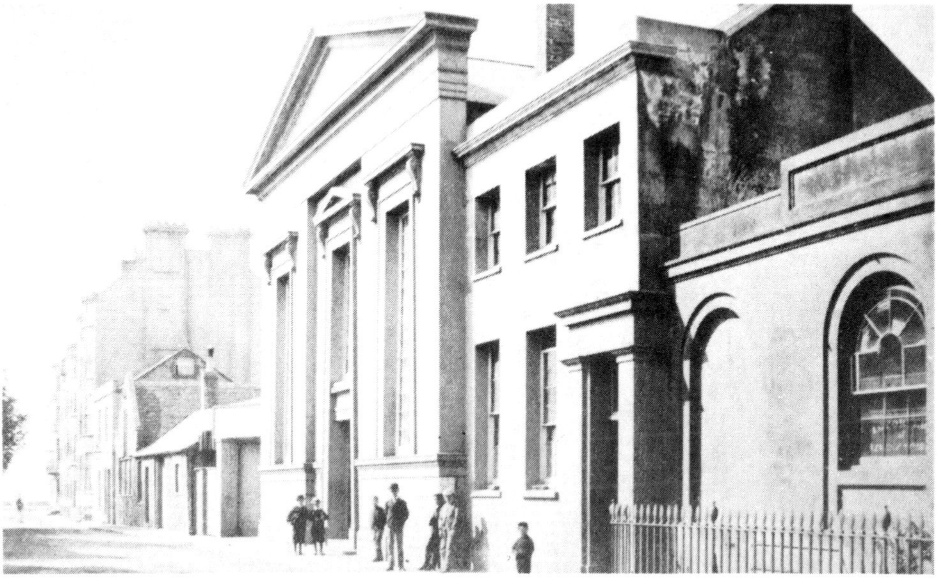

THE WESLEYAN CHAPEL in Bedford Row was designed by Charles Hyde and opened in 1838. It was the town's second Wesleyan chapel. The original was a smaller one in Marine Place. The Bedford Row chapel was later renamed Bedford Hall and used by Patching and Company as an auction room.

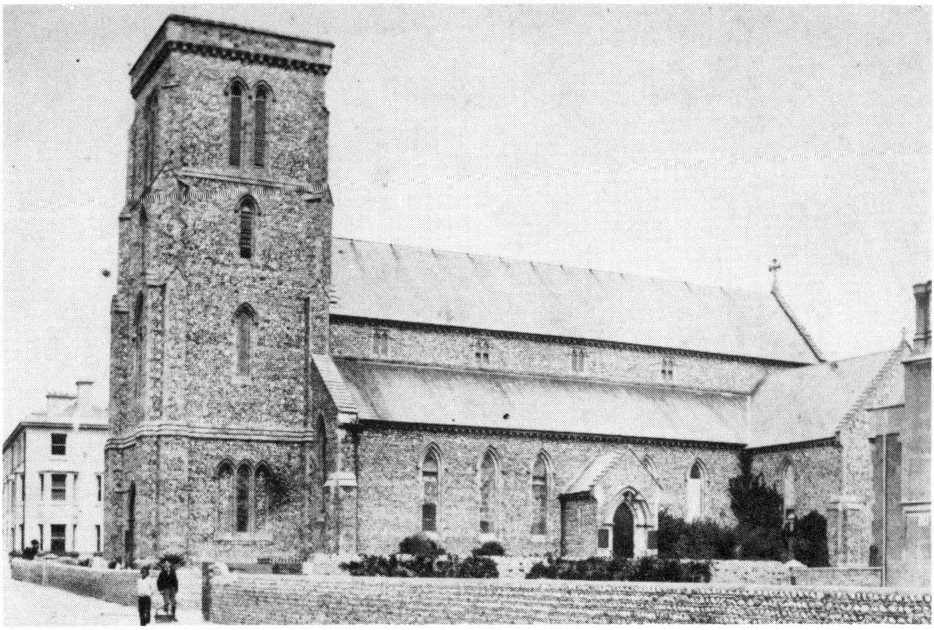

CHRISTCHURCH, with its fine flint walls, was built in 1841 and became the parish church of Worthing in 1855.

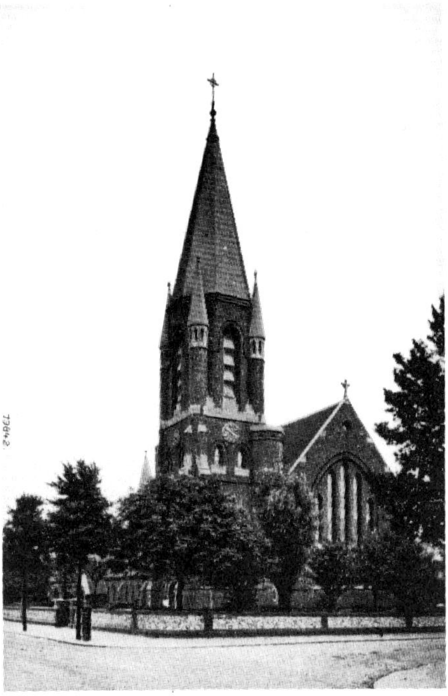

HOLY TRINITY CHURCH in Shelley Road opened in 1883 and is unusual among local churches in being built of red brick. The tower was added in 1887. In the late nineteenth century Worthing was spreading to the west and Holy Trinity was built for the people in the new Gratwicke Estate.

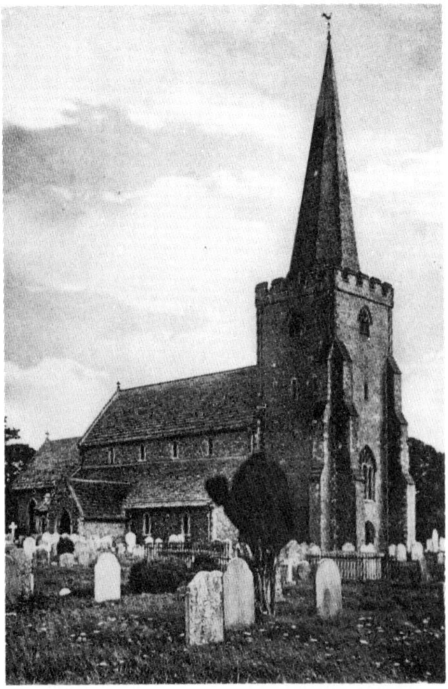

THE NAVE IS THE OLDEST PART of St Andrew's church in Tarring and was built in the late thirteenth century. The chancel and tower were added in the early fifteenth century and the vestry in 1853.

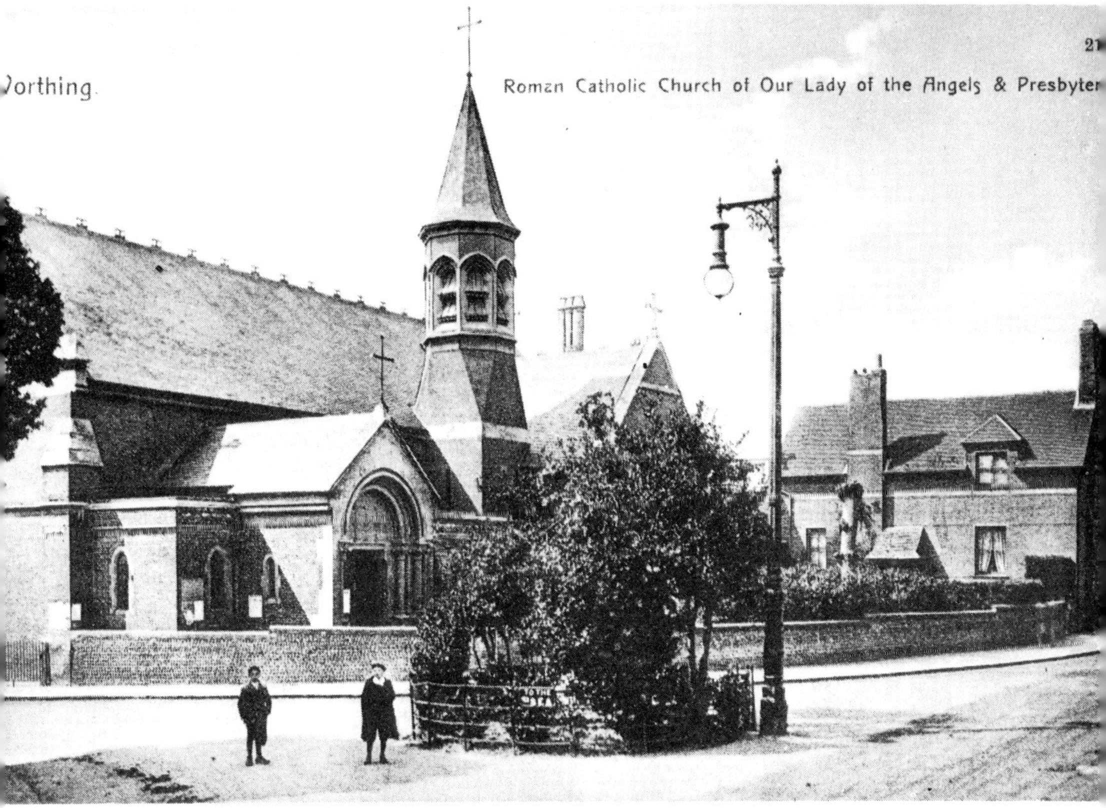


THE CHURCH OF ST MARY OF THE ANGELS in Crescent Road was founded by Thomas Gaisford of Offington and is attached to the Convent of Our Lady of Sion. The church and convent opened in 1864. This was the first Roman Catholic church in Worthing.

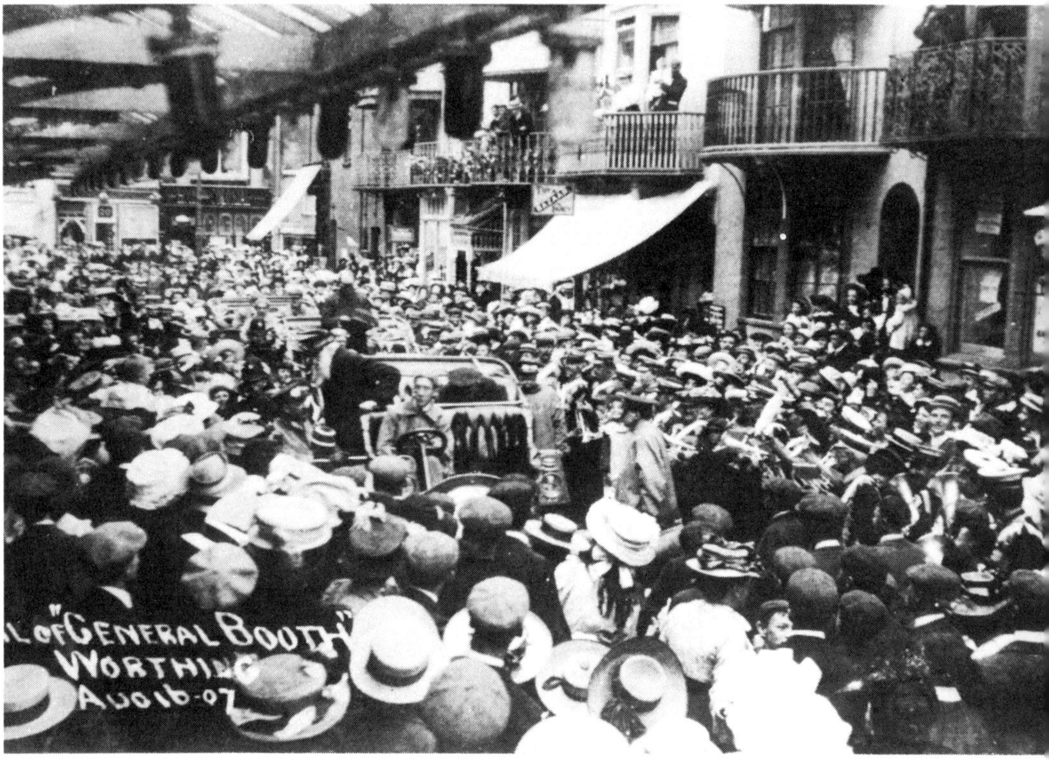


WHEN THE SALVATION ARMY WAS STARTED BY GENERAL BOOTH it was opposed by many people who felt threatened by its militant moral stance. There were demonstrations in a number of towns. In Worthing these were so bad the Home Secretary intervened and ordered that the disturbances be stopped once and for all. A small band of Salvationists arrived in Worthing to 'fight Satan' in 1883. They targetted the Worthing Excelsior Bonfire Club, a group already well-known for disorderly behaviour, and before long the Salvation Army could only operate with police support. For a while they had to suspend their Sunday parades. In April 1884 Captain Ada Smith arrived to lead the Salvation Army in Worthing. She refused to be intimidated and re-introduced the parades. Their opponents, calling themselves the Worthing Excelsior Skeleton Army, became increasingly aggressive and matters came to a head. On 17 August there were serious riots outside Montague Hall where the Salvation Army held their meetings. The ironmongers shop owned by George Head, a Salvation Army supporter, was attacked, and he fired on the mob. Three days later, after some of the Skeleton Army had appeared in court, the mob got out of hand. The police were joined by thirty-nine dragoons from Brighton and the Riot Act was read. The rioters only dispersed after the dragoons had charged into the crowd. The Salvation Army was accepted in time but periodic problems continued in Worthing until 1888. This picture shows General Booth arriving at Montague Hall on 16 August 1907.

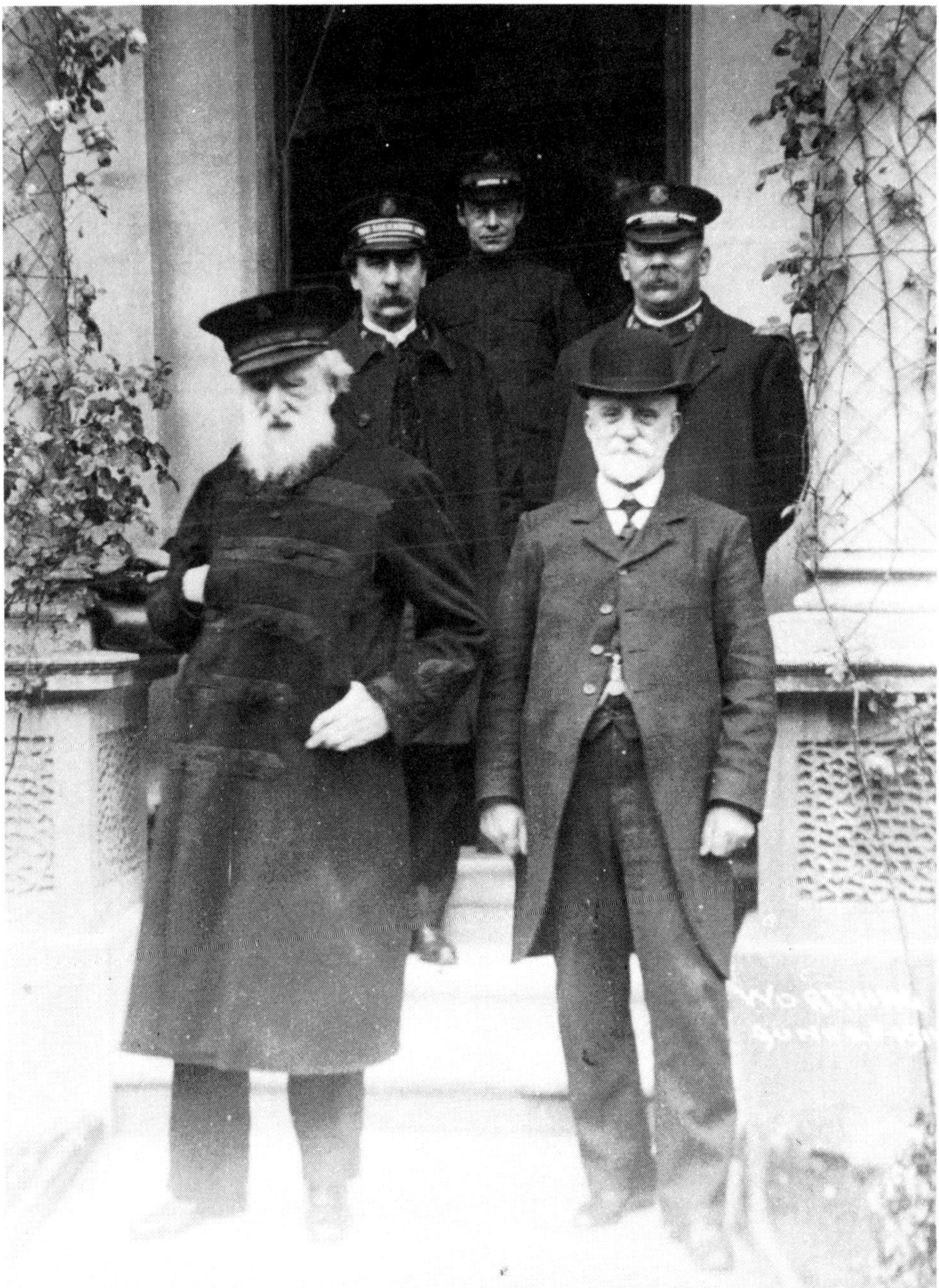


GENERAL BOOTH VISITED WORTHING again in 1911 and is seen on the left of this picture, by now a very old man. He is beside Mr Bentall, of Bentalls shop in South Street, and three Salvation Army officers.

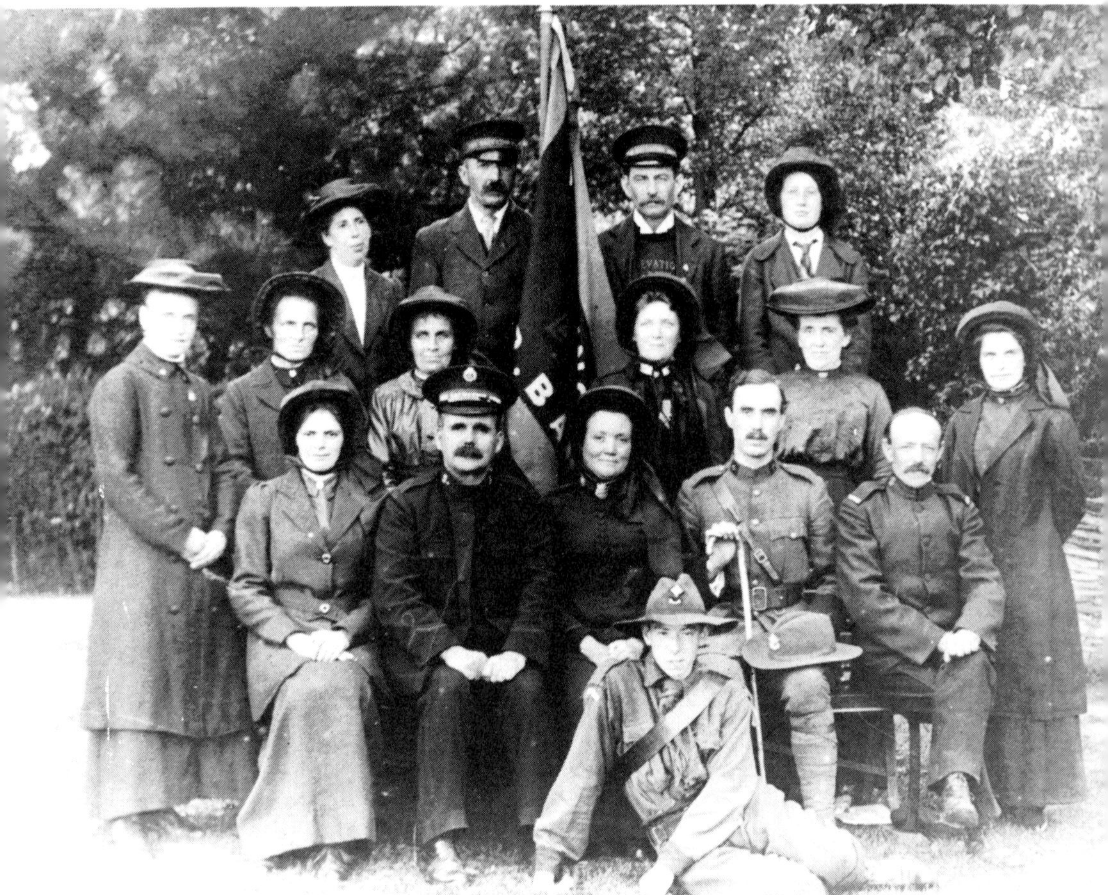

THE SALVATION ARMY'S FOLLOWING in Worthing grew and in 1912 a new citadel was opened in Crescent Road. This group consists of leaders of the Young People's League *c.* 1912.

## SECTION TEN

# Transport

THE SS *WORTHING BELLE* was one of a number of steamers which plied between coastal resorts around a hundred years ago. Owned by the Brighton, Worthing and South Coast Steamboat Company, she was built on the Clyde in 1885 and until 1901 she was called the *Diana Vernon*. In 1913 she was sold to Turkey.

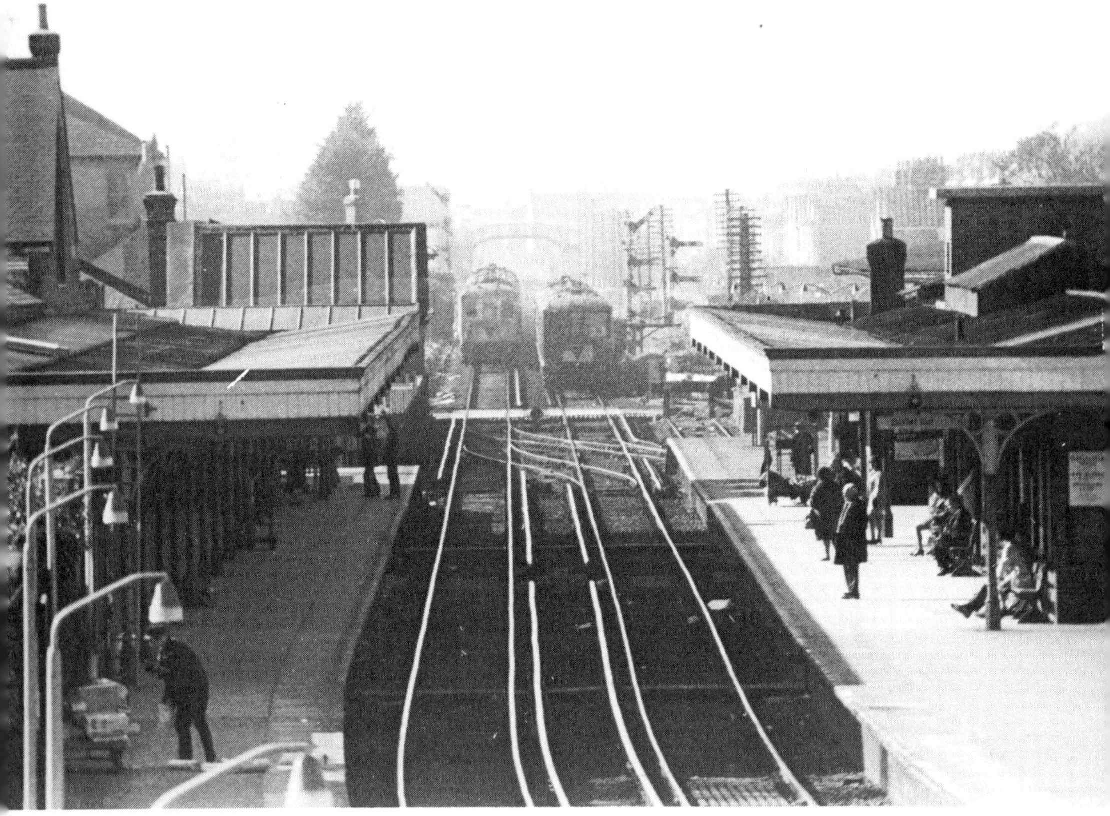

THE RAILWAY CAME TO WORTHING in 1845. A new station was built beside the first one in 1868. Rebuilt in 1911 it is still in use today. West Worthing station was added in 1889 and in 1933 the line was electrified.

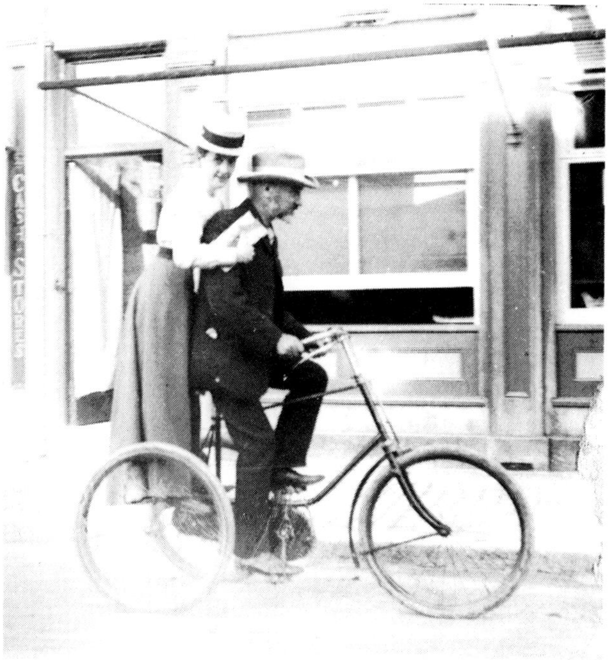

THE GENTLEMAN ON THIS TRICYCLE may be a member of the well-known Simpson family. Pictured in 1901, he appears to be concentrating hard on what he is doing, while his lady passenger has time to look, but not smile, at the camera.

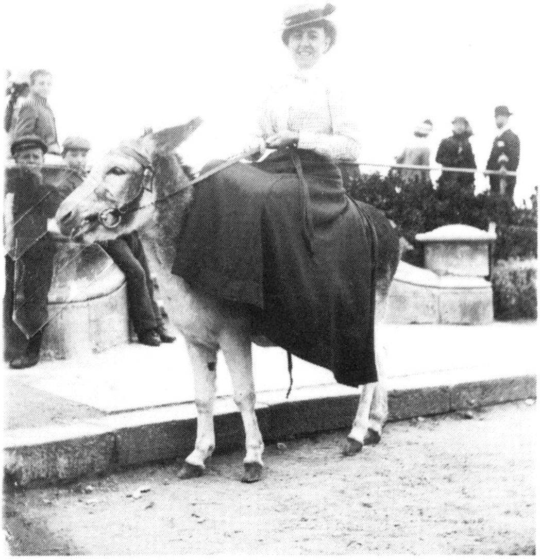

DONKEY RIDES have long been a popular part of seaside holidays. In nineteenth-century Worthing donkeys were also used to pull bath chairs from hotels to the beach. 'Jerusalem Ponies' appears to have been a local nickname for donkeys.

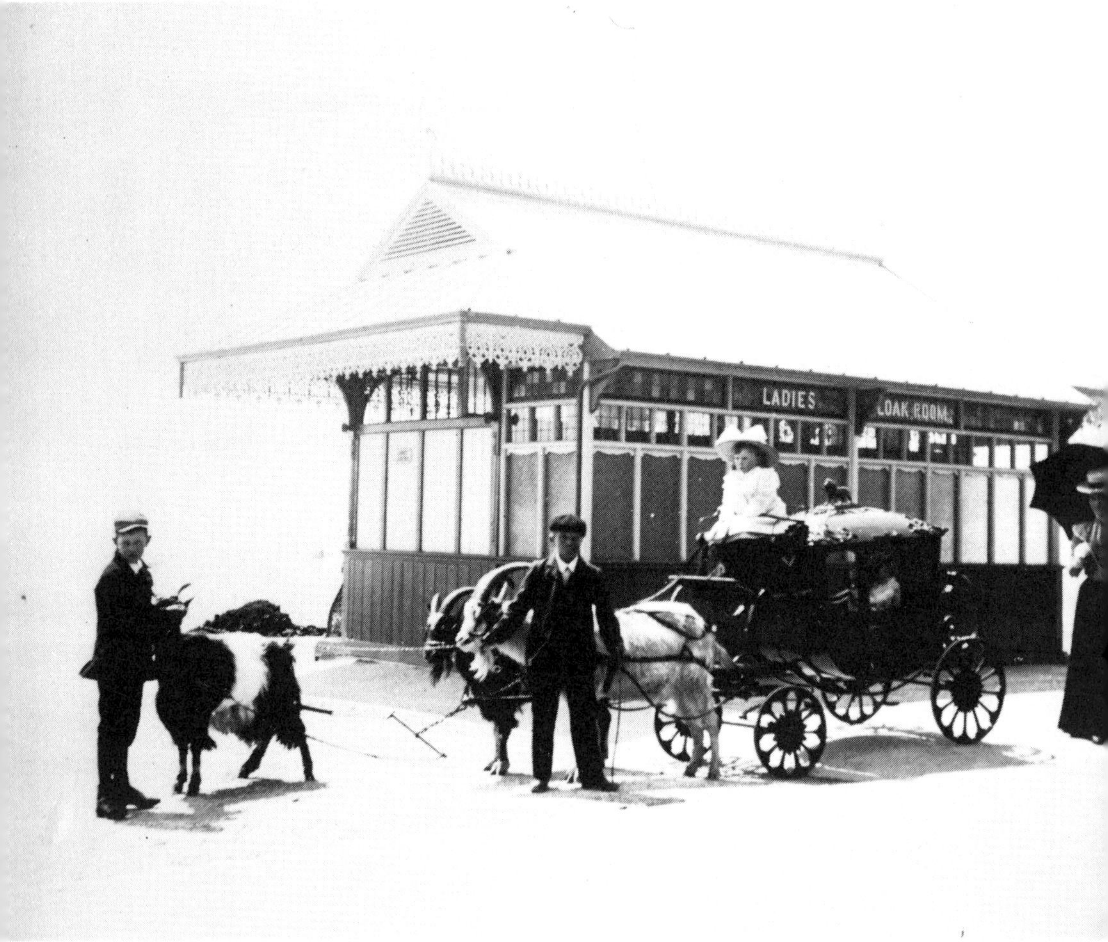


GOAT CARTS WERE A FEATURE OF WORTHING SEAFRONT for many years, giving rides to visitors. At times there were great debates in the council about how they could judge if the goats were fit enough to work. This elaborate 'Cinderella' coach was one of those which worked along the seafront.

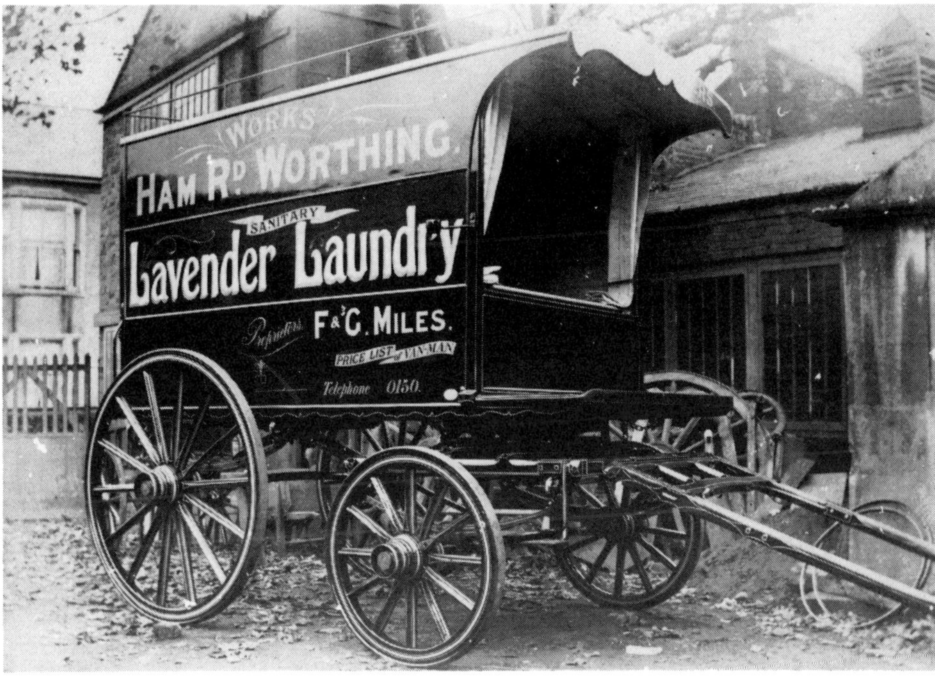


THIS WAGGON IS A FINE ADVERTISEMENT, not only for the Lavender Sanitary Laundry run by F. and C. Miles, but also for its makers, J. Boon and Sons.

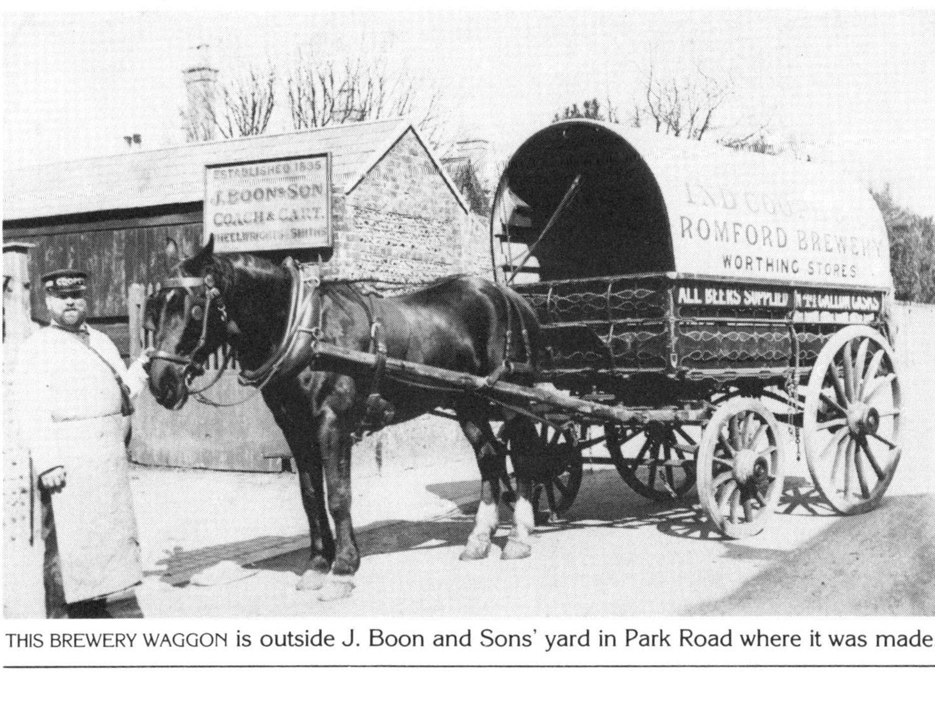


THIS BREWERY WAGGON is outside J. Boon and Sons' yard in Park Road where it was made.

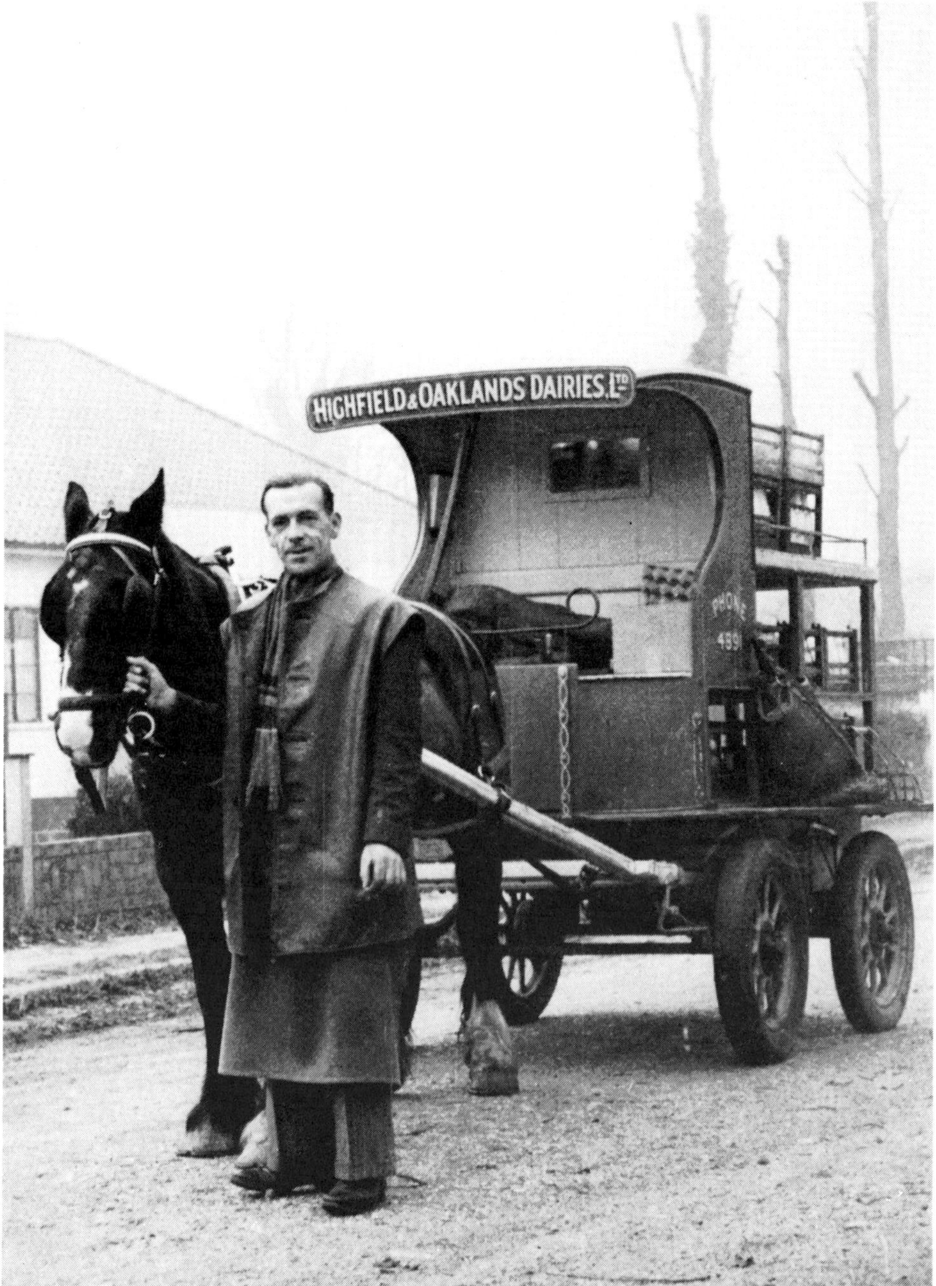


MR WELLS, pictured here with his horse and milk float, was a milkman for the Highfield and Oaklands Dairies Ltd.

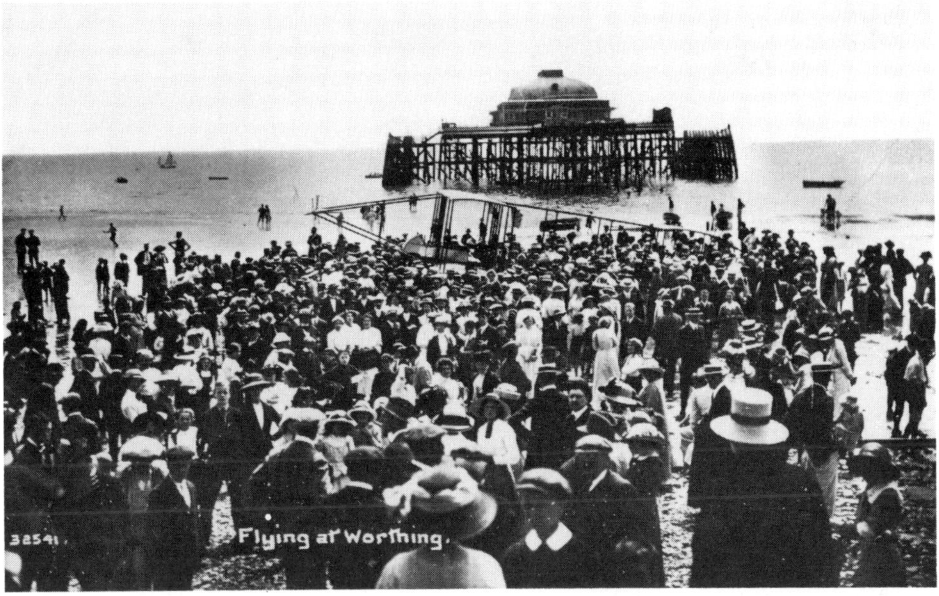


IN THE EARLY YEARS OF FLYING many planes landed on Worthing beach and at one time there were plans for a flying boat service from the seafront. As the ruined pier shows, this plane visited Worthing between 1913 and 1924, and as usual the plane drew a large crowd.

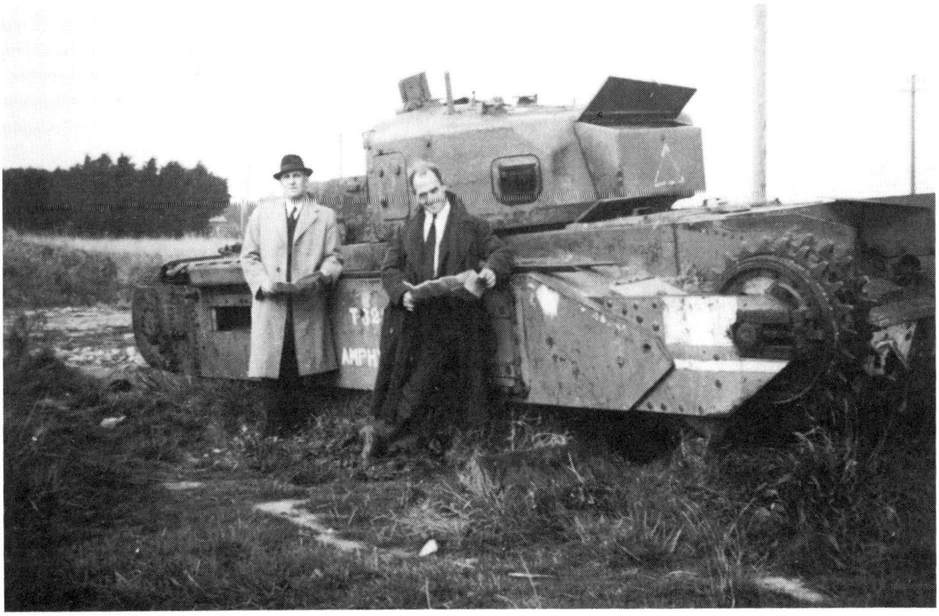

THE BACK OF THIS PHOTOGRAPH OF AN AMPHIBIOUS VEHICLE is labelled 'Being buried somewhere near Worthing 1945–6.' No one seems to know why it should have been buried or where it rests.

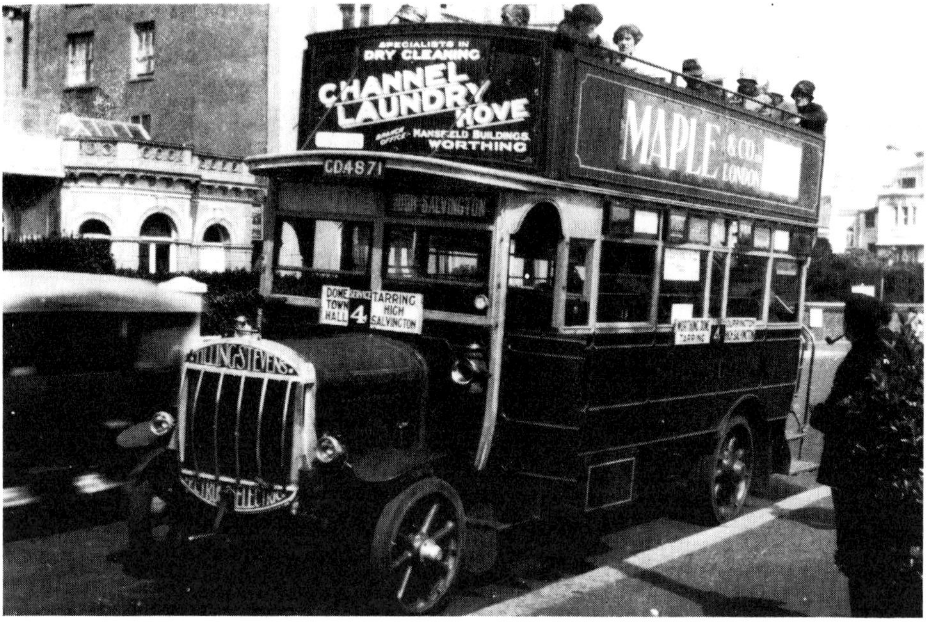


BUSES HAVE BEEN A USEFUL PLACE for showing advertisements for many years. This open-top Southdown bus is on Marine Parade, near Steyne Gardens.

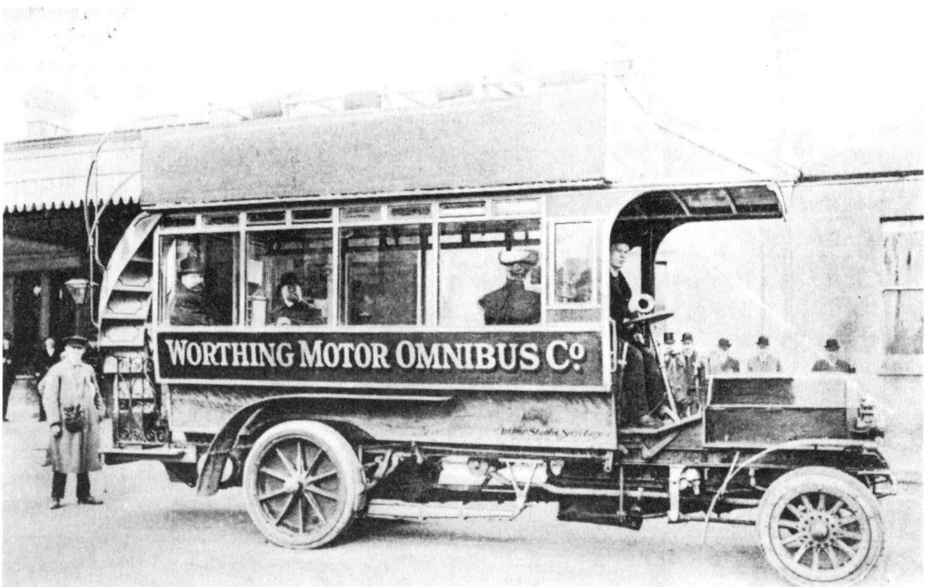


WORTHING MOTOR OMNIBUS COMPANY was founded in 1904 and competed, on local routes, with J. Town's buses. It later amalgamated with the Sussex Motor Road Car Company Ltd. The bus shown here is outside Worthing station.

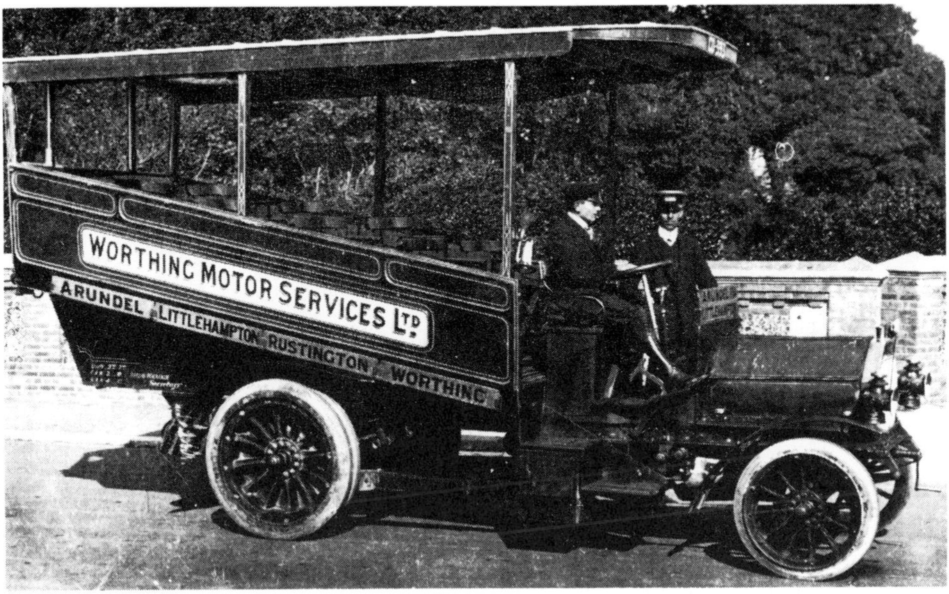


WORTHING MOTOR SERVICES LTD took over the Sussex Motor Road Car Company Ltd in 1909. In 1910 they adopted a green livery for the buses. This peculiar, sloping bus was on the Arundel to Worthing route.

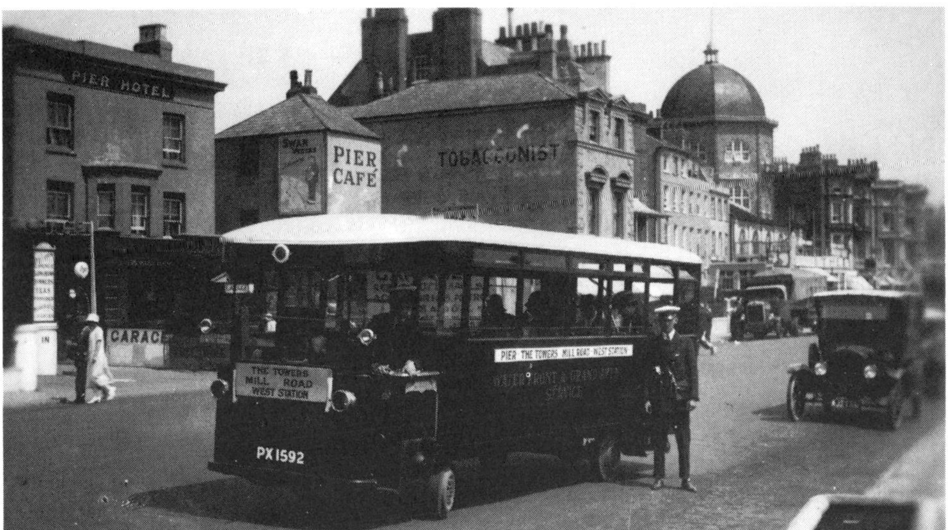


TRAMOCARS WERE SMALL SINGLE-DECK ELECTRIC BUSES with tram-like controls. They were made by Shelvoke and Drury. They were introduced by W.R. Gates in 1924 and ran from Splash Point to Grand Avenue. The service was successful and was soon extended. The Tramocars were red with gold lettering. In 1938 Tramocars were taken over by Southdown who later replaced them with single-deck Leyland buses.

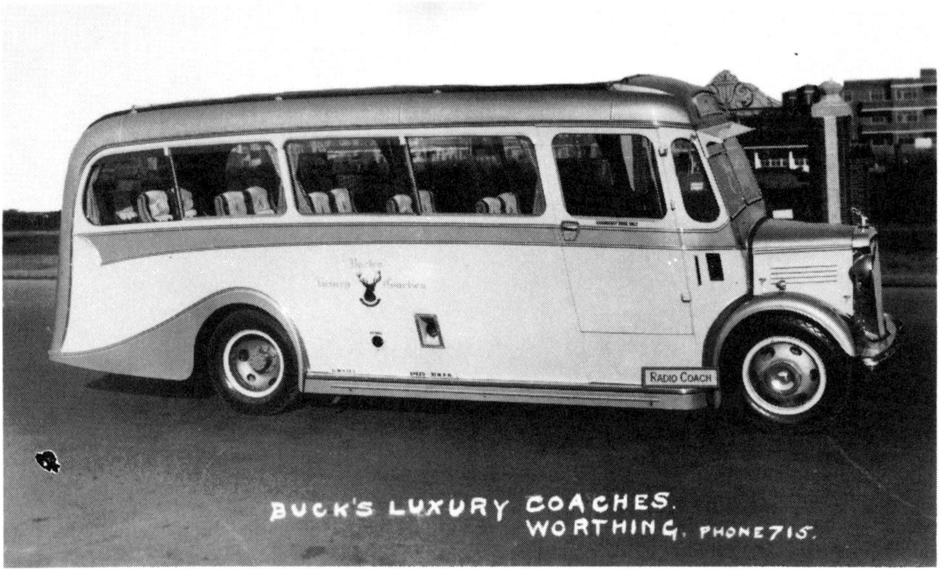


BUCKS LUXURY COACH COMPANY produced this card to advertise their buses. This Bedford coach was photographed outside Marine Gardens, *c.* 1935.

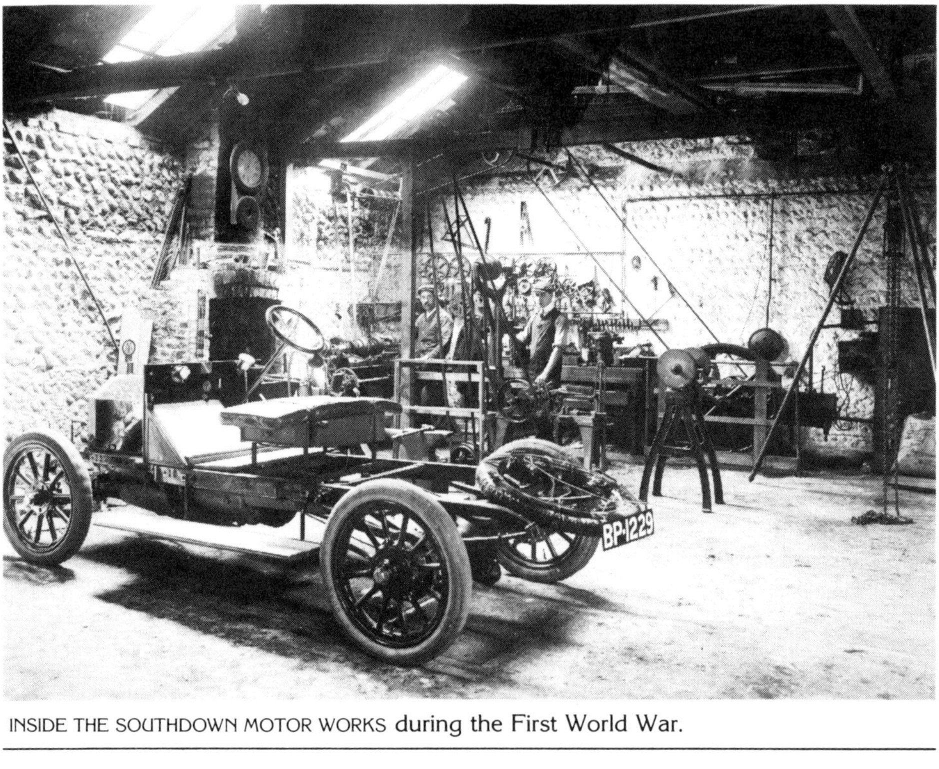


INSIDE THE SOUTHDOWN MOTOR WORKS during the First World War.

SECTION ELEVEN

# Events

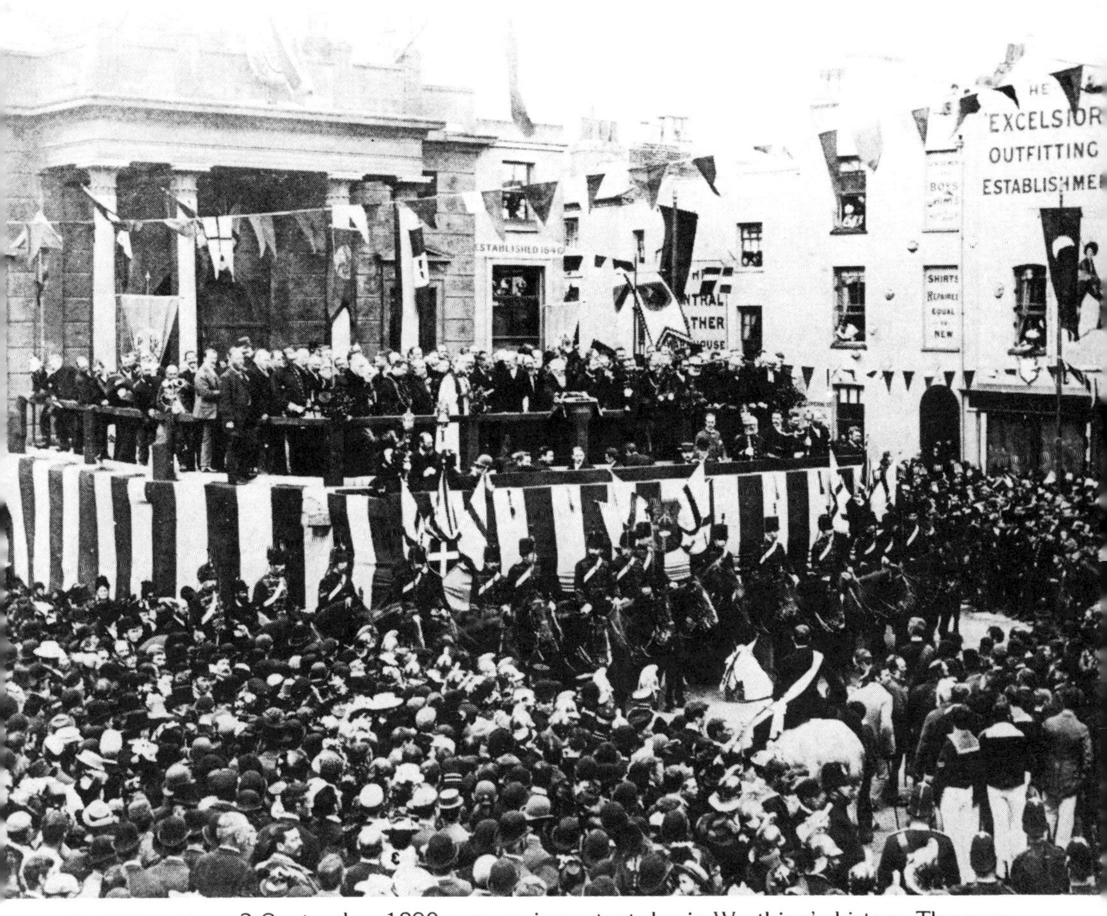


CHARTER DAY, on 3 September 1890, was an important day in Worthing's history. The new charter, giving the town borough status, was read to a huge crowd from the steps of the old town hall and a variety of celebrations took place throughout the town.

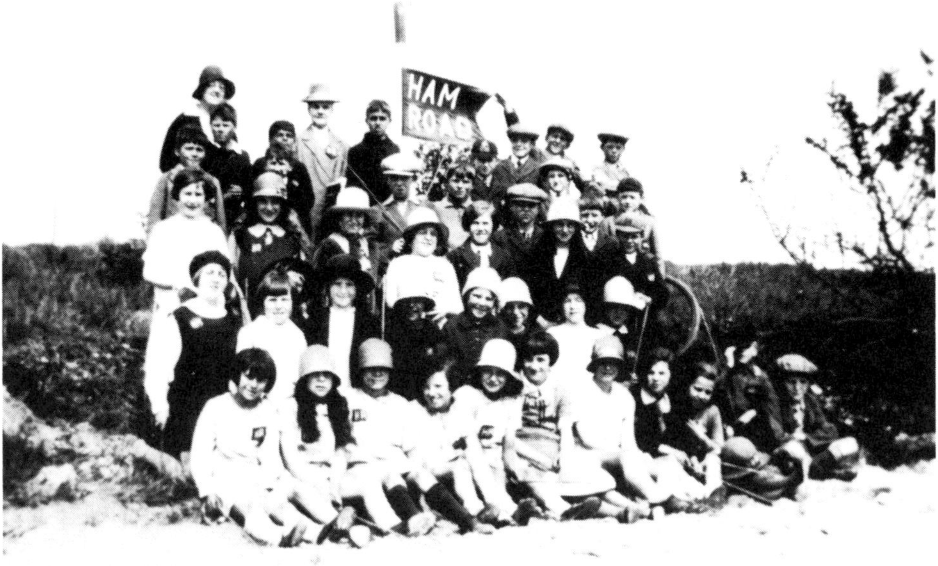


THE BOUNDARIES OF WORTHING were extended to include Goring and Durrington in May 1929. As part of the celebrations school children beat the bounds of the borough. This group is from Ham Road School. Their headmistress, Miss Anuige, is second from the left in the back row.

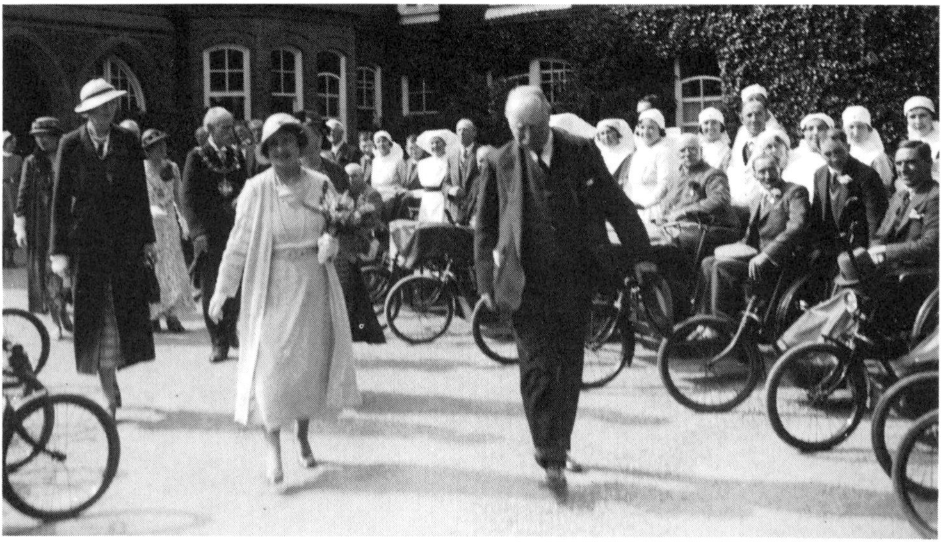

THE QUEEN ALEXANDRA HOSPITAL HOME FOR DISABLED EX-SERVICEMEN moved from Roehampton to Worthing in 1932. It was later renamed Gifford House. On 23 May 1934 it was visited by the Duchess of York, now the Queen Mother. In the picture the duchess is with Lord Leconfield and Councillor Duffield is with his wife, who is wearing a floral dress.

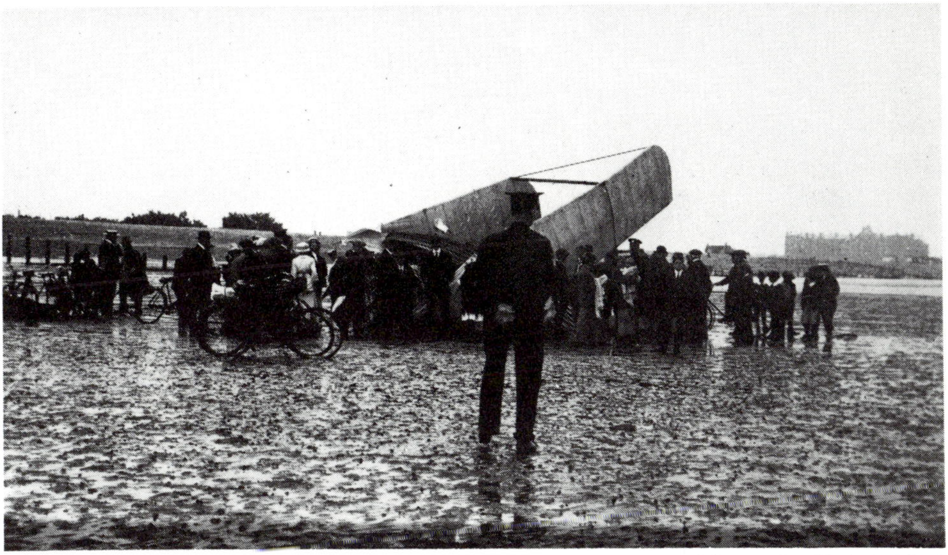

SEVERAL PLANES CAME TO GRIEF on Worthing beach in the early days of flying. On 22 July 1914 a naval plane crashed at Worthing on its way from Portsmouth to Felixstowe. Piloted by Flight Commander Rathbone, and carrying one passenger, it developed engine trouble and was badly damaged when it hit the sea just beyond the Metropole Hotel. The plane was taken to pieces and returned to Portsmouth by train.

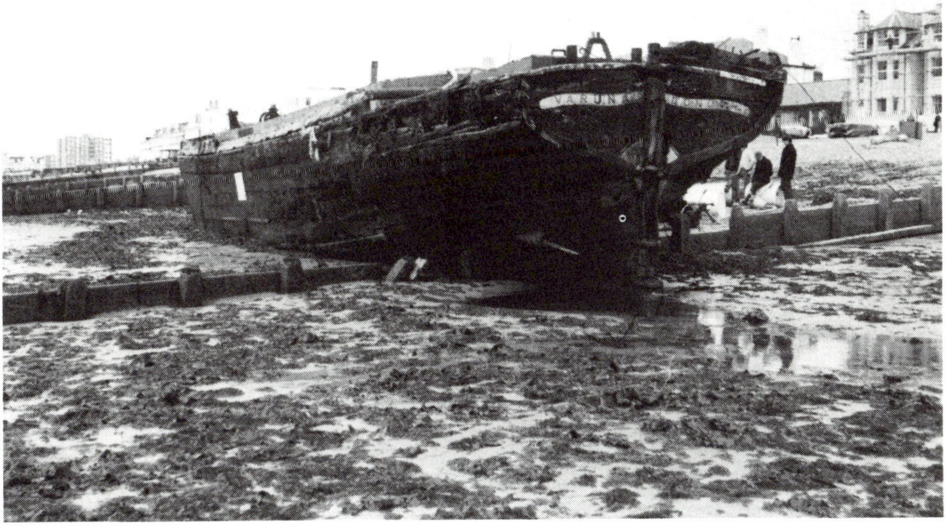

THERE HAVE BEEN A NUMBER OF SHIPWRECKS on Worthing beach. One of the more recent happened on 17 July 1970. A fifty-nine ton Thames barge, the *Varuna*, collided with a German ship, the *Tine*, opposite the Berkeley Hotel. The owner of the barge, Bryn Harwood, and his family were rescued and the boat towed to the beach.

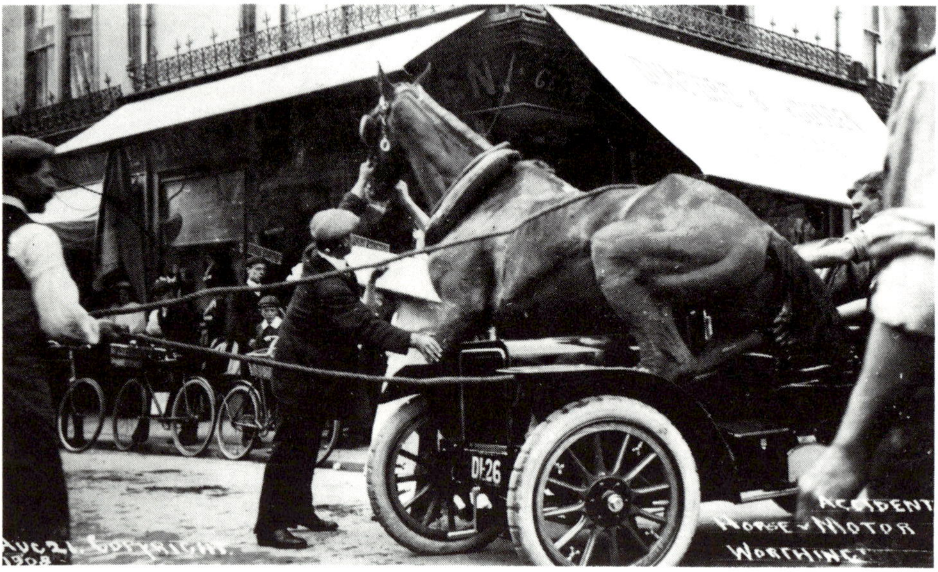


SOME HORSES FOUND IT DIFFICULT to get used to motor cars. Accidents were not unusual. This tradesman's horse was upset at the sight of Dr Le Riche's Rover in Montague Street in August 1908 and ended up on the car's bonnet. It had to be hauled off with ropes. The damage to the car was greater than to the horse.

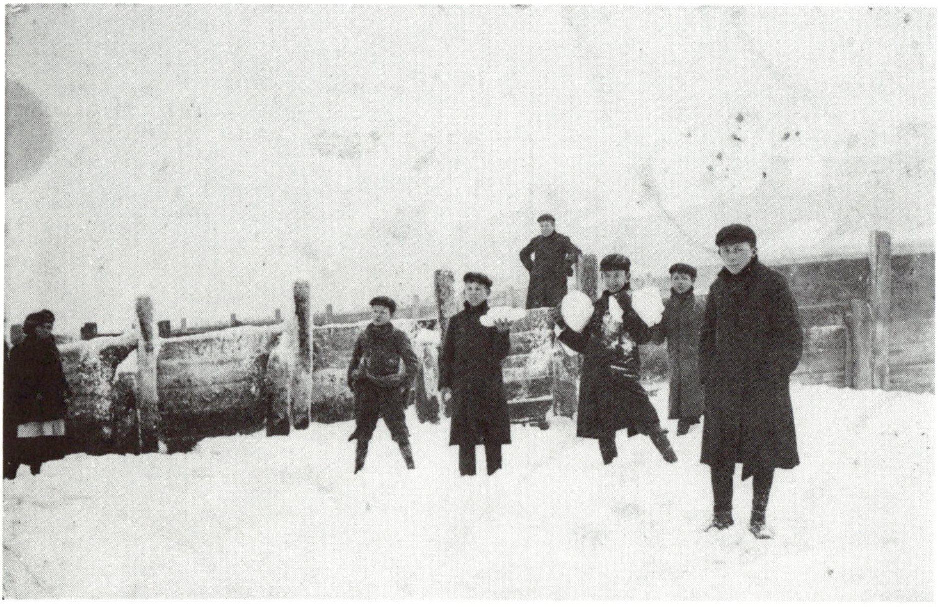

THE WINTER OF 1905/6 brought deeper than usual snow to Worthing. These boys took advantage of the uncommon weather to make large snowballs on the beach.

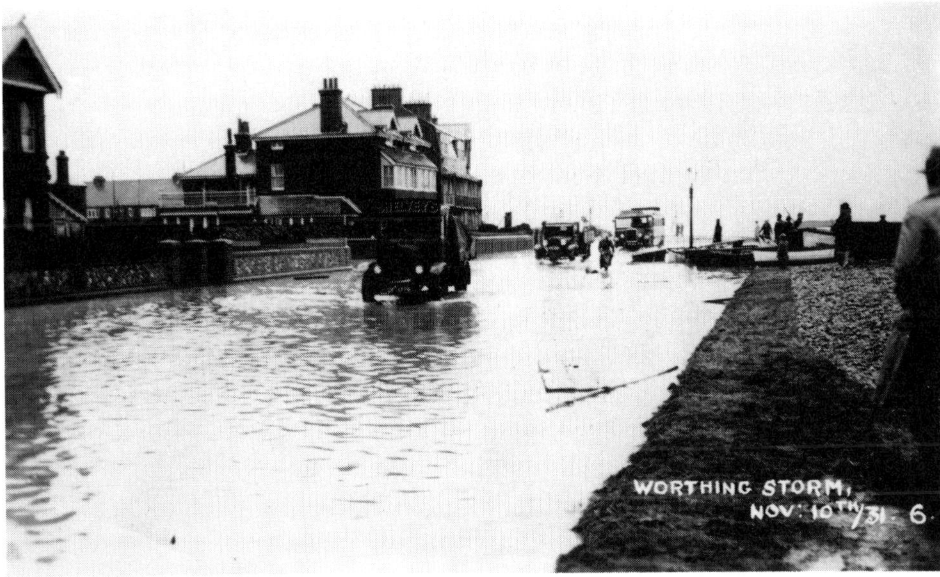


TIDAL FLOODS have been a periodic problem in Worthing and were much worse before the sea defences and promenade were built towards the end of the nineteenth century. In November 1931 a heavy storm brought severe flooding along Brighton Road and the seafront.

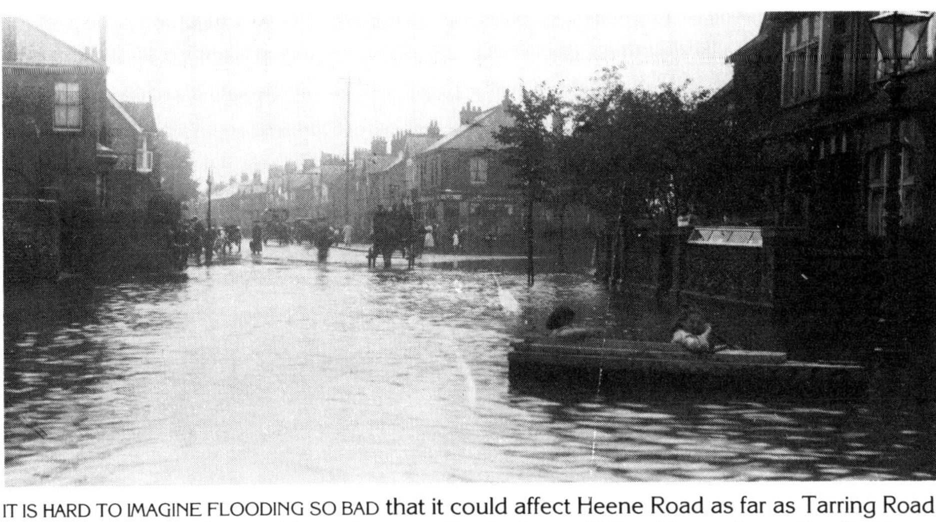

IT IS HARD TO IMAGINE FLOODING SO BAD that it could affect Heene Road as far as Tarring Road, let alone that people would need to use boats there. This picture shows the floods on 1 September 1915.

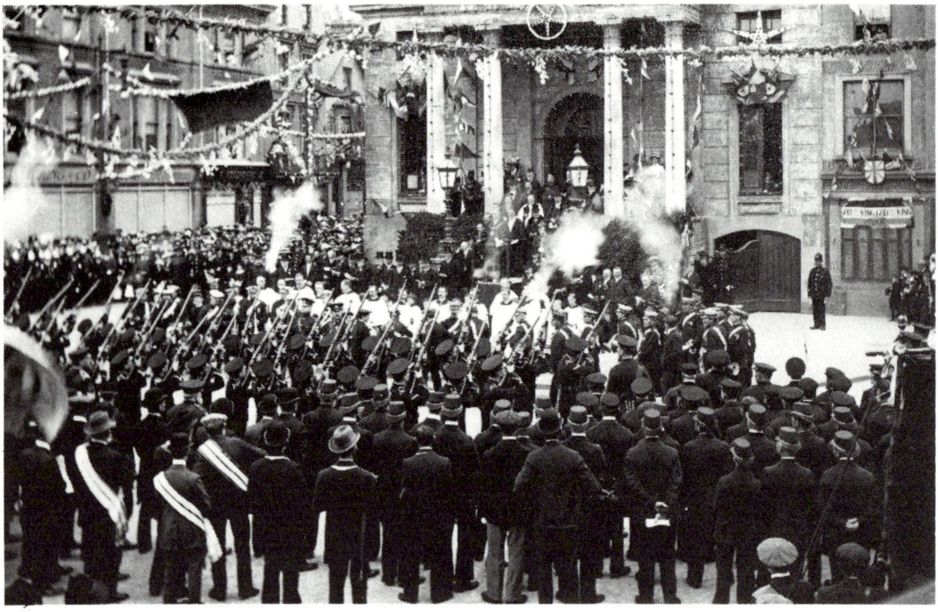

THE CORONATION OF KING GEORGE V in 1911 was a cause for great celebration throughout the country and Worthing was no exception. The streets were festooned with flags and bunting and there were speeches, parades and events like this demonstration by local firemen.

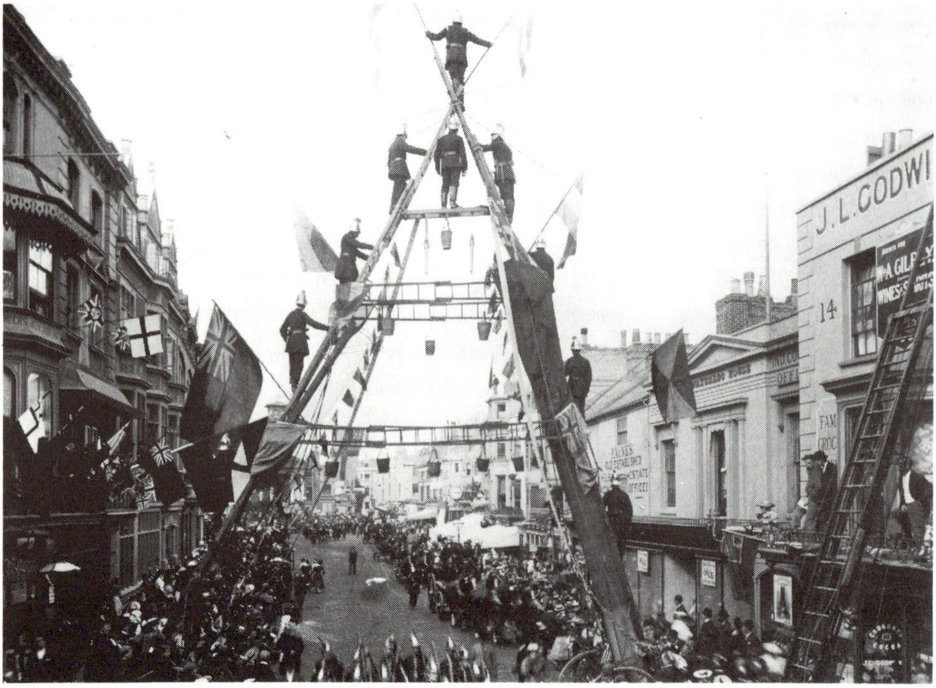

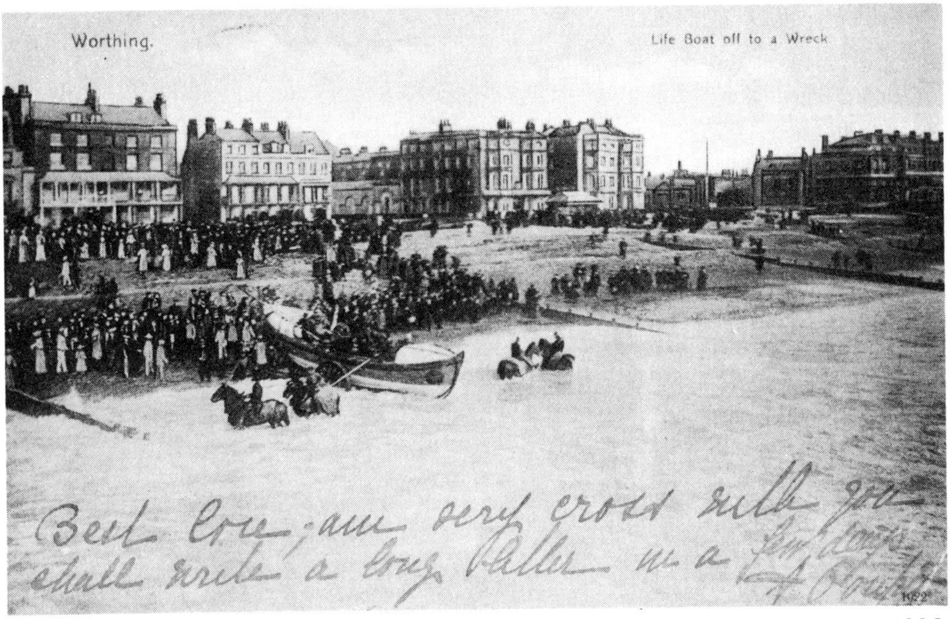


THE LAUNCHING, BY MEN AND HORSES, OF WORTHING'S LIFEBOAT, the *Richard Coleman*, in 1906. The sender of the card wrote on it that she was 'very cross' with the recipient for some reason which is not explained.

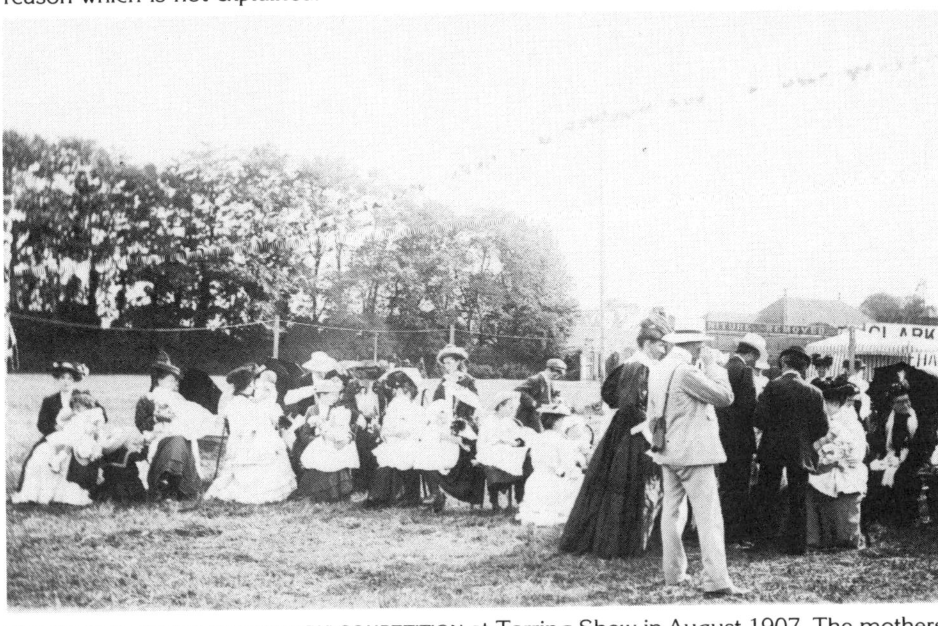

THE JUDGING OF THE 'BONNY BABY' COMPETITION at Tarring Show in August 1907. The mothers and babies are all dressed in their best clothes, and the people on the right appear to be the judges.

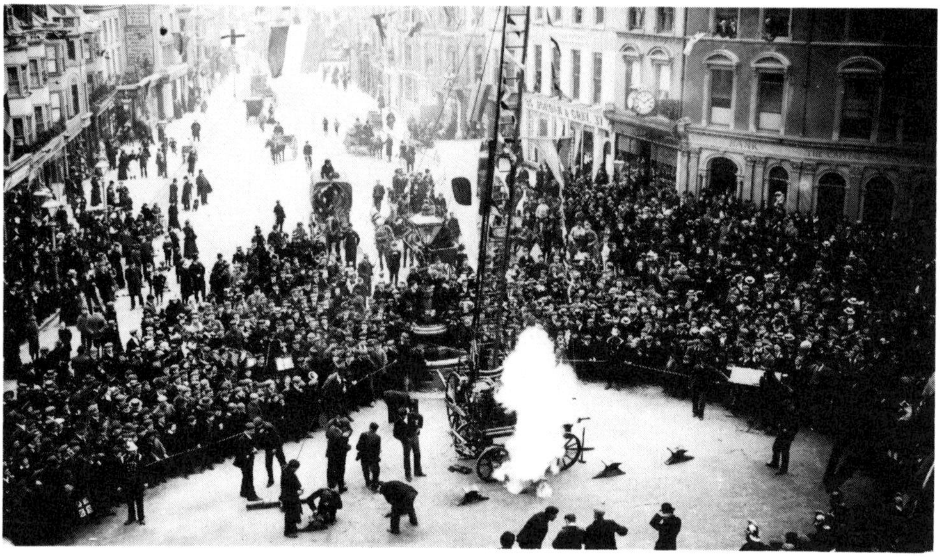

'LADYSMITH DAY 1 March 1900' reads the label on this photograph which shows crowds in South Street watching a display by members of the local fire service. The celebrations were to mark the relief of Ladysmith during the South African War.

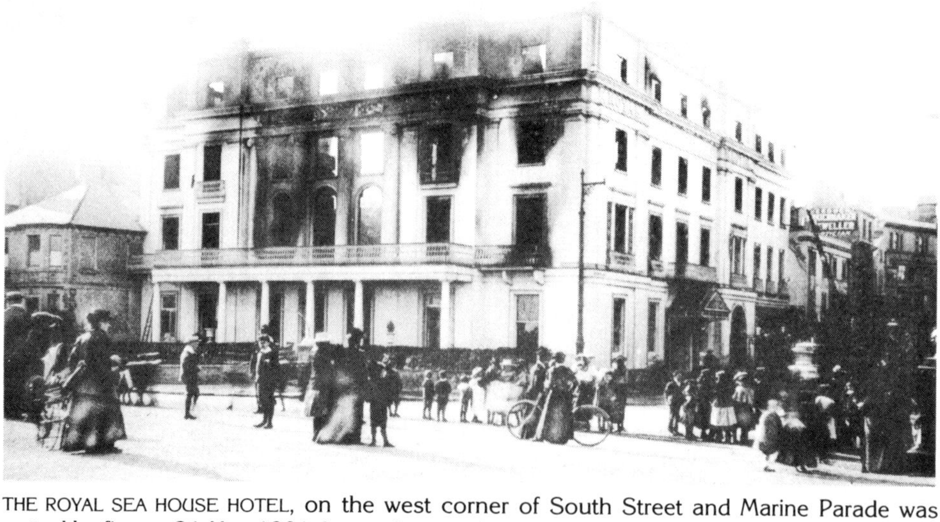

THE ROYAL SEA HOUSE HOTEL, on the west corner of South Street and Marine Parade was gutted by fire on 21 May 1901. It stood empty for many years, enclosed by hoardings which formed a prime site for bill-posters. One local bill-poster advertised for trade with the slogan, 'By paste we flourish'.

SECTION TWELVE

# People

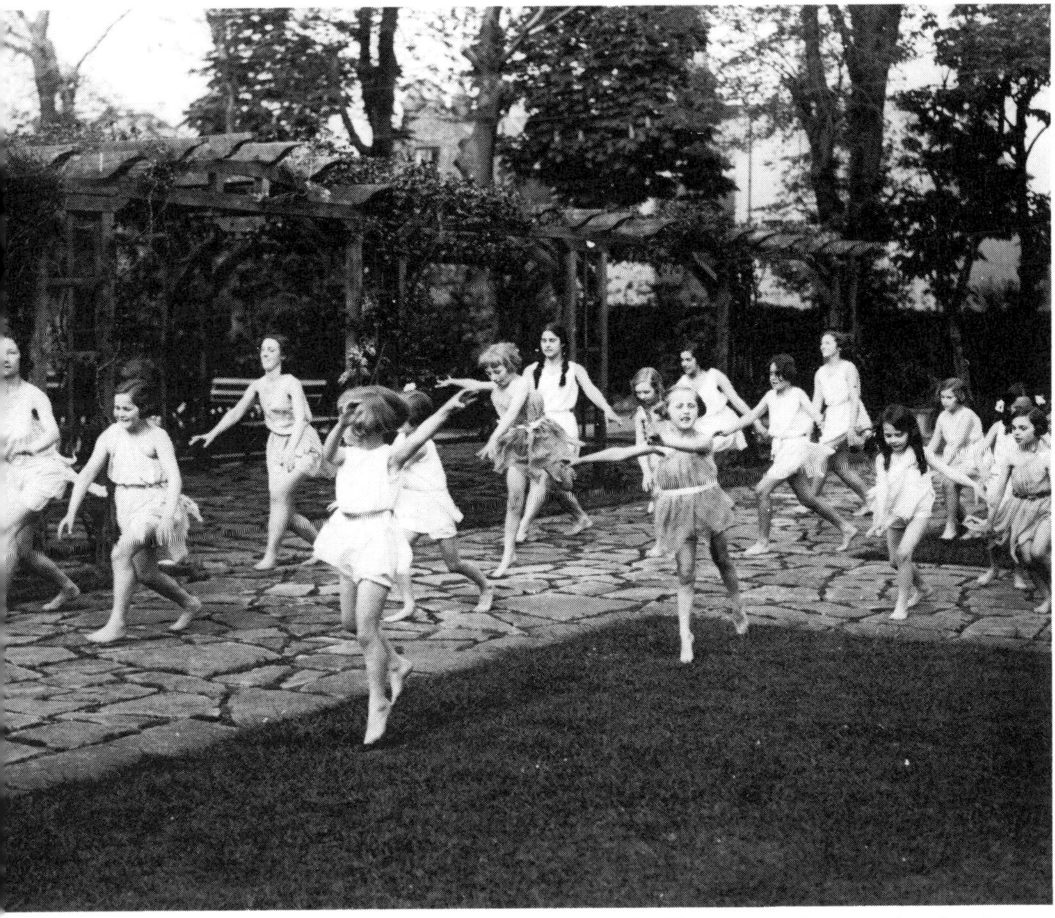

GREEK DANCING WAS VERY POPULAR in the 1920s and '30s. This action photograph, taken in a local park, shows just how much pleasure it gave to girls of all ages.

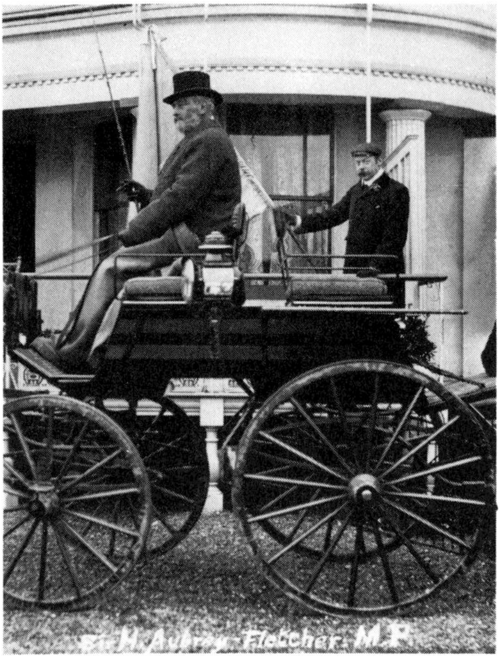


SIR HENRY AUBREY FLETCHER was the MP for mid-Sussex between 1885 and 1910. He lived at Ham Manor in Angmering. His wife was a very active member of the local Primrose League.

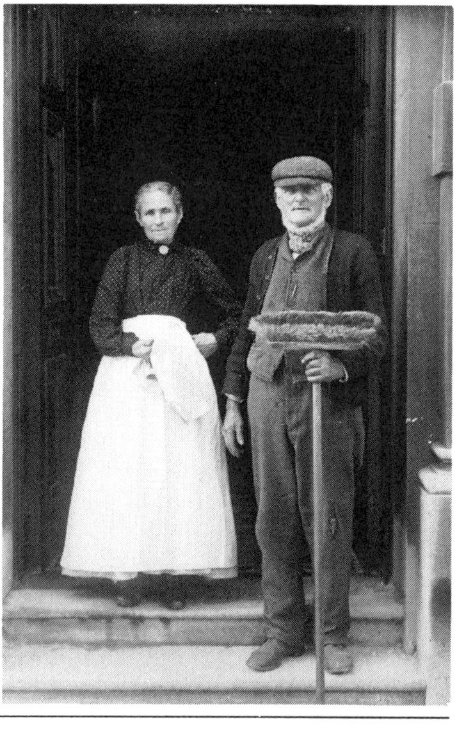

MR AND MRS THOMAS BROWN, *c.* 1890, on the steps of the old town hall. Mr Brown was a cleaner there and verger at the chapel of ease

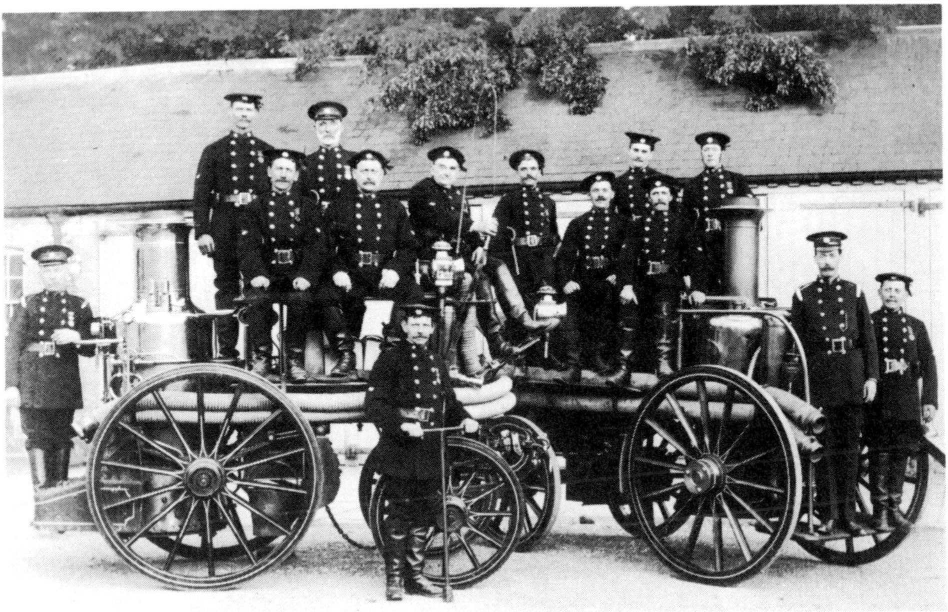

FOURTEEN MEMBERS OF THE LOCAL FIRE BRIGADE with two steam appliances. They are posing in the yard of the East Worthing fire station in Selden Road, *c.* 1900.

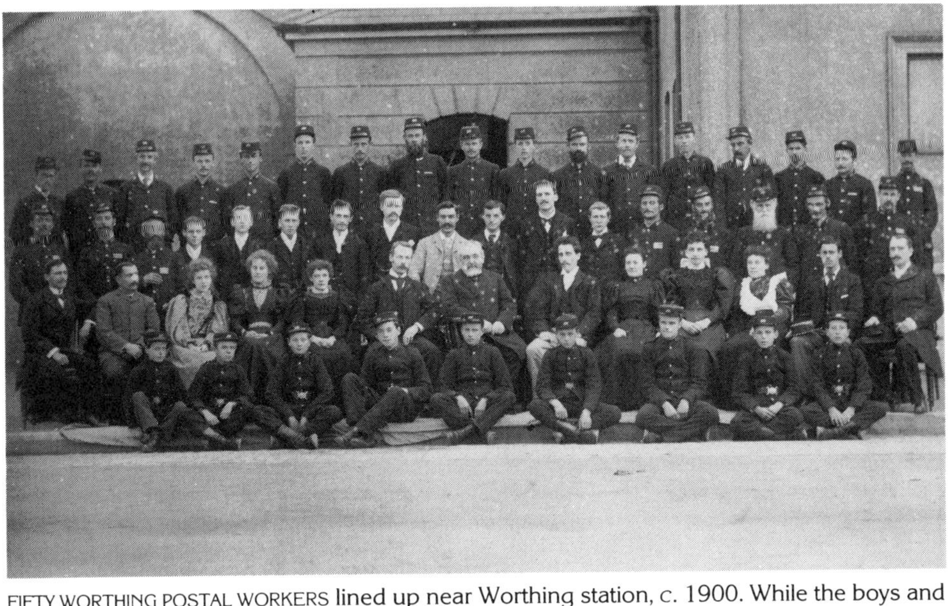

FIFTY WORTHING POSTAL WORKERS lined up near Worthing station, *c.* 1900. While the boys and postmen have their uniforms, the clothes worn by the other staff show quite a lot of variation which helps to indicate each person's relative status in the office.

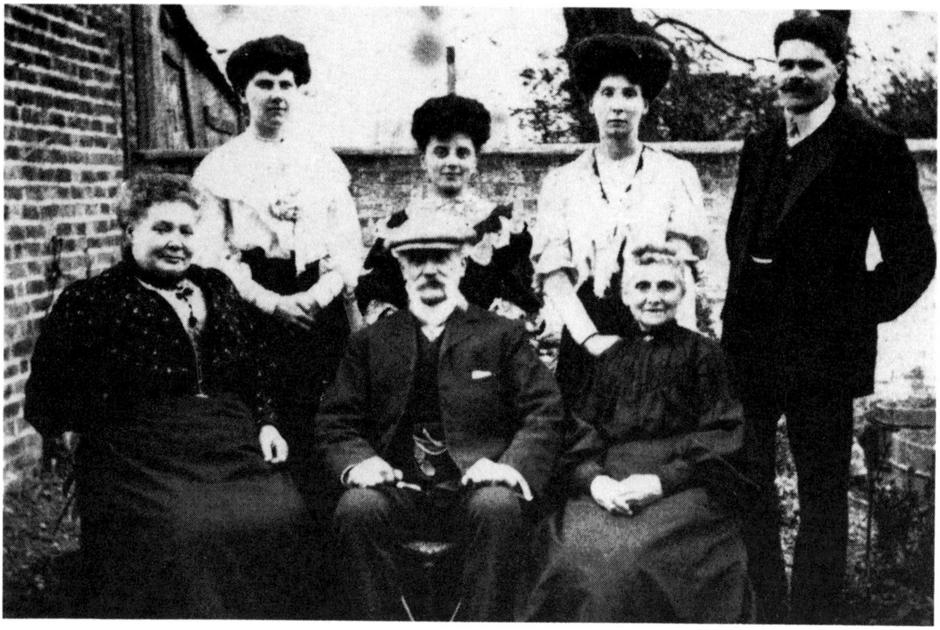

SEVEN MEMBERS OF THE LUCAS FAMILY in their garden, *c.* 1906. They owned a bakery and a drapers shop in Chapel Road and the younger members of the family, including Albert Lucas junior, on the right of the back row, were keen amateur actors.

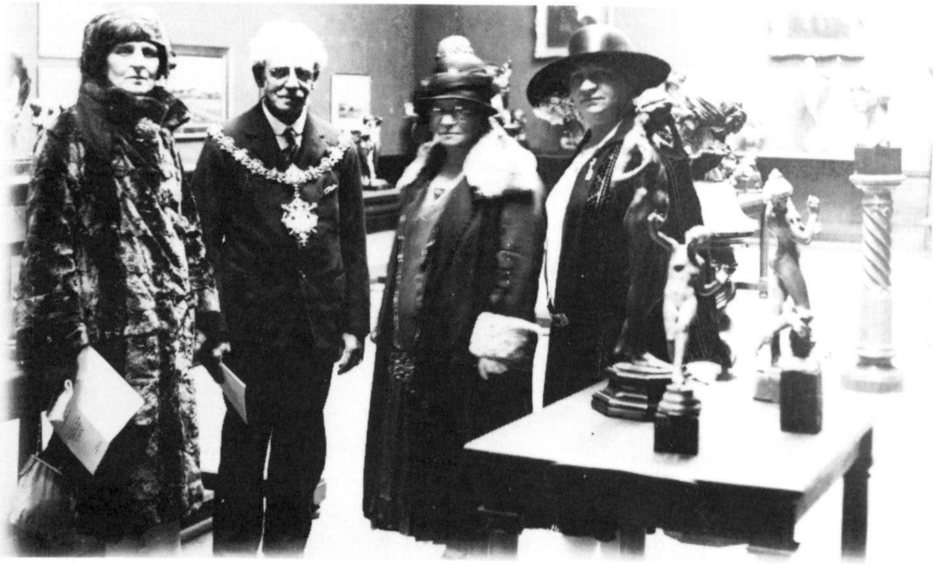

THE TOWN'S REMARKABLE LIBRARIAN, Marian Frost, is the lady on the right of this picture. She helped raise the money for the library and museum to be built. For many years she was also curator of the museum and is seen here in the art gallery with the mayor, mayoress and another lady, *c.* 1925.

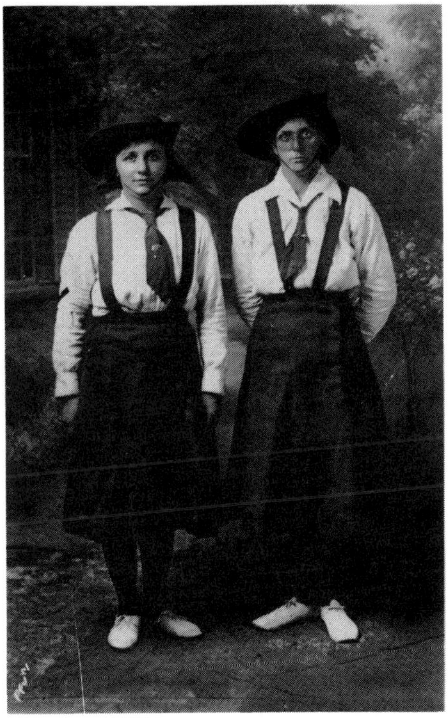

TWO GIRL GUIDES photographed between 1910 and 1920 by Otto Brown of Worthing.

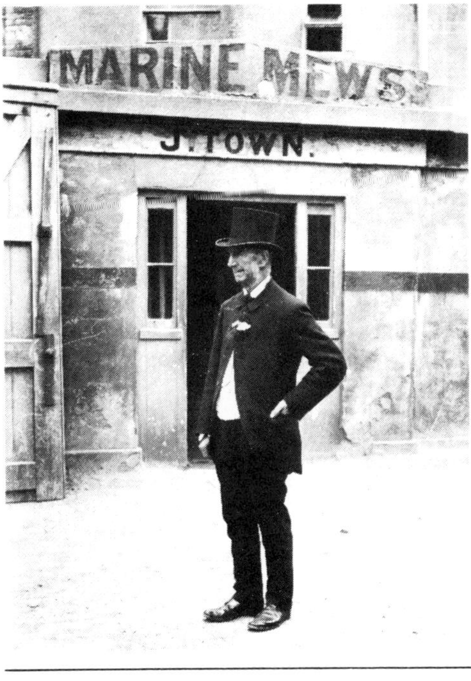


JAMES TOWN set up his business in Worthing in 1849 with a donkey and cart which he hired out at 9d (4p) an hour. He quickly expanded the business until he had thirty men working for him and premises in Steyne Mews and Marine Mews. In the 1880s he had ten horse buses, on which the fare from Heene to Broadwater was 6d (2½p). He died in 1912.

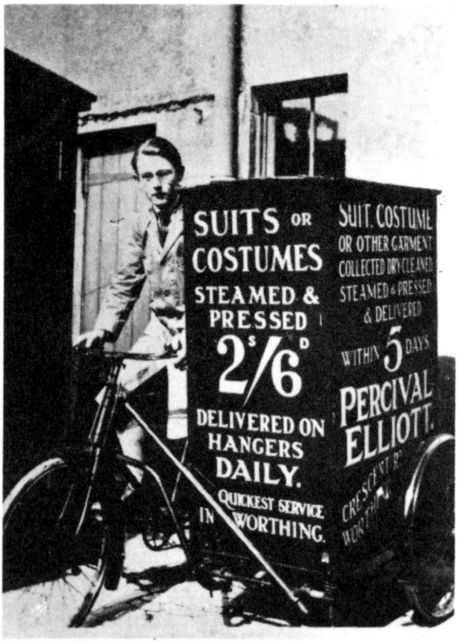


A DELIVERY BOY WITH HIS BICYCLE and huge mounted box advertising the services of his employer Percival Elliot.

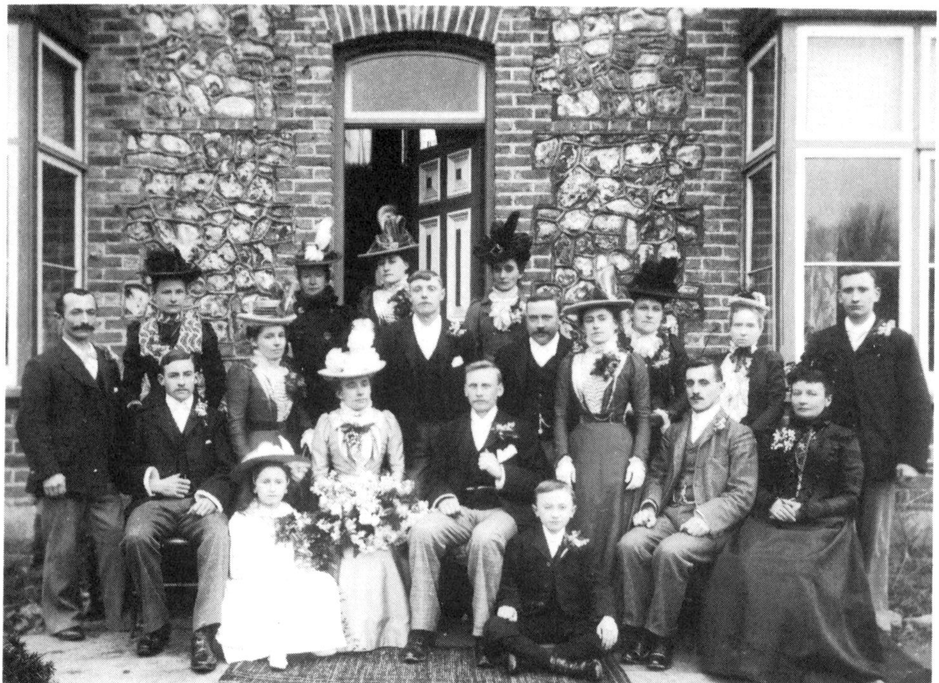

CHARLOTTE RICH got married in 1901. The wedding party is posing outside Jefferies House in Goring which was named after the naturalist, Richard Jefferies, who once lived there.

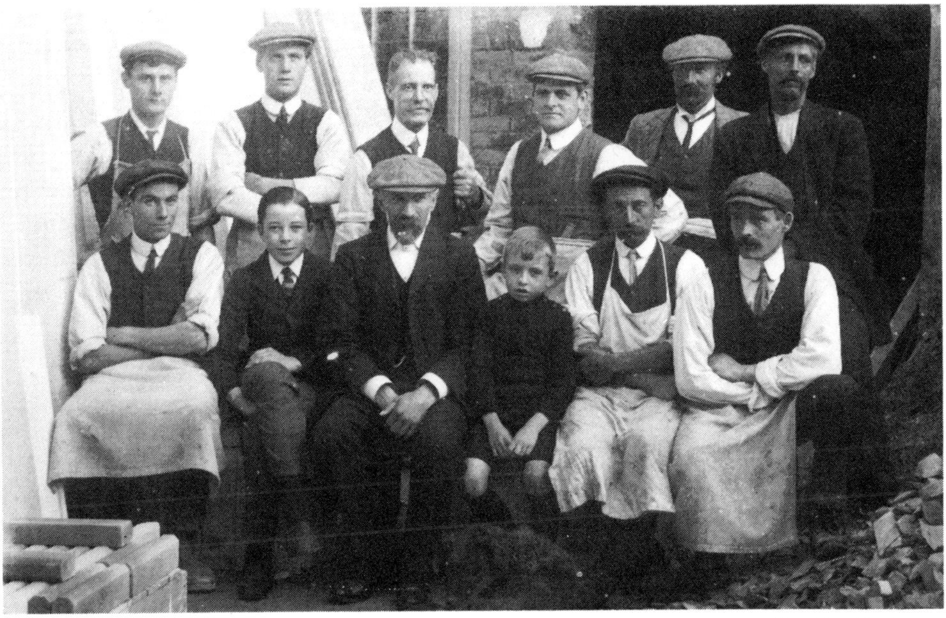

A GROUP OF WORKMEN FROM TATES, the stonemasons, who had the Carrara Marble Works in North Street. This picture was taken *c.* 1910.

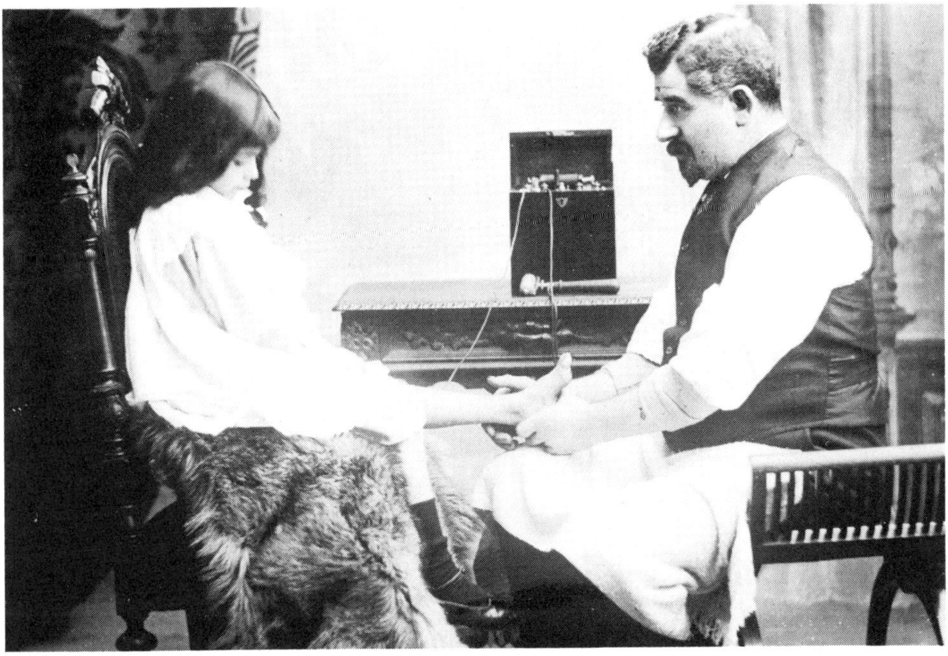

THE NAME OF THIS THERAPIST and the details of the treatment he is giving are unknown. The back of the photograph, taken between 1900 and 1910, is labelled 'W. West Worthing'.

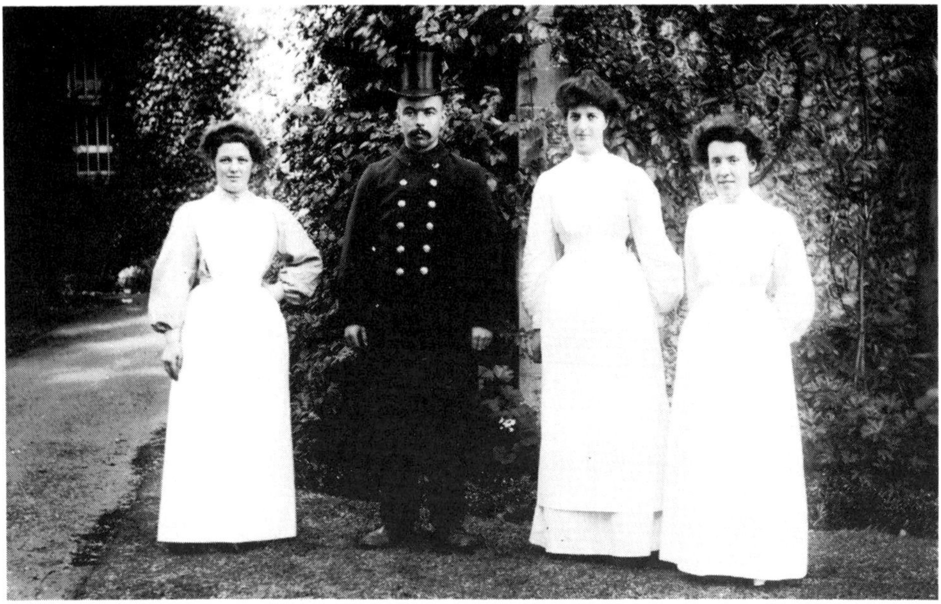

THIS COOK, coachman (Charles George Townshend) and two housemaids were employed at Chios, Colonel Rodoconachi's house in Manor Road.

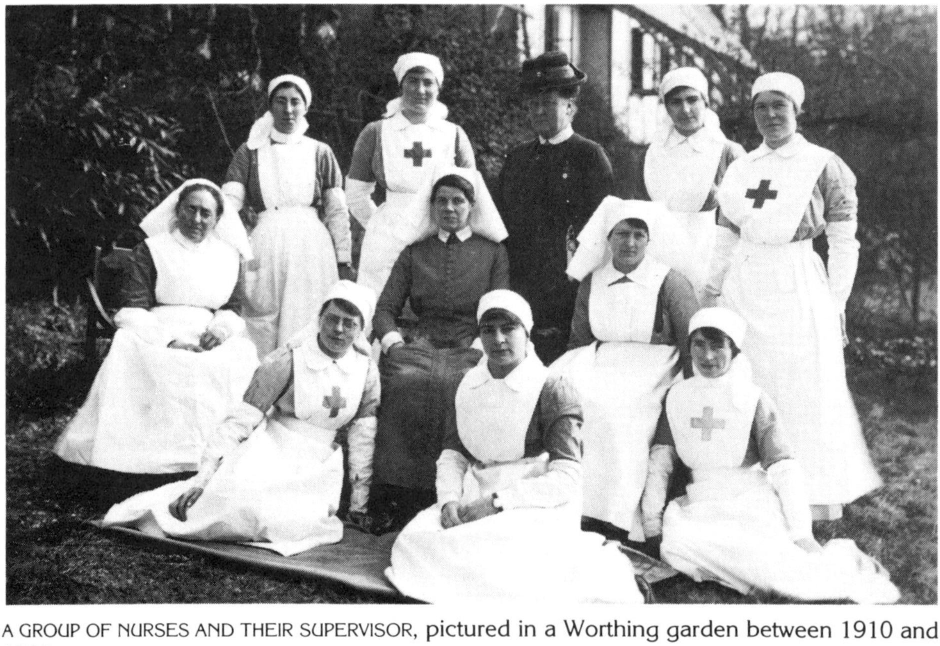

A GROUP OF NURSES AND THEIR SUPERVISOR, pictured in a Worthing garden between 1910 and 1920.

SECTION THIRTEEN

# Streets and Buildings

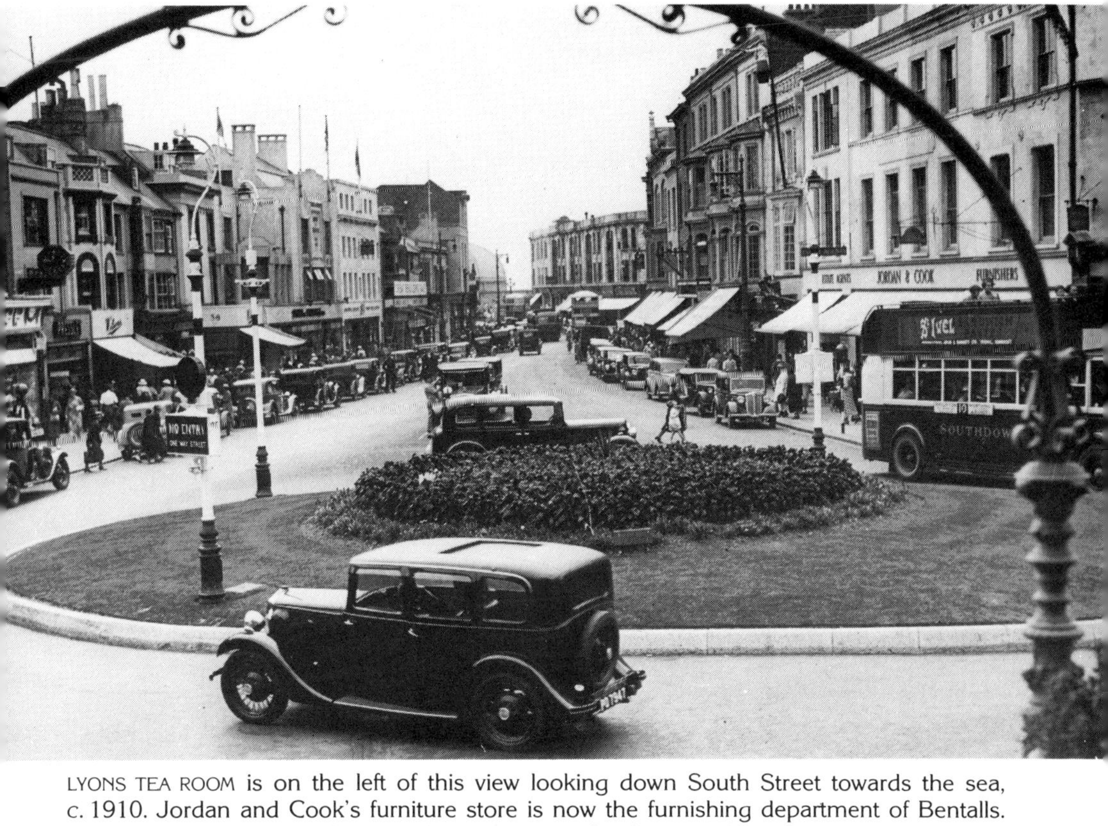


LYONS TEA ROOM is on the left of this view looking down South Street towards the sea, c. 1910. Jordan and Cook's furniture store is now the furnishing department of Bentalls. Parking was clearly a problem in the town centre by the time this picture was taken. This view was taken from in front of the old town hall.

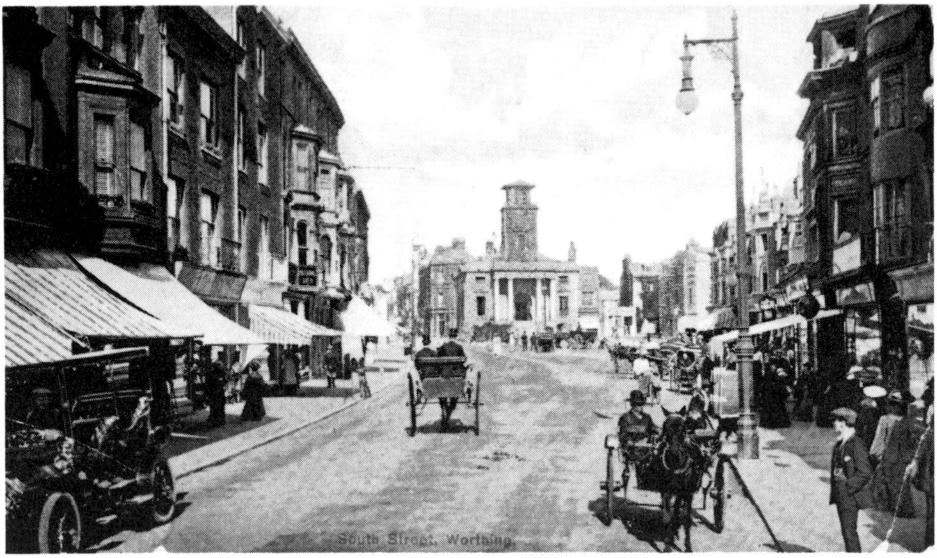


THIS PICTURE OF SOUTH STREET, *c.* 1908, shows both horse-drawn and early motor vehicles.

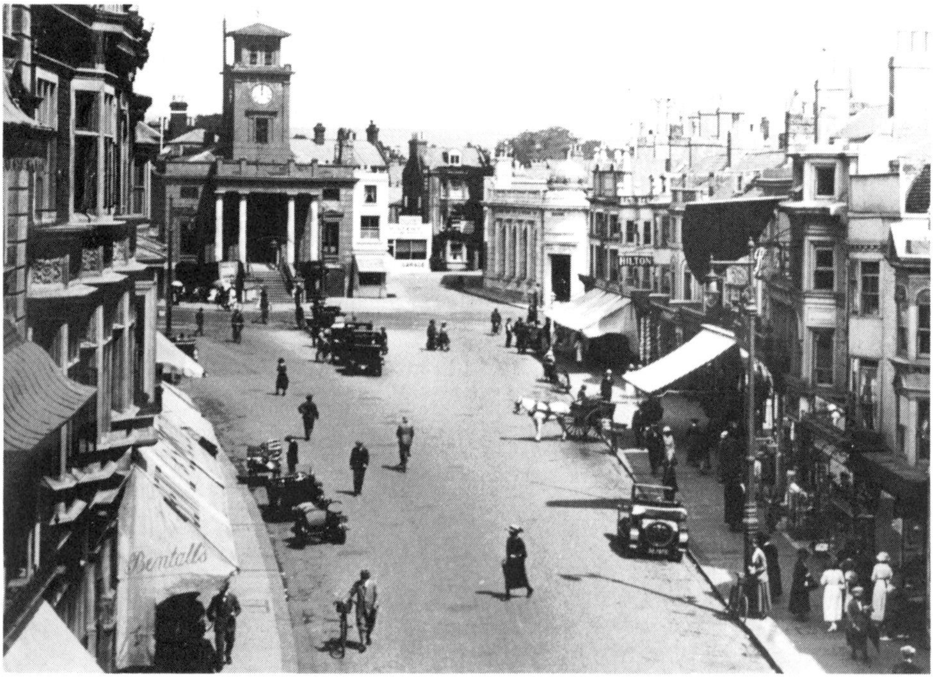


THE OLD TOWN HALL was built in 1835 in the heart of Worthing and stood on the corner of South Street and Warwick Street. It was built on land donated by Sir Timothy Shelley, who was one of the town's first commissioners. The building stood until 1968 but the council moved out in 1933.

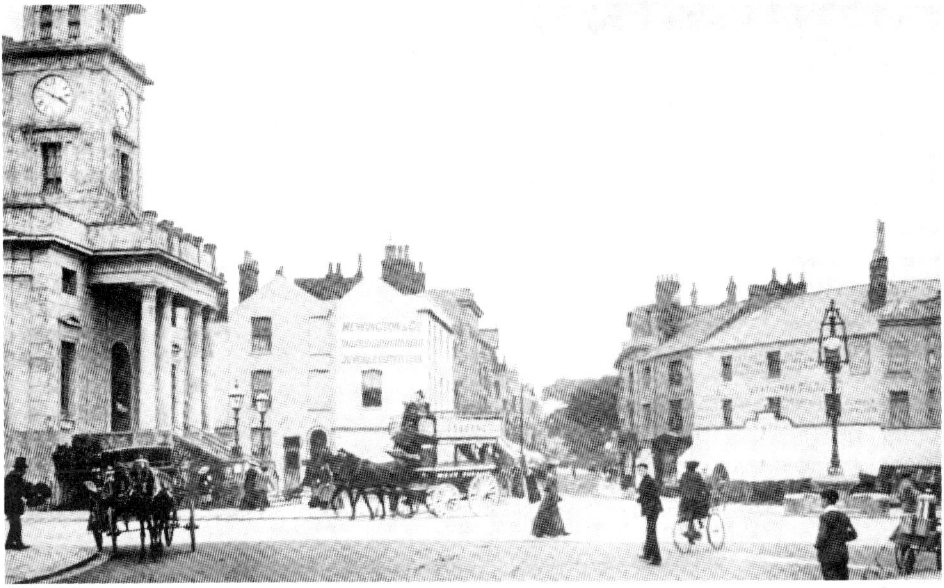

THE COMMERCIAL HEART OF WORTHING was in Warwick Street and South Street by the beginning of the twentieth century. As the cart on the right shows, milk was still delivered from churns and not in bottles or cartons. Miss Carter's popular nineteenth-century library was in Warwick Street.

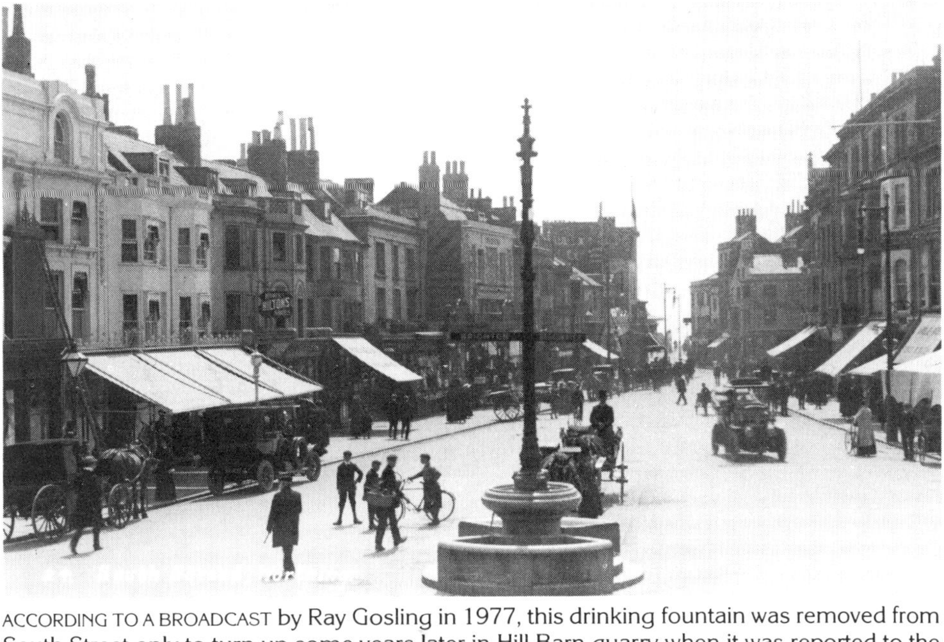

ACCORDING TO A BROADCAST by Ray Gosling in 1977, this drinking fountain was removed from South Street only to turn up some years later in Hill Barn quarry when it was reported to the museum as part of a Roman temple.

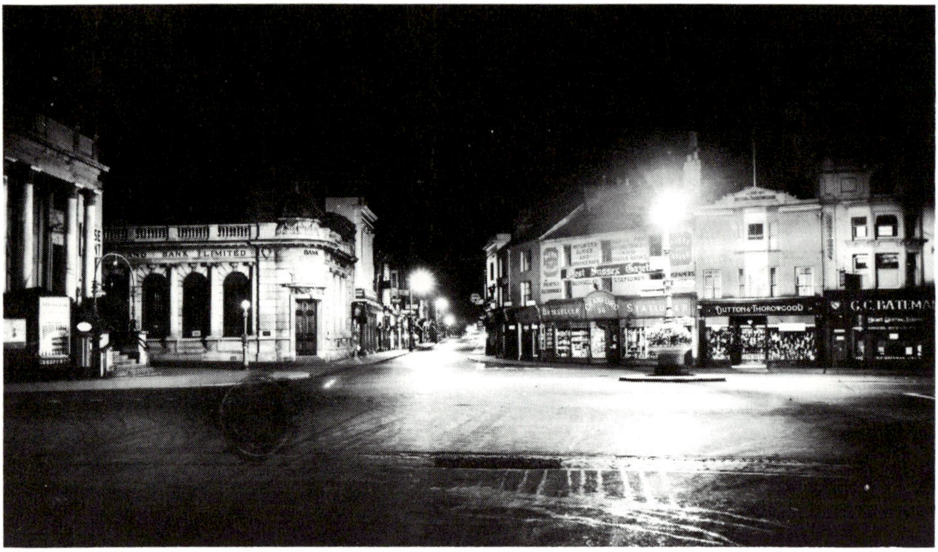

THE NAMES AND ADVERTISEMENTS ON THE SHOPS on the corner of Warwick Street and South Street show up sharply in this unusual night view. The Midland Bank, built in 1921, is still there but the old town hall has been demolished and the site is now part of the Guildbourne shopping centre. The space in the centre of this picture is now filled by a roundabout.

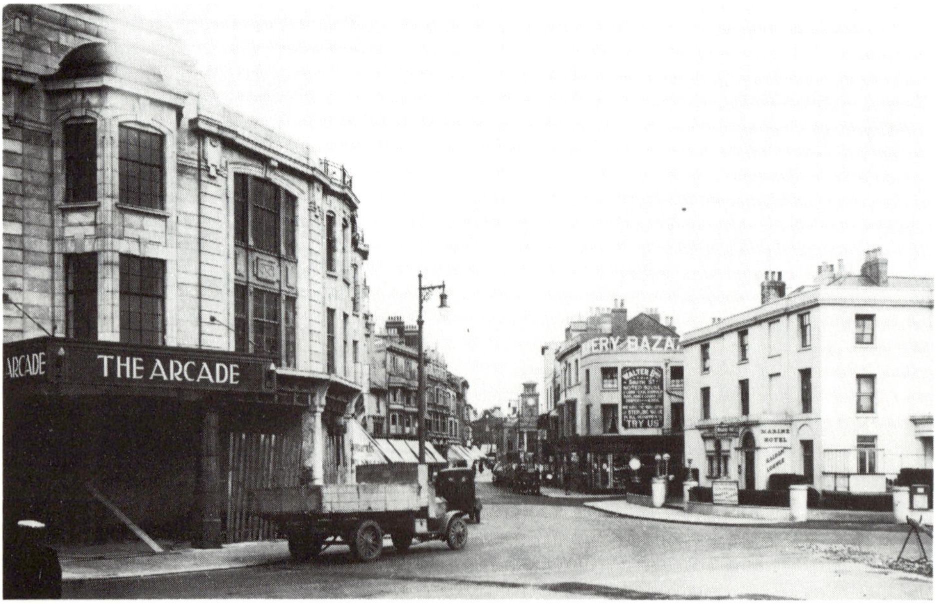


ARCADES WERE BUILT in a number of south coast towns in the 1920s. In Worthing the arcade was built on the site of the old Royal Sea House Hotel, on the corner of South Street and Marine Parade. This site had been derelict since fire gutted the hotel in 1901. This picture was taken in 1925 before the arcade was completed. The Marine Hotel is on the right.

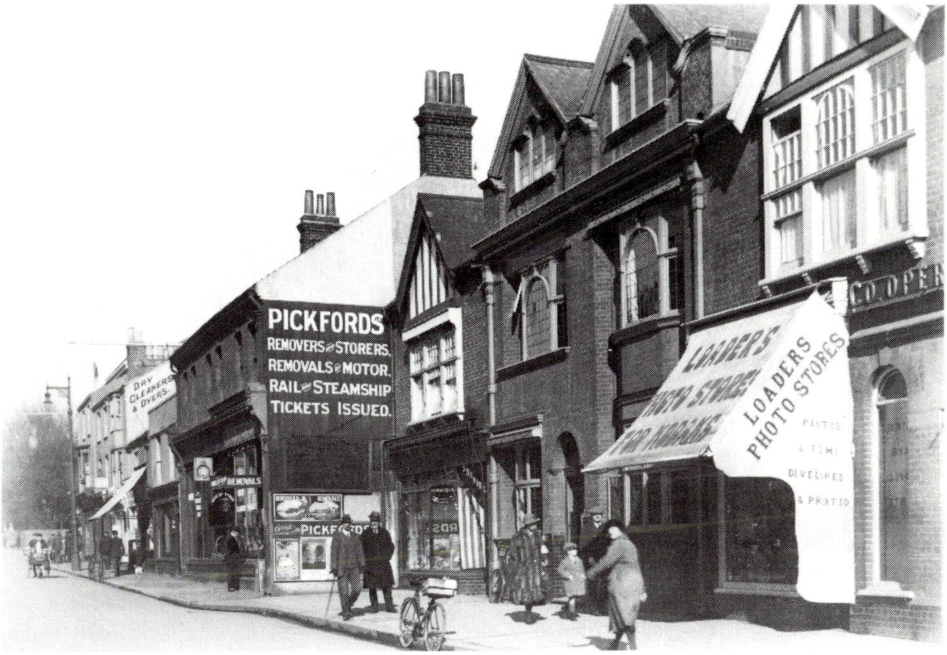


THE EAST SIDE OF CHAPEL ROAD in February 1922. Pickfords no longer have an office there from which they issue steamship tickets and Loader's Photo Store has been taken over by Fotosound.

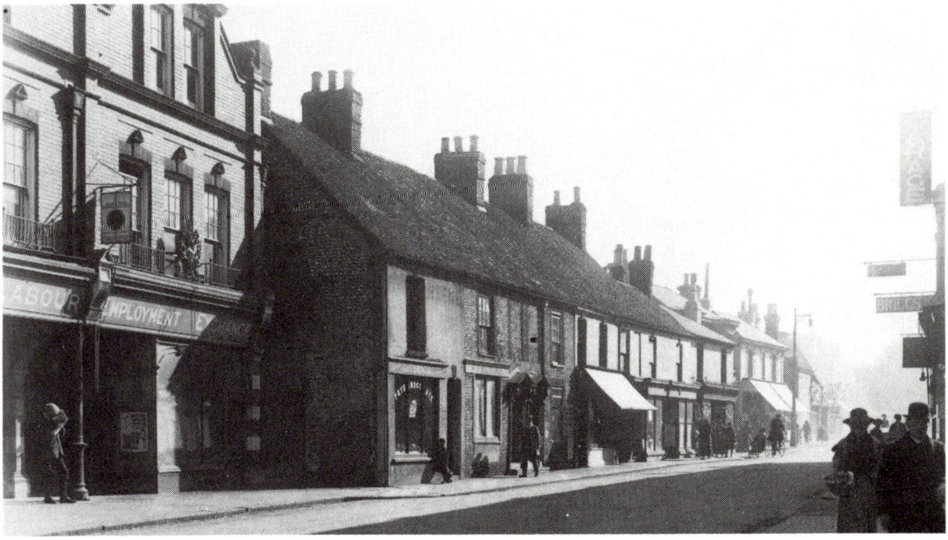


LABOUR AND EMPLOYMENT EXCHANGES have long since been replaced by job centres and DSS offices, but the problems related to unemployment remain very much the same. This labour exchange was in the northern part of Chapel Road in the 1920s. The office later moved to Clifton Road.

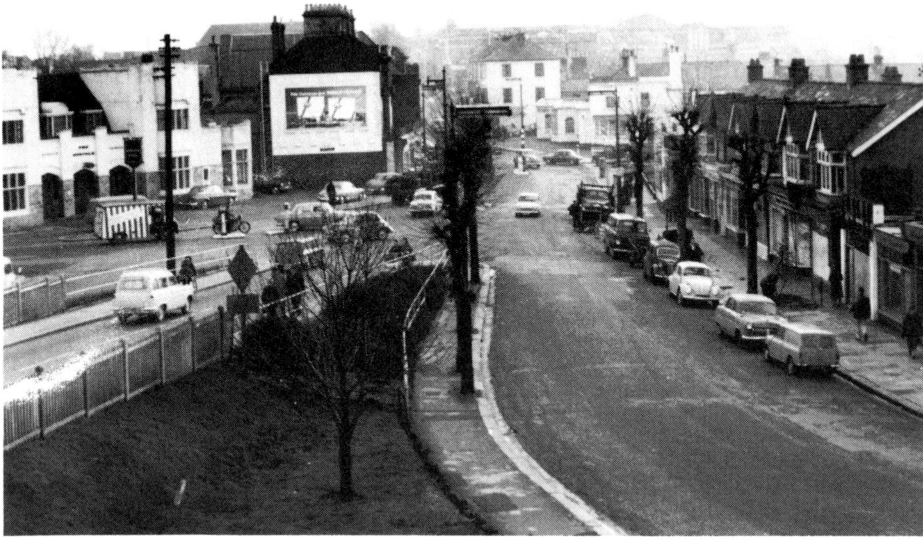

THE VIEW SOUTH FROM BROADWATER BRIDGE in the early 1960s. The road layout has been changed considerably since then, but the hotels are still there. Teville Gate shopping centre and multi-storey car park now occupy the area to the right of this scene.

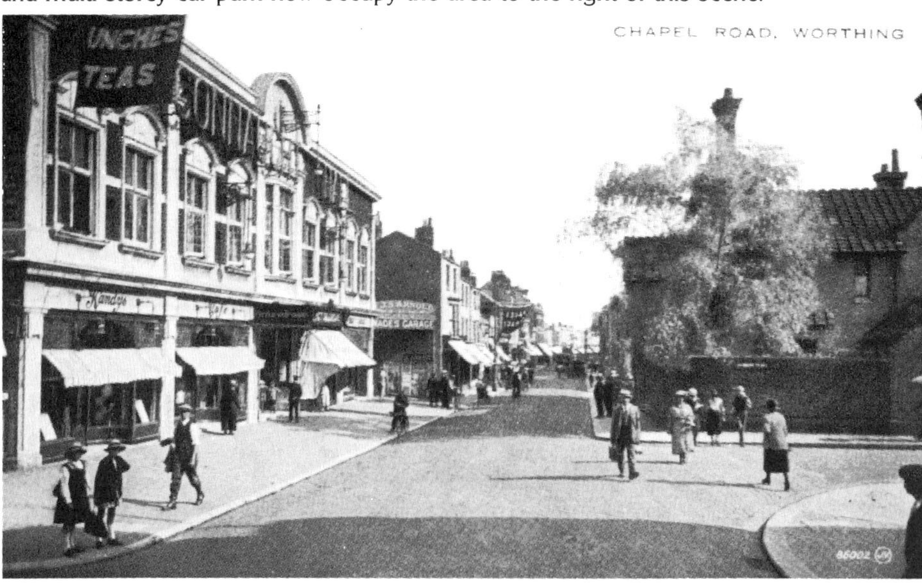


THIS VIEW ALONG CHAPEL ROAD from near the present post office looks very peaceful. The tree and house on the right-hand corner are on the site of the present gas showroom. The large letters above Kandy's Café identify the building as the Connaught Hall.

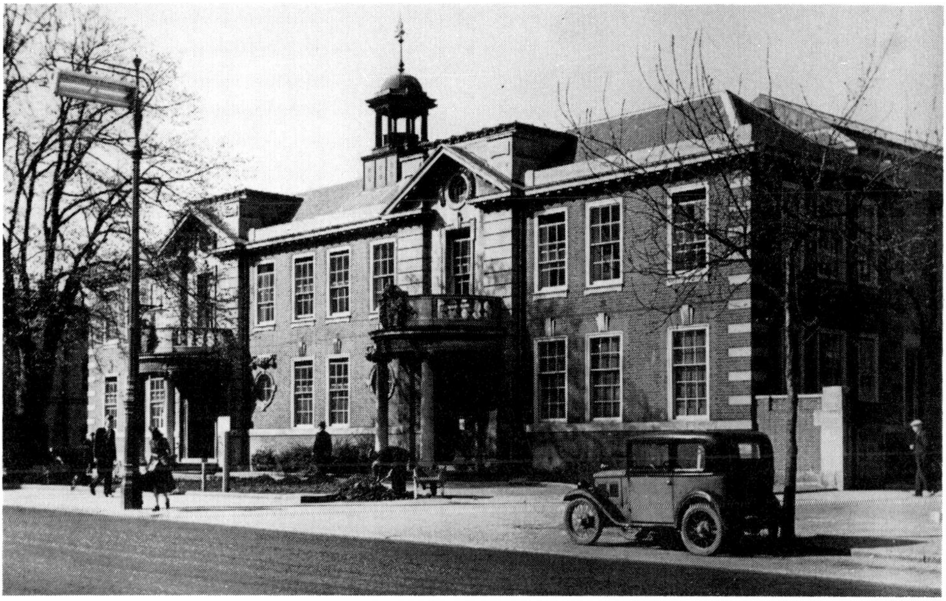

WORTHING MUSEUM AND LIBRARY was built in 1908. The librarian, Marian Frost, persuaded Andrew Carnegie to help pay for the building. The remainder of the cost was contributed by an anonymous donor who was later identified as the first mayor of Worthing, Alfred Cortis. In 1974 the library moved to a new building in Richmond Road and the museum was able to expand into some of the vacated space. The left-hand portico has, sadly, been demolished since this picture was taken in the 1950s.

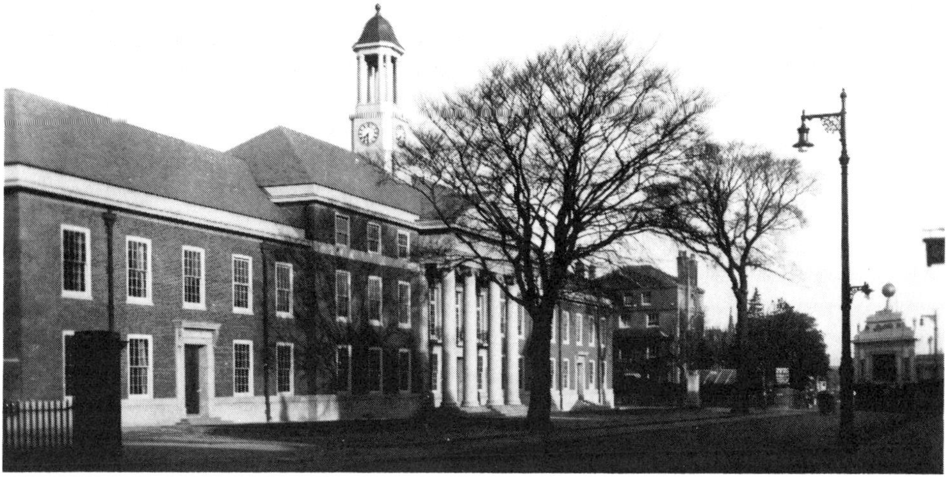

THE NEW TOWN HALL in Chapel Road was designed by Charles Voysey and opened by HRH Prince George, later the Duke of Kent, on 22 May 1933. The council obtained a grant towards the cost of the building from the Unemployment Grants Commission on the condition that ninety per cent of the workmen used was taken from the ranks of the unemployed.

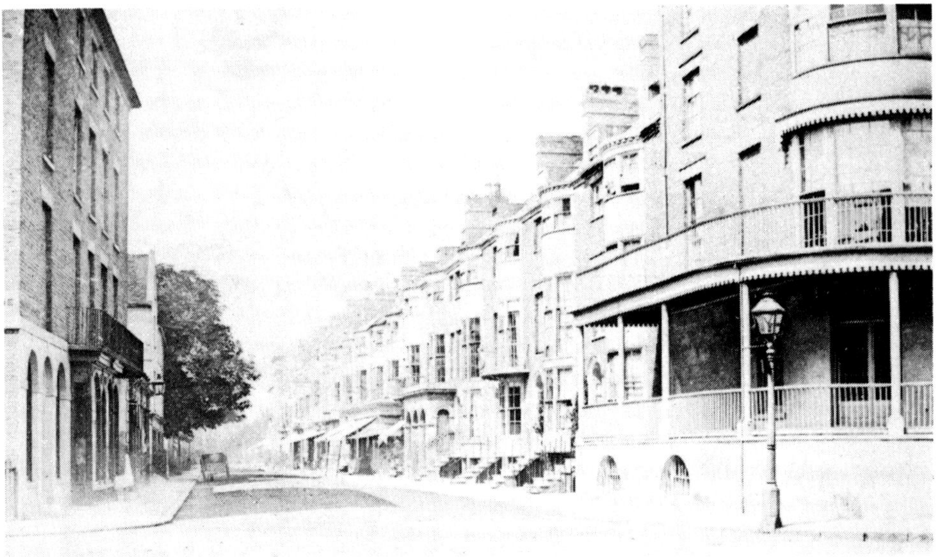

WARWICK STREET was one of the busiest roads in Worthing in the nineteenth century. The north side was built around 1807. Colonnade House, on the right-hand corner, was part of the Warwick House Estate. In 1888 Colonnade House was gutted by a fire which started in the School for Young Ladies at No. 3. Colonnade House is now occupied by the offices of the *Brighton Evening Argus*.

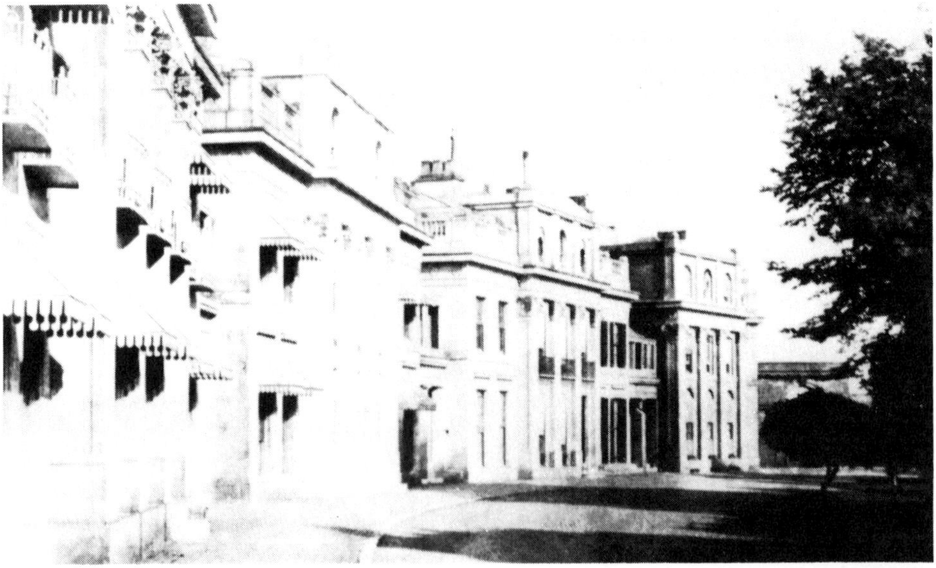

PARK CRESCENT was built by Amon H. Wilde in 1828 as part of a much larger scheme. An economic slump caused him to abandon the project and it was never completed. The grounds were renamed Amelia Park in 1990 to mark the centenary of the Borough of Worthing.

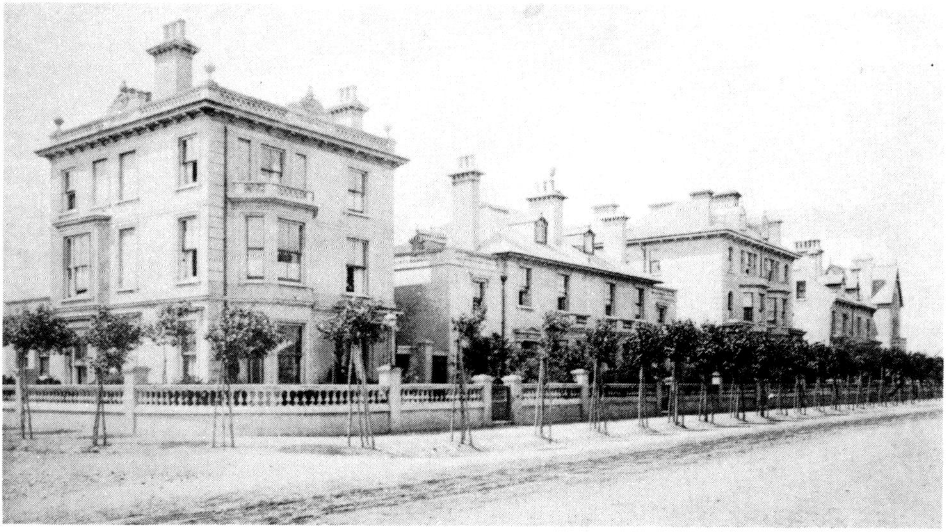

THIS VIEW OF THE ELEGANT VILLAS on the western side of Heene Road was taken around 1890. The saplings are now tall, mature trees.

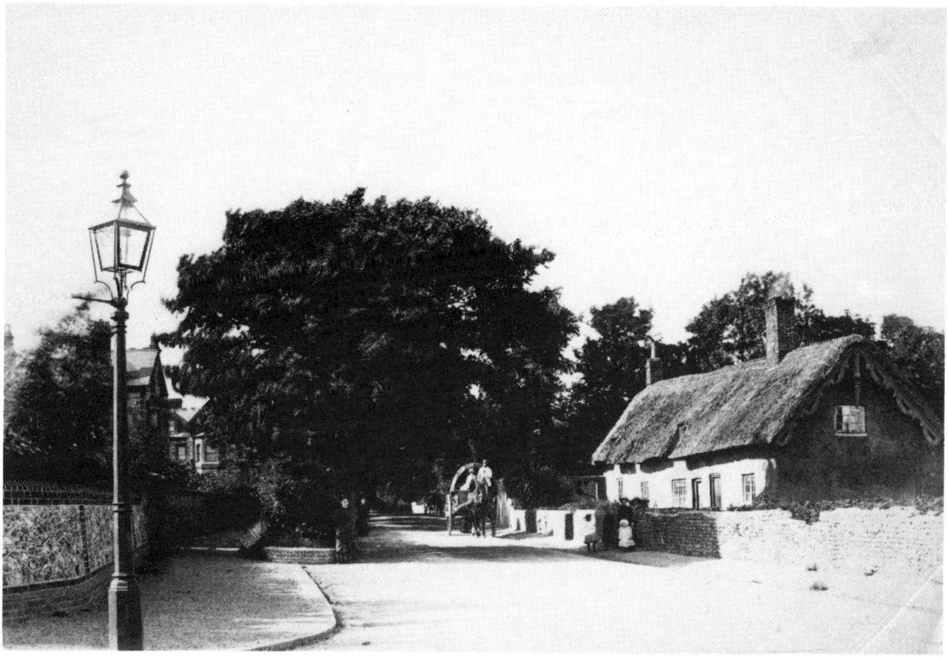

THIS THATCHED HOUSE WAS IN HEENE ROAD. The area was still rural around the start of the twentieth century. Today it is fully built up.

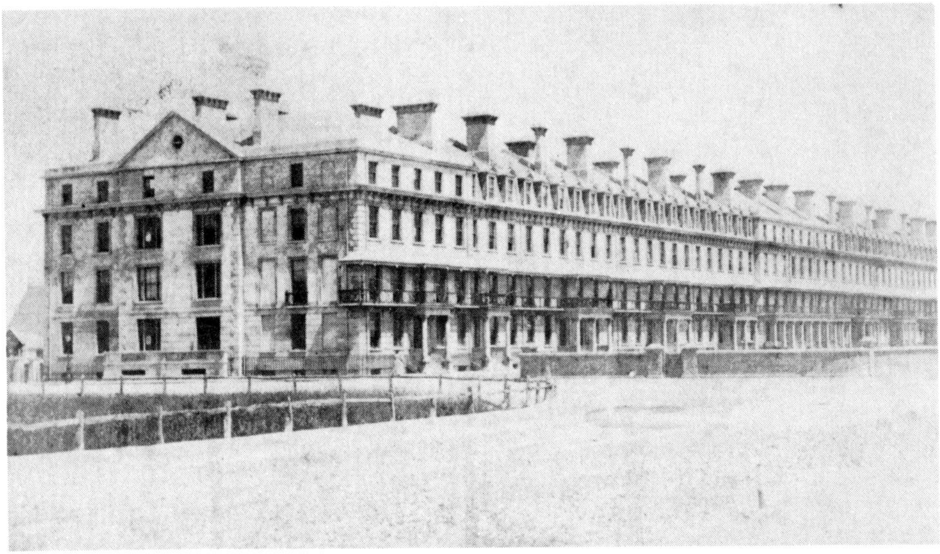

HEENE TERRACE was built as eighteen four-storey houses in 1865, at a time when the West Worthing Esplanade was being built. The houses are yellow brick with stucco dressings. This photograph was taken not long after the terrace was completed.

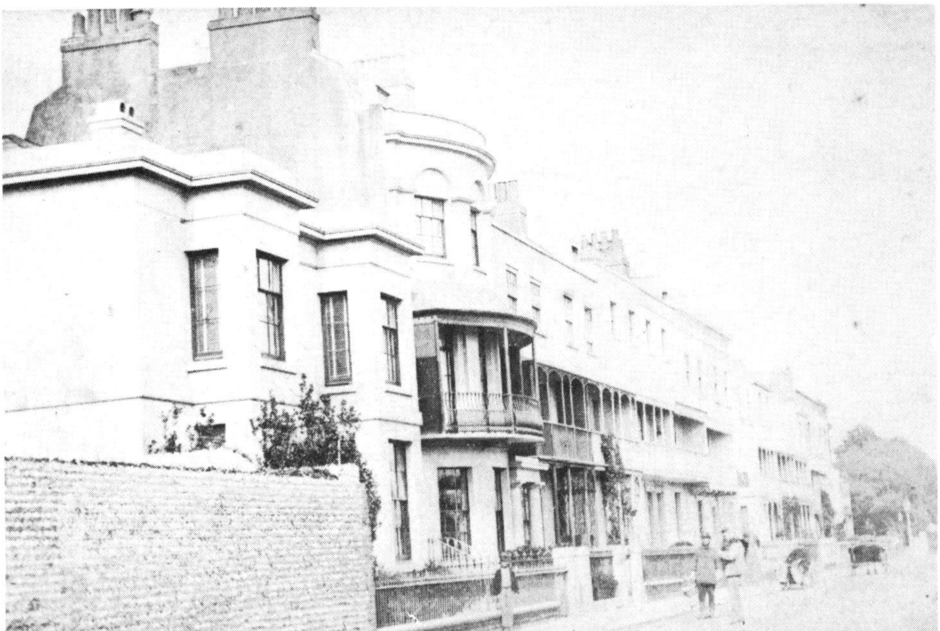

AMBROSE PLACE, one of the most elegant and attractive roads in Worthing, was built between 1810 and 1826. It was named after Ambrose Cartwright, who was one of the architects involved in its construction. It is still a lovely sight and largely unspoiled.

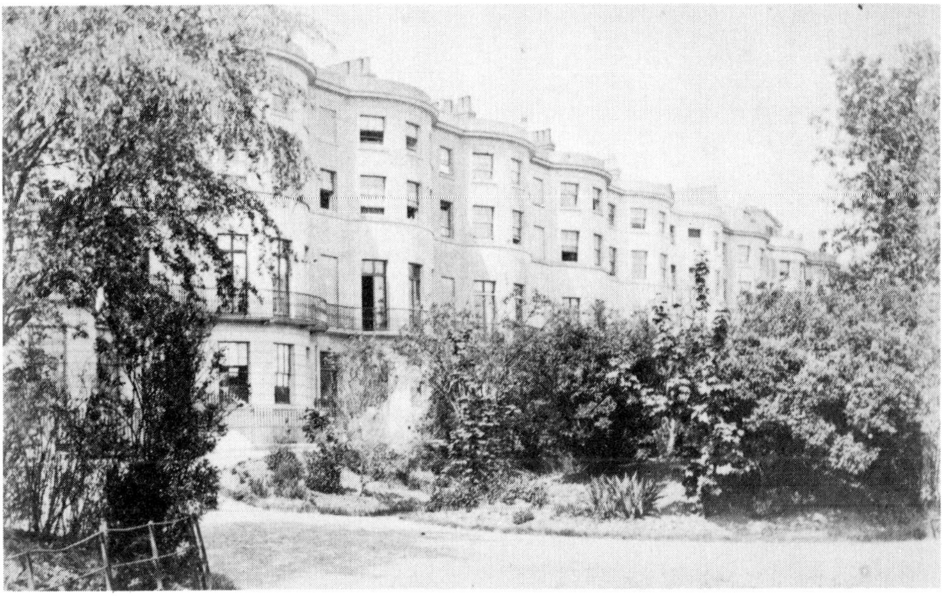

LIVERPOOL TERRACE was designed by Henry Cotton and built between 1814 and 1826. It is one of the most graceful sections of Worthing still standing. It is also one of the oldest. The area in front of the terrace was a pleasure garden with a Gothic rural bower, a bowling green and archery ground. The land on which it was built was formerly called London Fields.

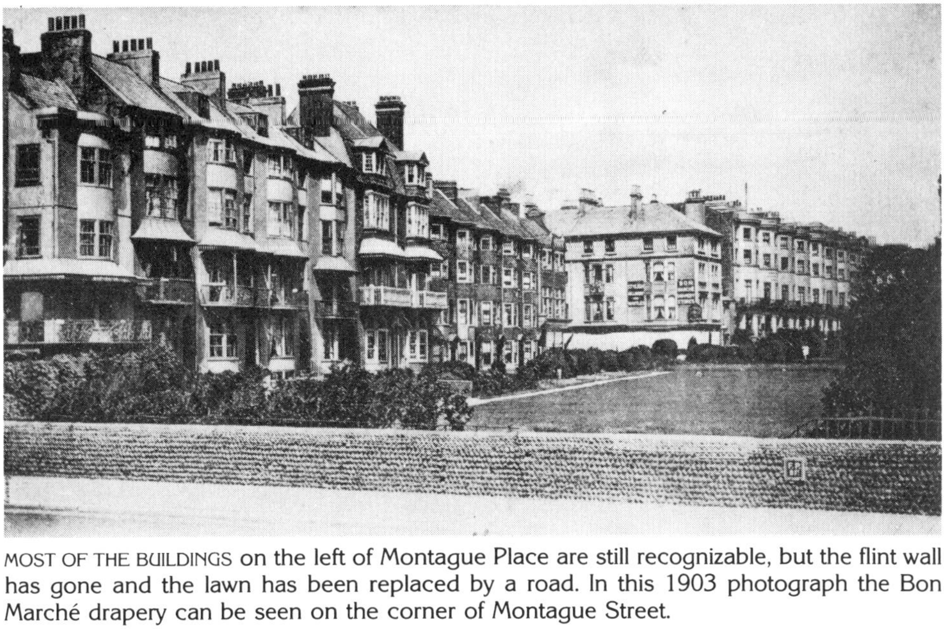

MOST OF THE BUILDINGS on the left of Montague Place are still recognizable, but the flint wall has gone and the lawn has been replaced by a road. In this 1903 photograph the Bon Marché drapery can be seen on the corner of Montague Street.

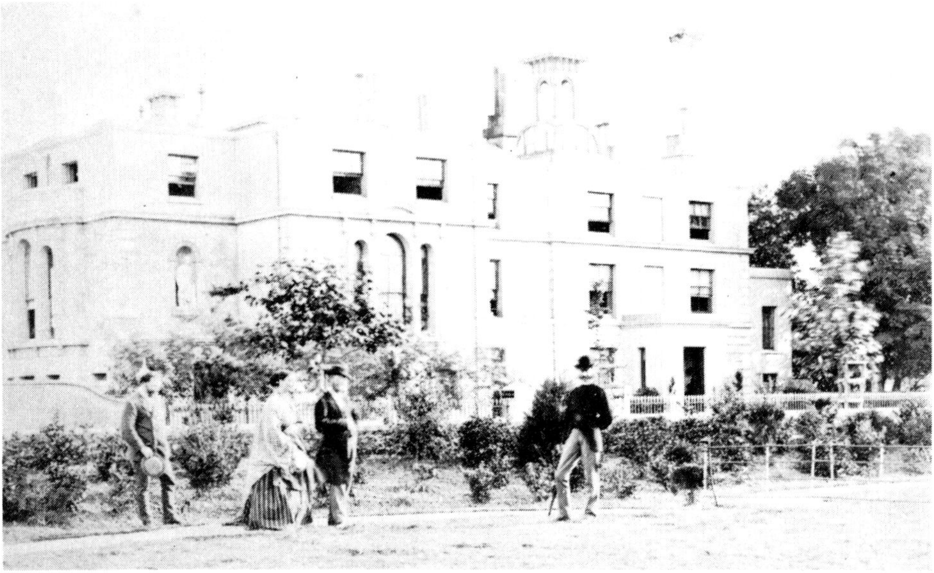

BEACHFIELD, ON BRIGHTON ROAD, was originally only a four-room house, built *c.* 1840 by a brickmaker called Pope. Like its surviving neighbour, Beach House, it was designed by John B. Rebecca. It was enlarged by a schoolmaster who renamed it College House. It was used as a school for some years, but was demolished in 1961, about a hundred years after this picture was taken. The Aquarena is now on this site.

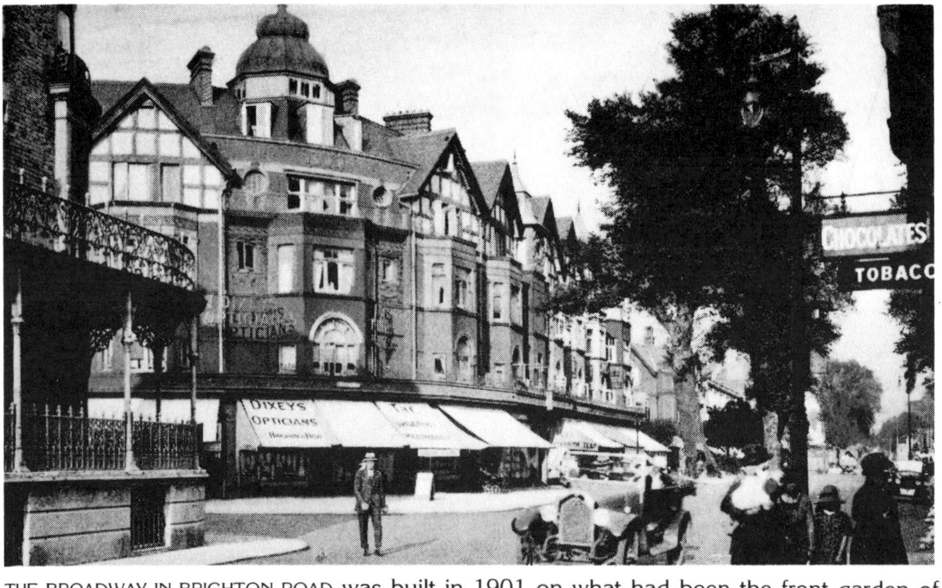


THE BROADWAY IN BRIGHTON ROAD was built in 1901 on what had been the front garden of Warwick House. It faces Steyne Gardens and is decorated with elaborate panels of plaster which are in need of renovation.

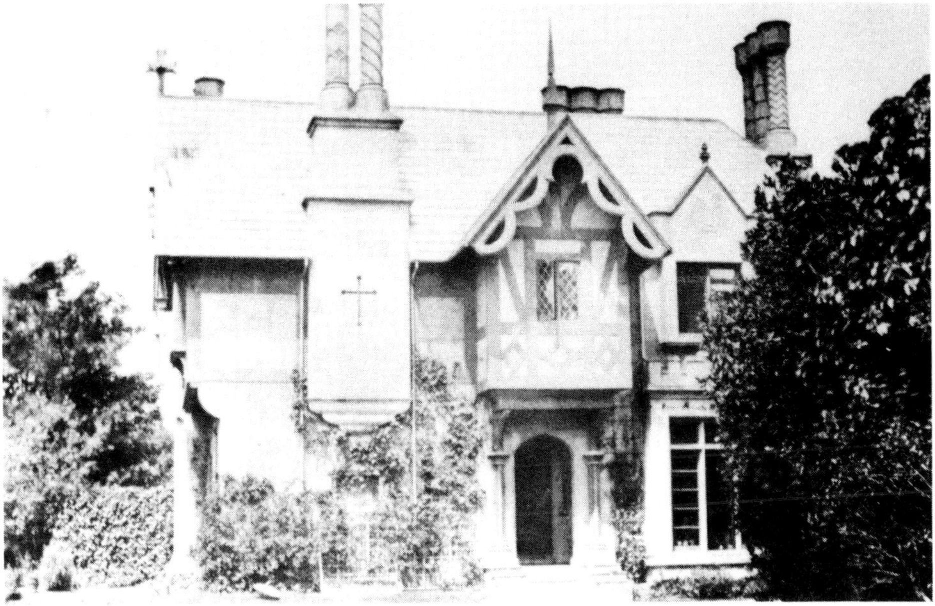

GOTHIC LODGE IN RICHMOND ROAD is now called Tudor Close. It was built *c.* 1840 in a Tudor Gothic style. This picture was taken *c.* 1860.

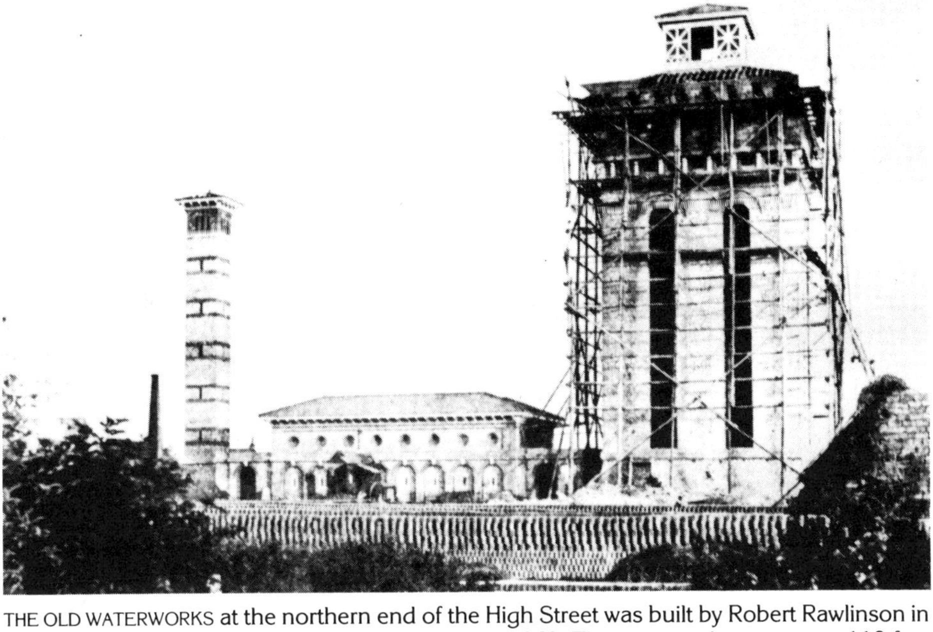

THE OLD WATERWORKS at the northern end of the High Street was built by Robert Rawlinson in 1857. He was also responsible for the first pier in 1862. The waterworks tower was 110 feet high and held 110,000 gallons. In 1896 it was replaced by a new water station in Broadwater. It was demolished in 1922.

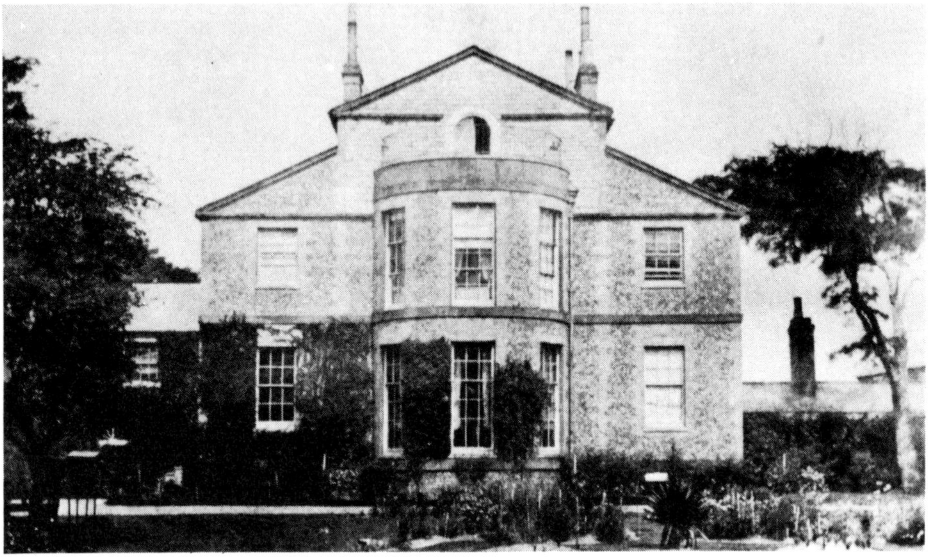

WARWICK HOUSE used to face Steyne Gardens from the north and was the main residence in Worthing in the late eighteenth century. At that time it was let out to famous and wealthy visitors for up to twenty-five pounds a week. Princess Amelia stayed there when she visited Worthing in 1798.

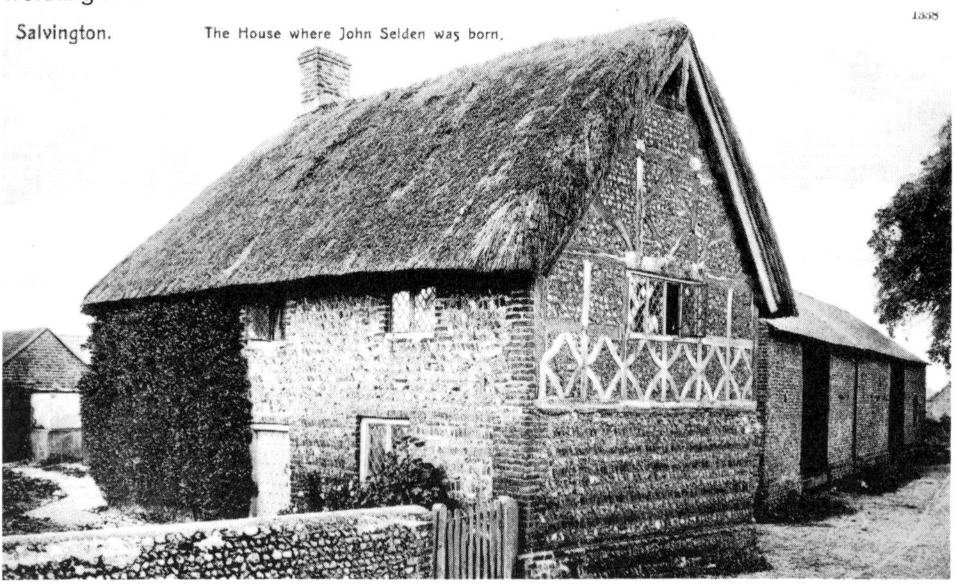


JOHN SELDEN WAS AN AUTHOR, lawyer and philosopher who was born in this cottage in Salvington in 1584. He was well known in his own lifetime. He carved a Latin inscription in the lintel over the front door which, translated, read 'Walk in and welcome, honest friend – repose; thief, get thee gone, to thee I'll not unclose.' His cottage became a local landmark, but was tragically demolished in 1963.

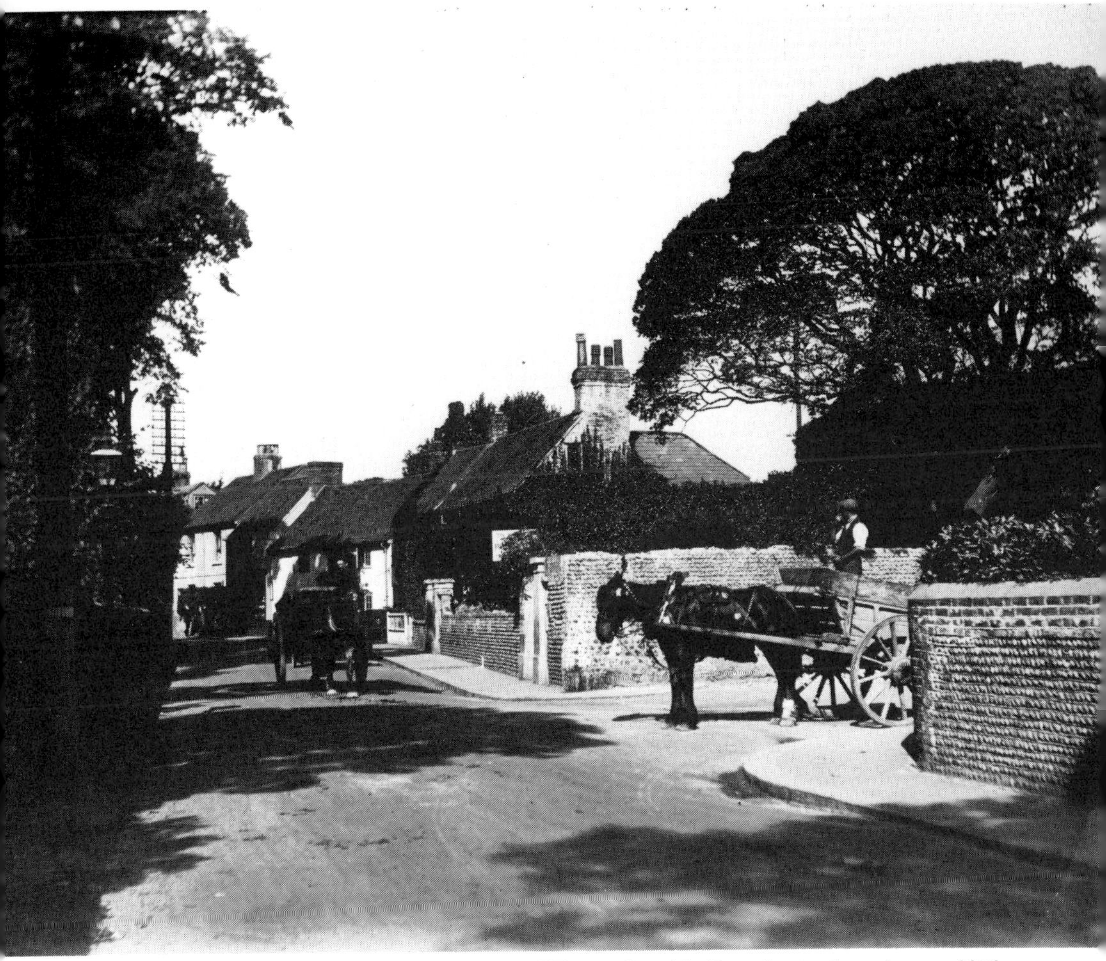

THE JUNCTION OF BROADWATER STREET EAST and Forest Road in Broadwater has changed little since this photograph was taken in September 1914.

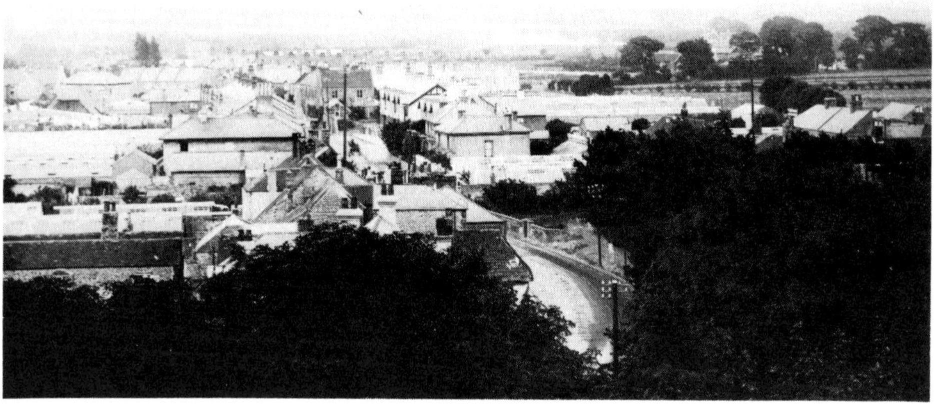

THE ROWS OF GLASSHOUSES shown in this view from Broadwater church tower at the beginning of the twentieth century were part of the area's thriving fruit and vegetable growing industry.

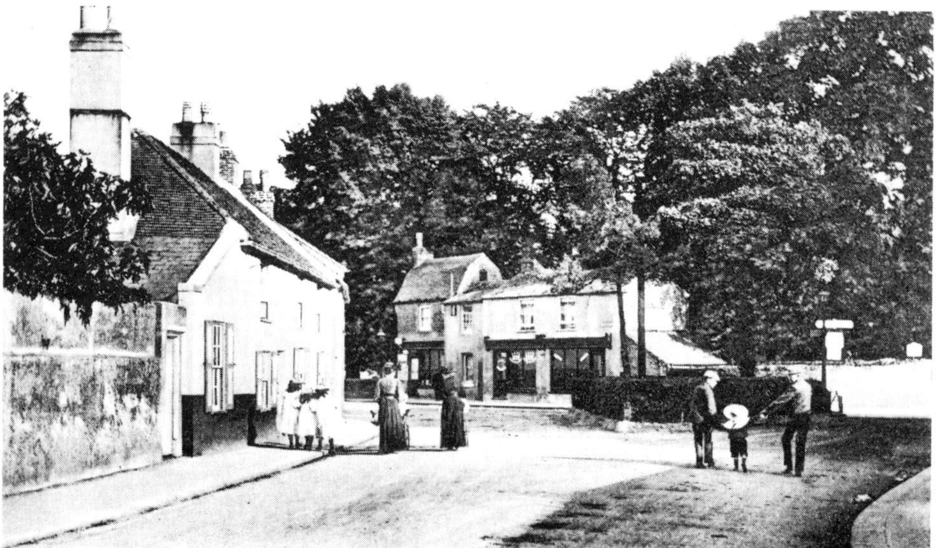

THE BUILDINGS ON THE FAR SIDE OF BROADWATER STREET EAST in this picture are still there today, backing on to the churchyard. Several photographers produced versions of this view.

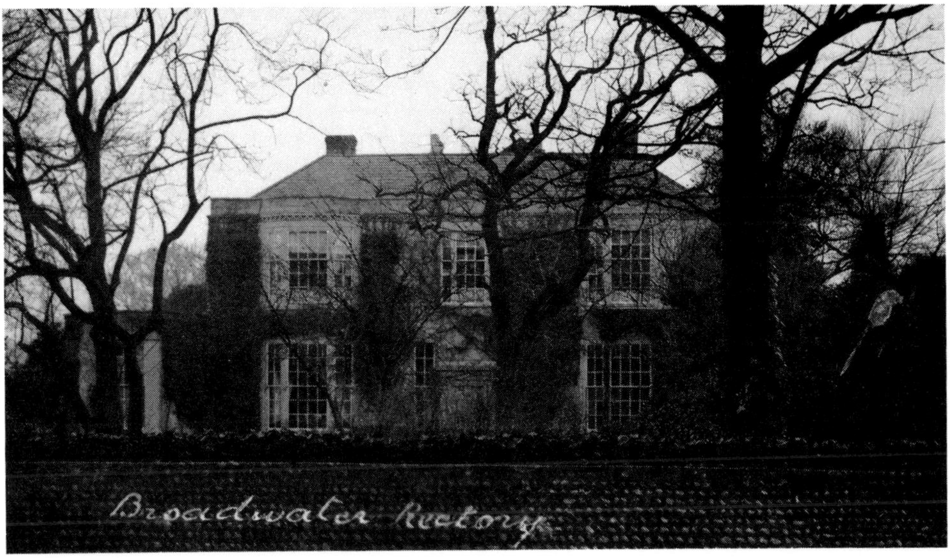


BROADWATER RECTORY was built opposite the church *c.* 1790, and was a handsome two-storey house. In 1924 the church gave it up and it passed into private hands, being renamed Muir House. It was demolished in 1959 and the site is now part of the ugly Broadwater Boulevard shopping precinct.

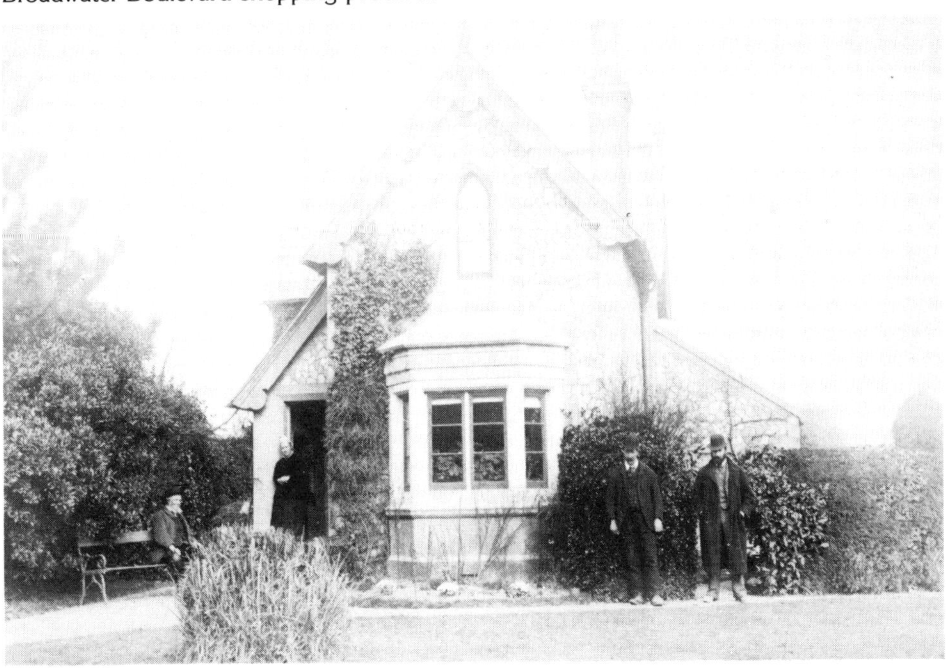

THE LODGE AT BROADWATER CEMETERY in South Farm Road, *c.* 1880. The people in the picture are not identified, but were probably the cemetery keeper and his assistants.

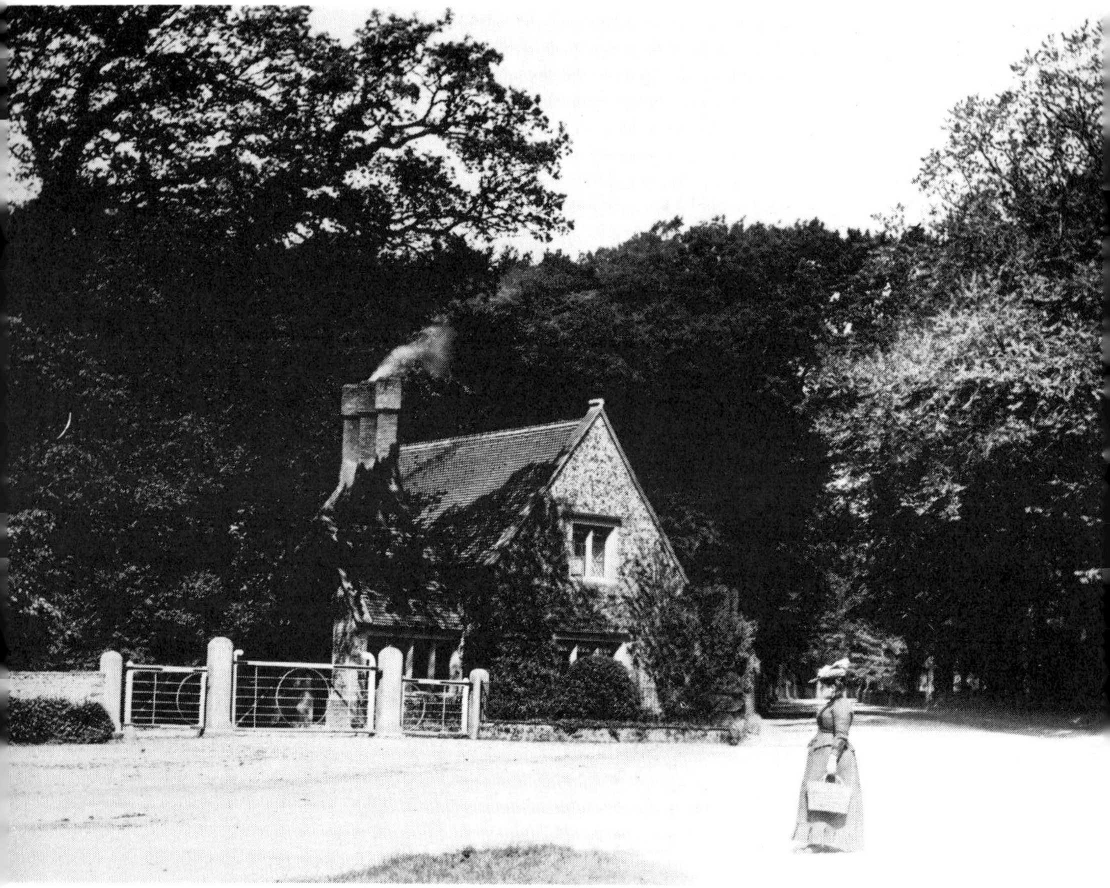

OFFINGTON LODGE on the boundary of the Offington Estate appears on many photographs from the turn of the century.

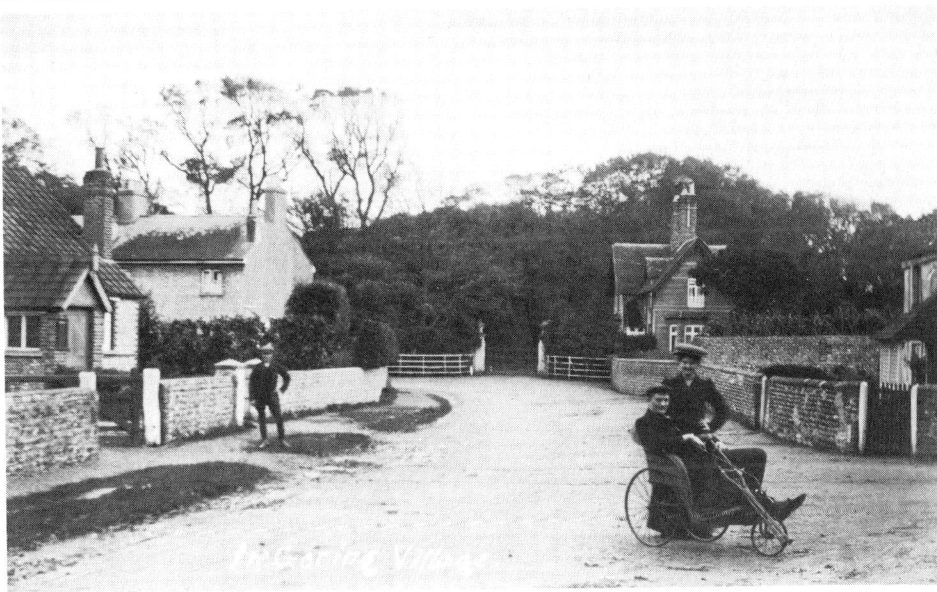

GORING around the turn of the century when it was still a village.

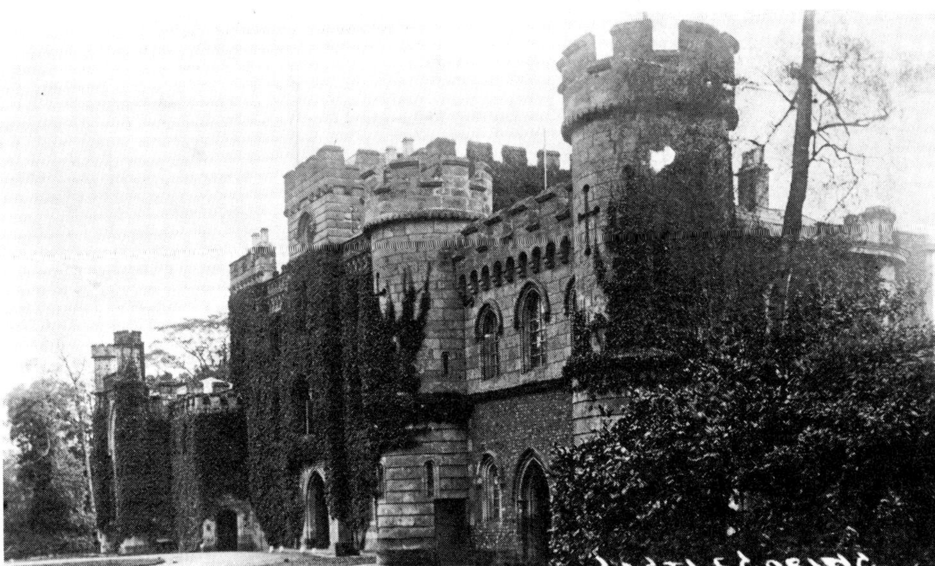


SIR BYSSHE SHELLEY, the grandfather of the poet, began building Castle Goring in 1790 but it was not completed for over twenty-five years. It has a Palladian front and a Gothic north face. By 1825 it was so dilapidated that it was known as 'Rat Castle'. It was then bought and repaired by Captain G. Petchell RN. It has recently been used as a centre for foreign students learning English.

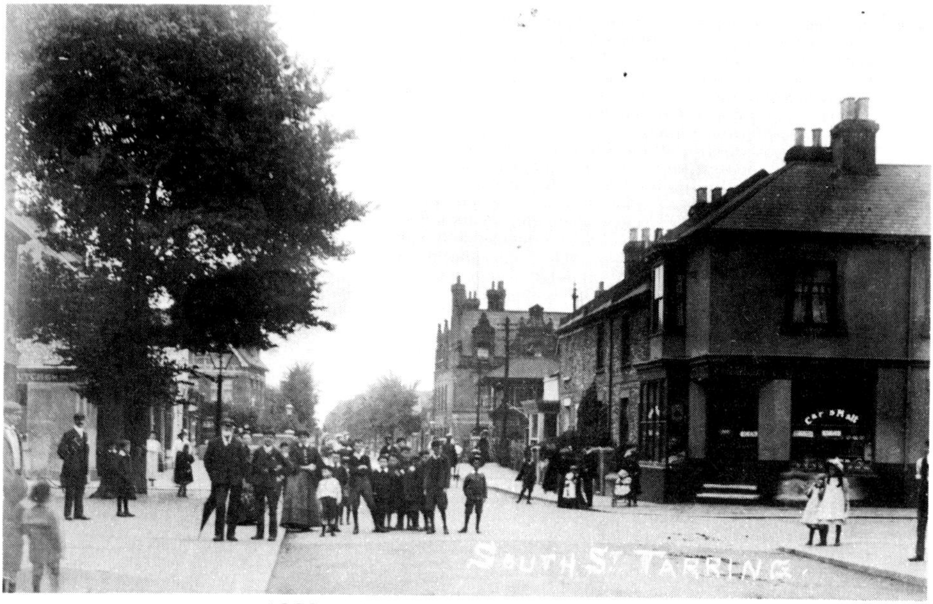


SOUTH STREET, TARRING, C. 1900, with the crowd clearly posing for the photographer.

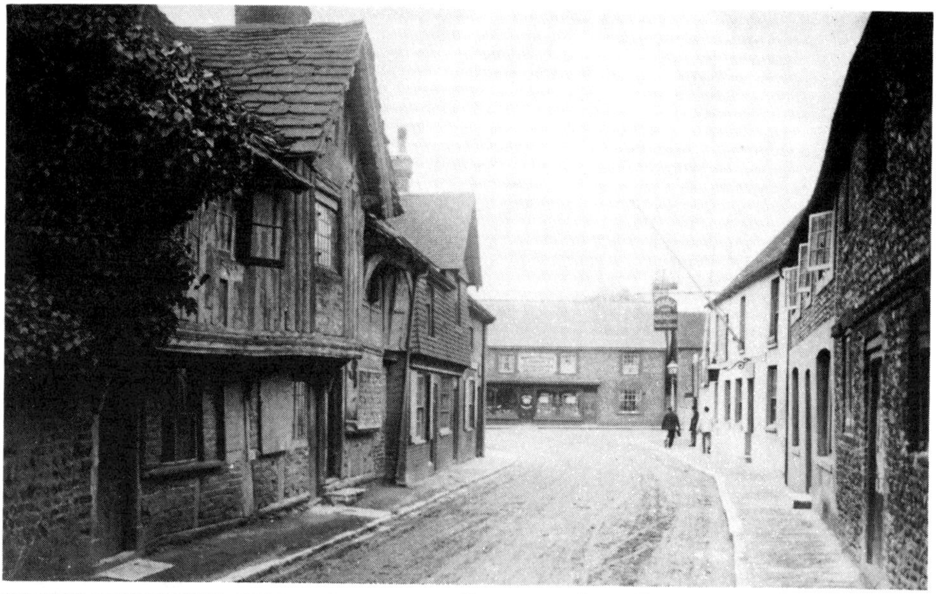

THIS ROW OF FIFTEENTH-CENTURY COTTAGES at Parsonage Row, Tarring was originally longer, but one section was demolished in 1895 to make way for Glebe Road. For some years the cottages were occupied by the Museum of Sussex Folklore, but they are now used as a restaurant. This picture, taken early in the twentieth century, also shows the George and Dragon public house.

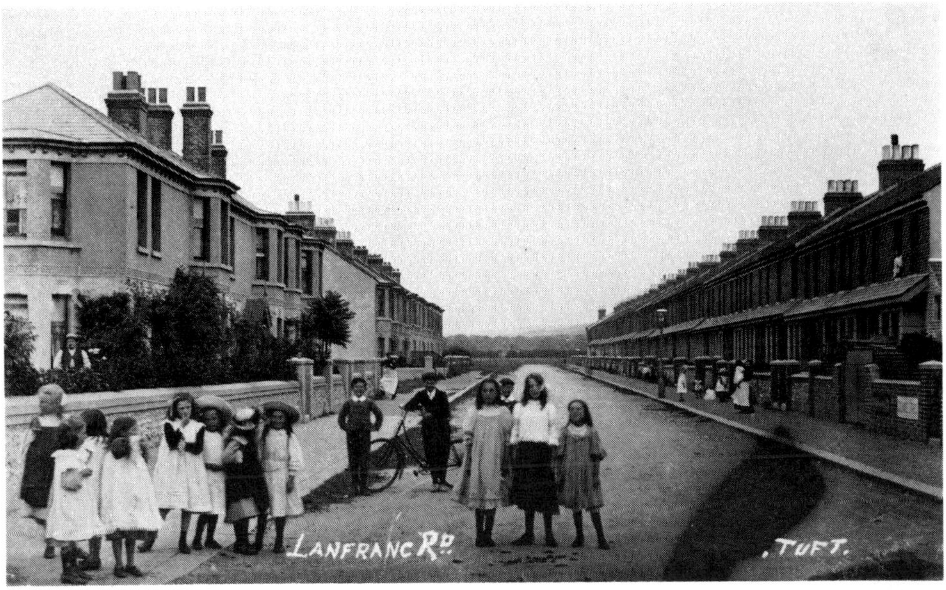


SOME OF THESE CHILDREN ARE NEATLY POSED for the photographer, while others seem to have been distracted and have turned away. They are in Lanfranc Road *c.* 1890. The road was named after an eleventh-century archbishop of Canterbury who was also lord of the manor of Tarring.

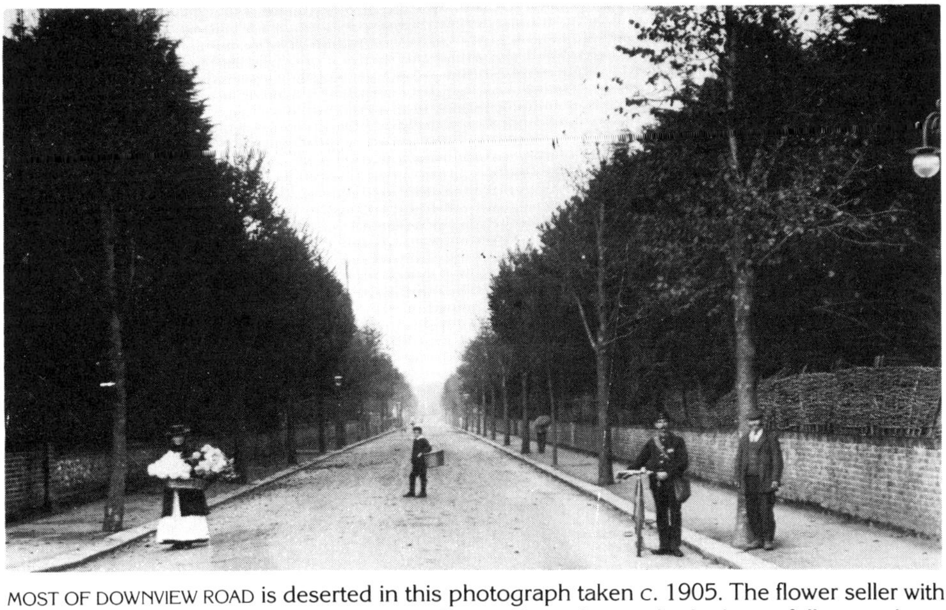

MOST OF DOWNVIEW ROAD is deserted in this photograph taken *c.* 1905. The flower seller with her heavy baskets, the postman, delivery boy and one bystander look carefully posed.

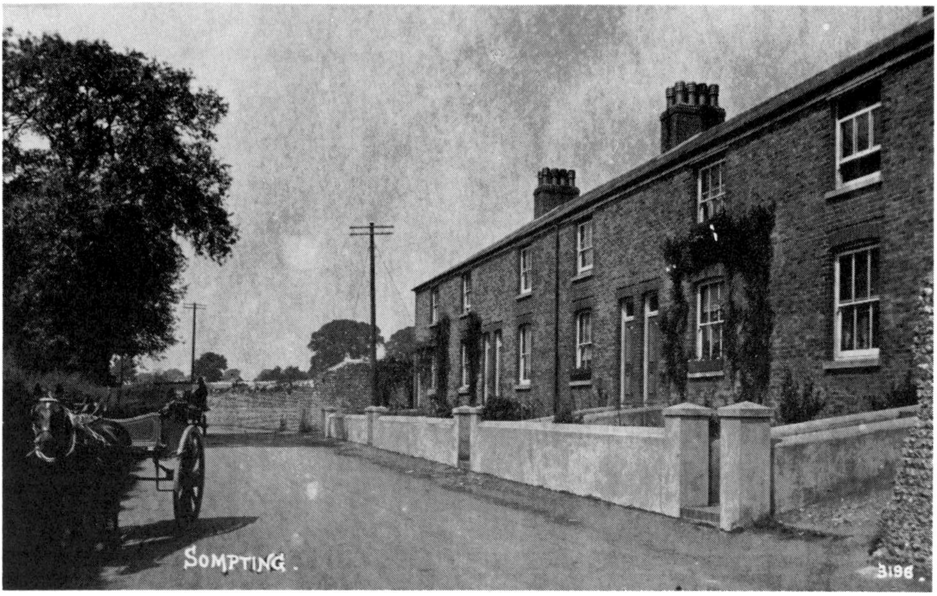


THIS PART OF WEST STREET, Sompting, has barely altered since this picture was taken early in the twentieth century.

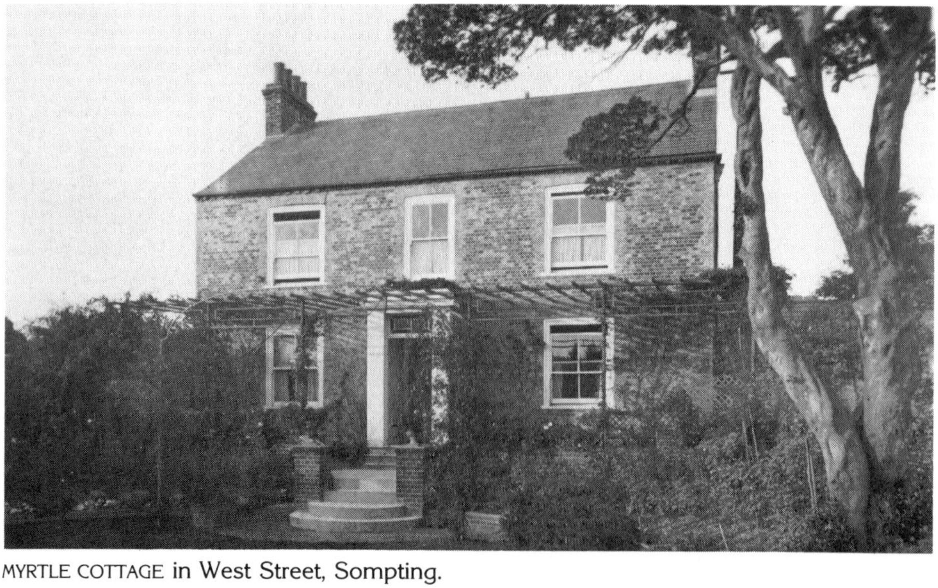

MYRTLE COTTAGE in West Street, Sompting.

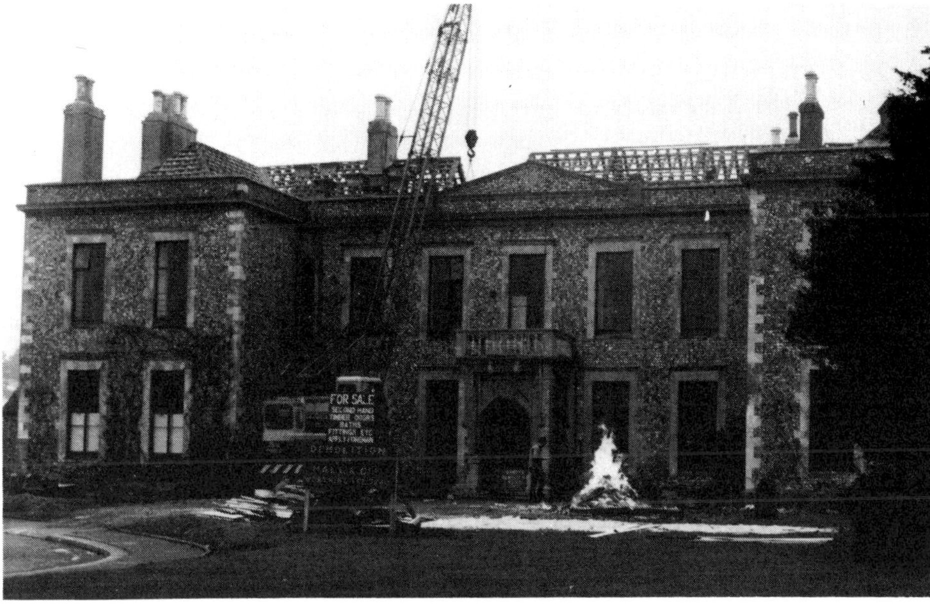


MANY BEAUTIFUL AND IMPORTANT BUILDINGS AROUND WORTHING have been pulled down, usually in the name of progress. The Tudor mansion of Offington Hall was demolished in 1808 and replaced by a Georgian house. In the mid-nineteenth century the Gaisford family built a Roman Catholic chapel there. In 1935 the house was turned into flats and in 1963 it was demolished.

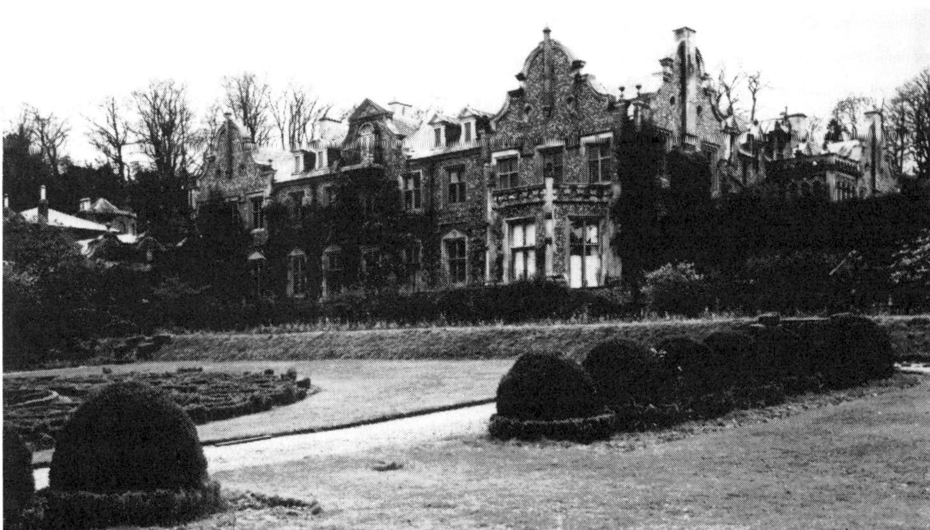

MUNTHAM COURT IN FINDON was built *c.* 1748 by Lord Montague. It was designed as a hunting lodge. In 1850 it was taken over by the Thynne family. It was, sadly, demolished in 1961. Part of the beautiful site is now occupied by the Worthing crematorium.

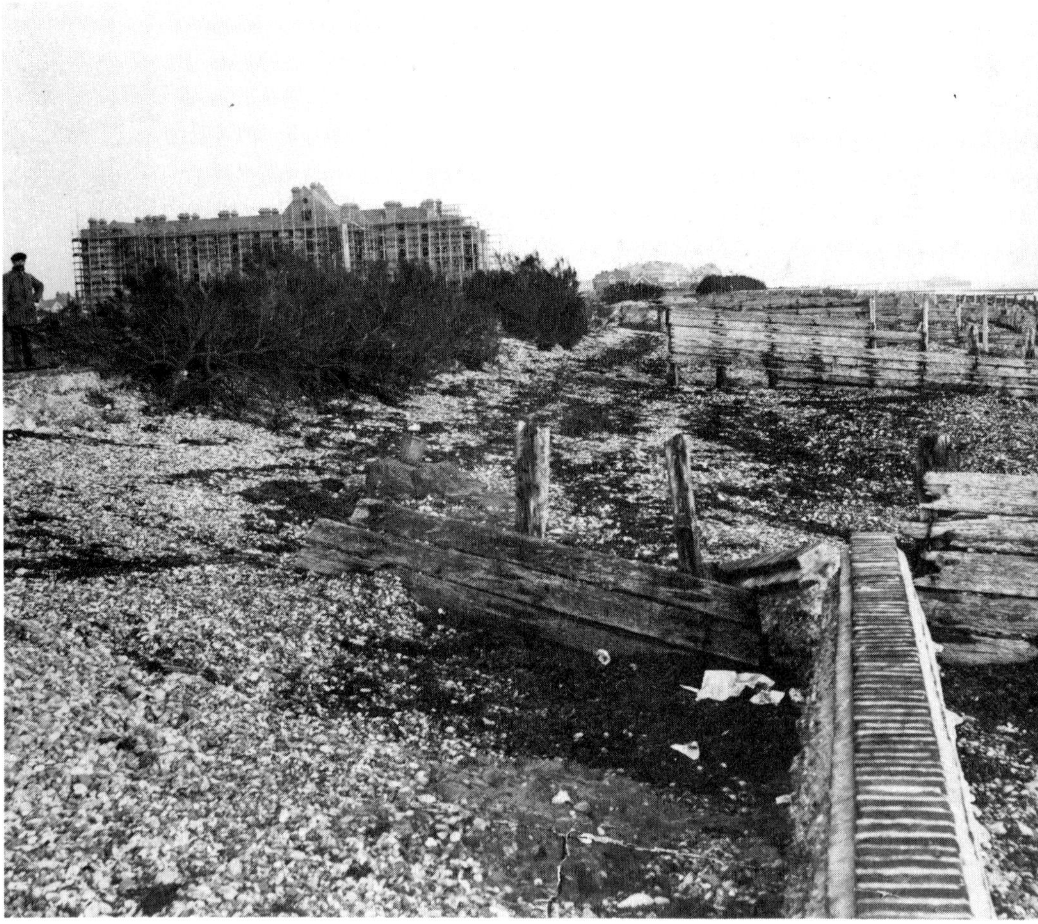

THE HOTEL METROPOLE was started in 1893 at the southern end of Grand Avenue. Development in West Worthing was only beginning then and there were even plans to build a second pier at the end of Grand Avenue. Funds ran out before the hotel was finished and the half-built shell was left until 1923. It was then finished as flats and called Dolphin Lodge, but to many local people it is known affectionately as 'Worthing's White Elephant'.

SECTION FOURTEEN

# Rural Life

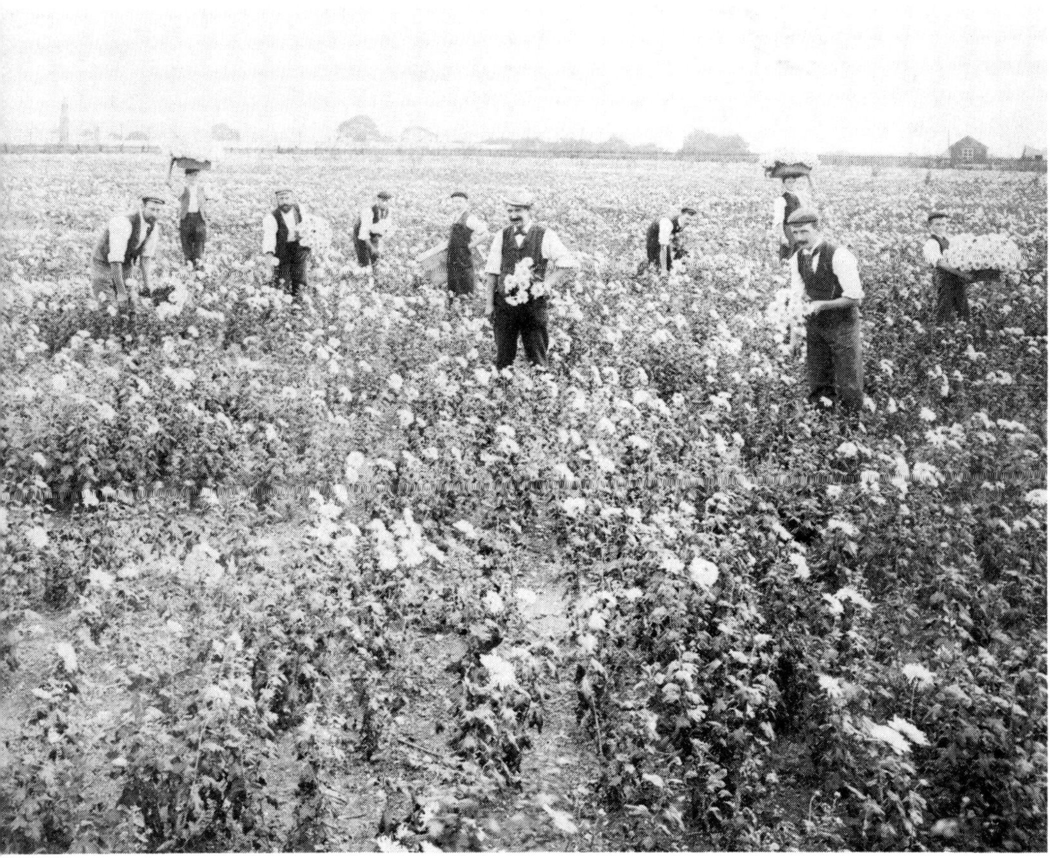

FLOWER GROWING was an important industry in the area until the 1950s. During the Second World War growers had great difficulties transporting their crops to market. These chrysanthemum pickers were photographed *c.* 1910. Chrysanthemum growing gave winter work to the nursery labourers. The largest glasshouse concern in the area was Piper's with 105 greenhouses.

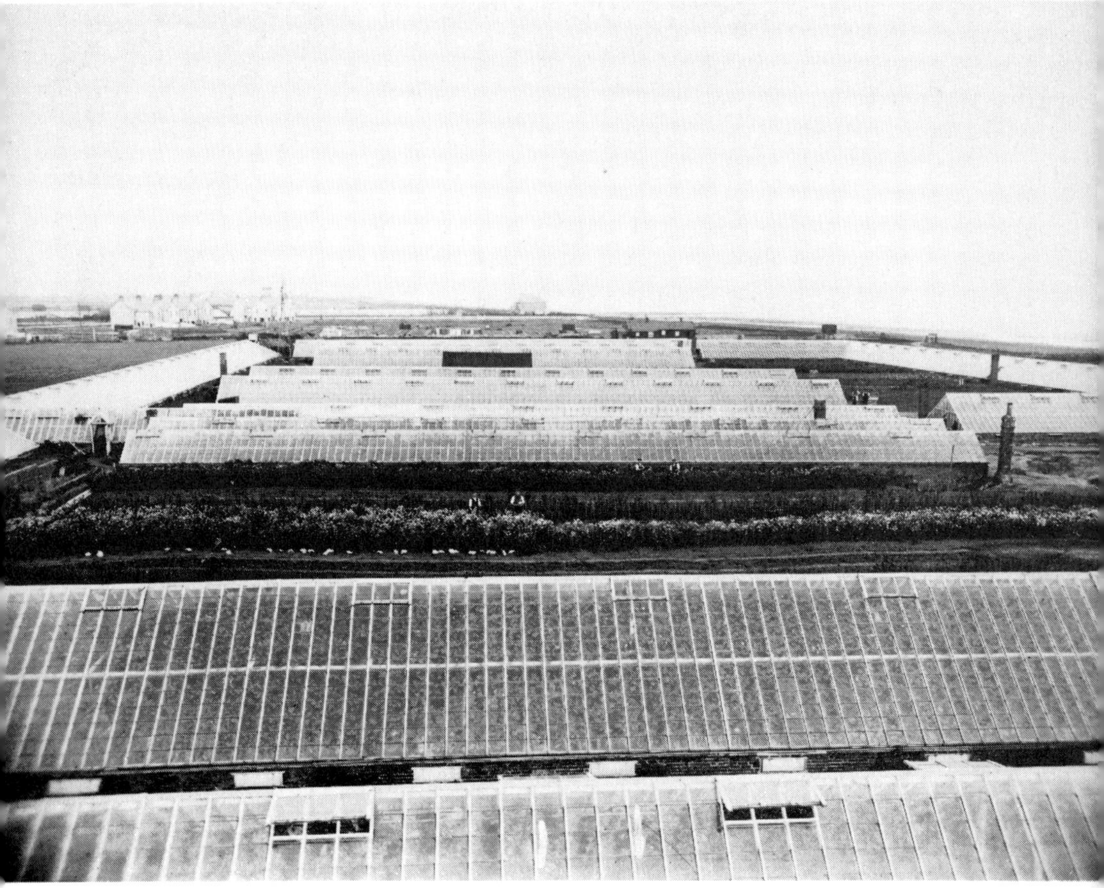

THESE ROWS OF GLASSHOUSES, seen before the First World War, show how extensive fruit and vegetable growing was around Worthing. The gentle climate enabled growers to produce high-quality unusual crops which were snapped up by London shops and restaurants.

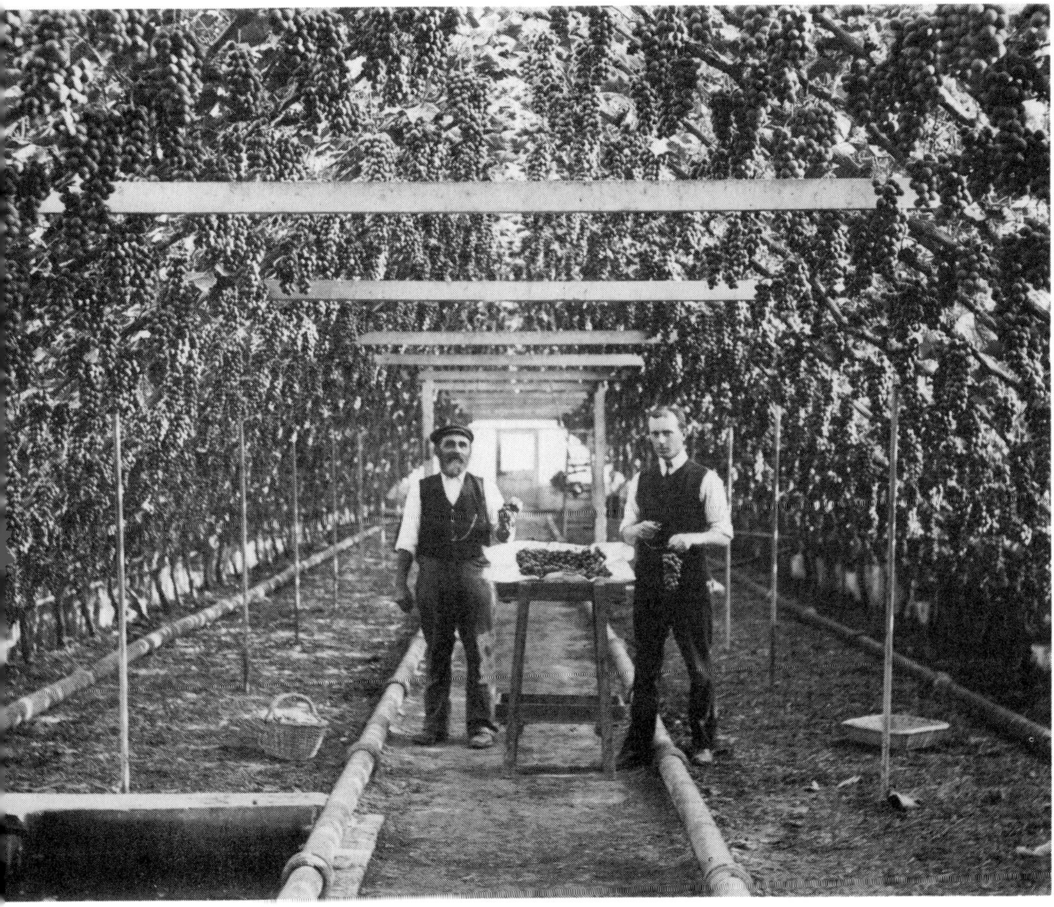

THE SUCCESS OF GRAPE GROWING along the coastal plain is shown in this photograph, taken *c.* 1910. During the First World War at least one local man was granted exemption from military service because he worked for a grape grower. The sale of grapes to the USA was a useful part of Britain's exports and produced much-needed income for the government.

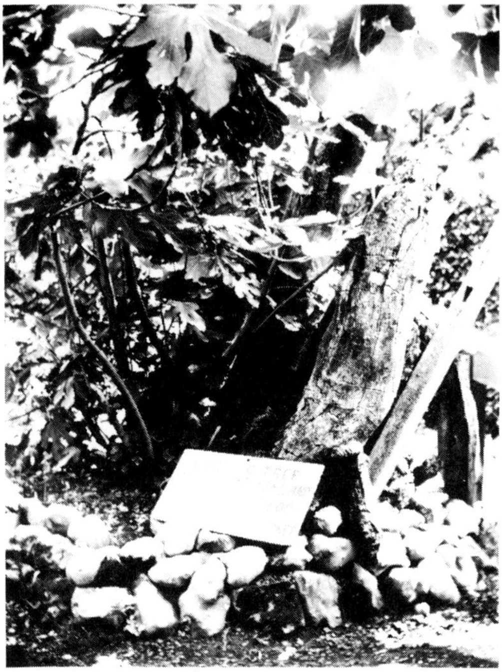

TARRING IS WELL KNOWN FOR THE FIG GARGENS in South Street. According to tradition the trees were planted by Thomas à Becket. However, in spite of the fact that Tarring was part of the archbishop's estates there is no evidence that he ever went there. Some of the trees were grown from cuttings taken in the parsonage garden in 1745. Until the Second World War Miss Humphries ran a tea garden in the orchard. Post-war building has been allowed to destroy a large part of the fig garden.

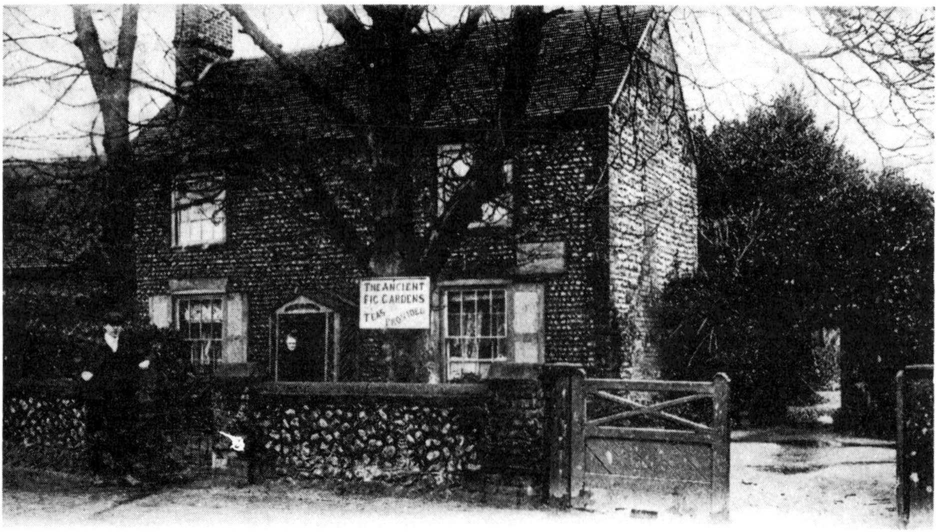

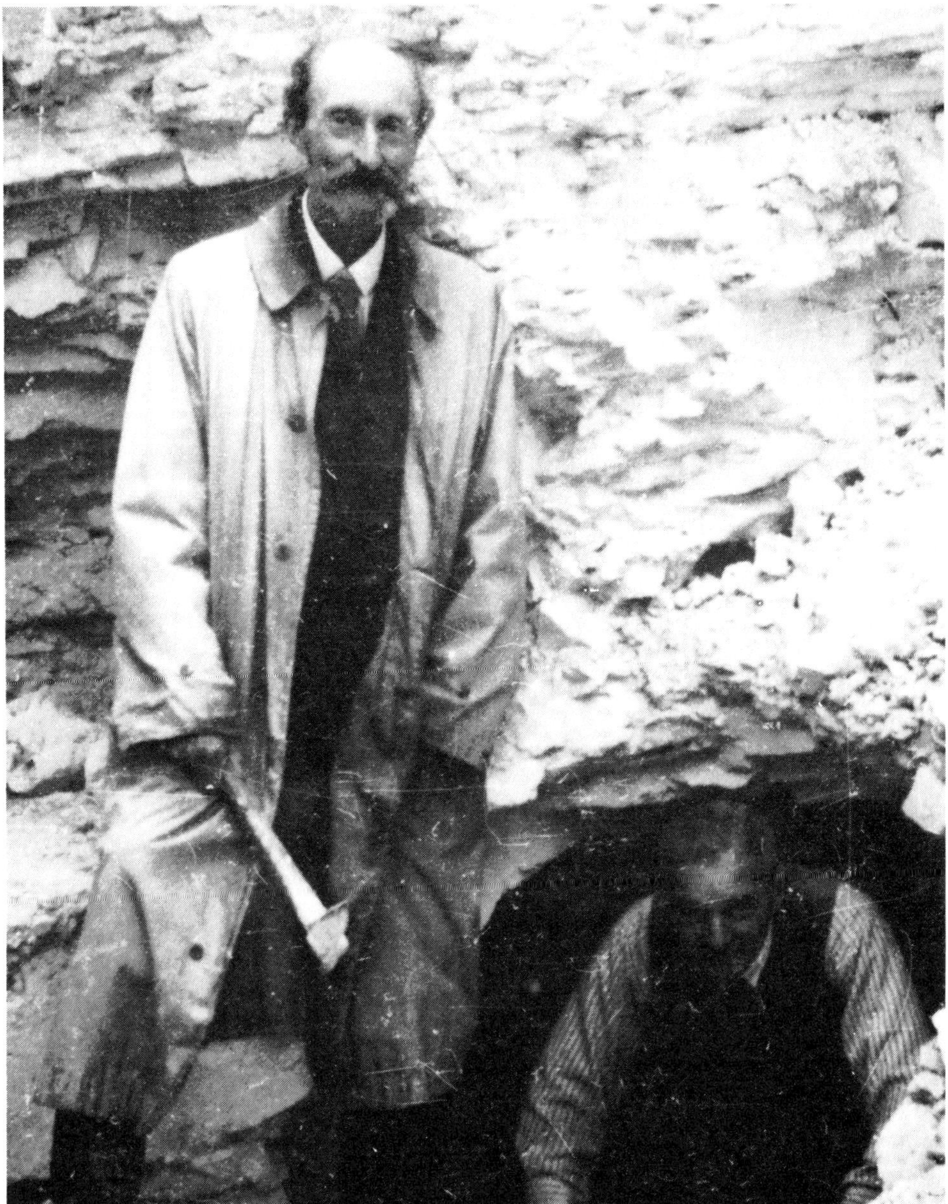

THIS PICTURE SHOWS TWO MEN who became friends through a shared interest in archaeology. They are shown during the re-excavation of one of the New Stone Age flint mines at Cissbury. The man down the mine is John Pull, a bank guard, who spent years investigating the mines. He was killed in a bank raid in 1960. The other man is Barclay Wills who studied and wrote about Sussex shepherds and their lives. Much of his collection of shepherding material is on show in Worthing museum.

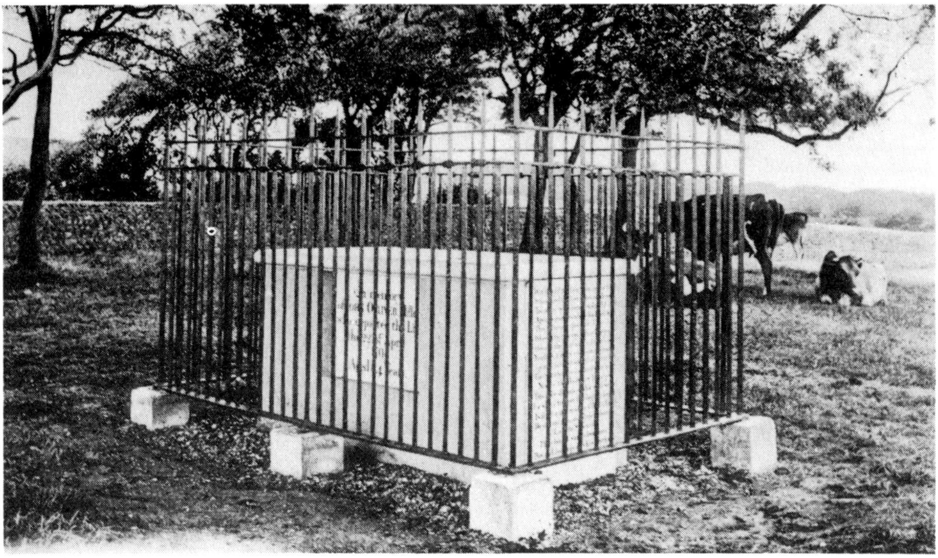

THE MILLER'S TOMB AT HIGHDOWN to the west of Worthing has drawn large numbers of visitors for two hundred years. John Olliver was an eccentric miller who lived in a cottage on the eastern edge of the hill. He used to write poetry and liked to sit in a summer house he built, reading his Bible and looking out over the coast. He built his tomb twenty-seven years before his death and kept his coffin on wheels under his bed, bringing it out to show visitors.

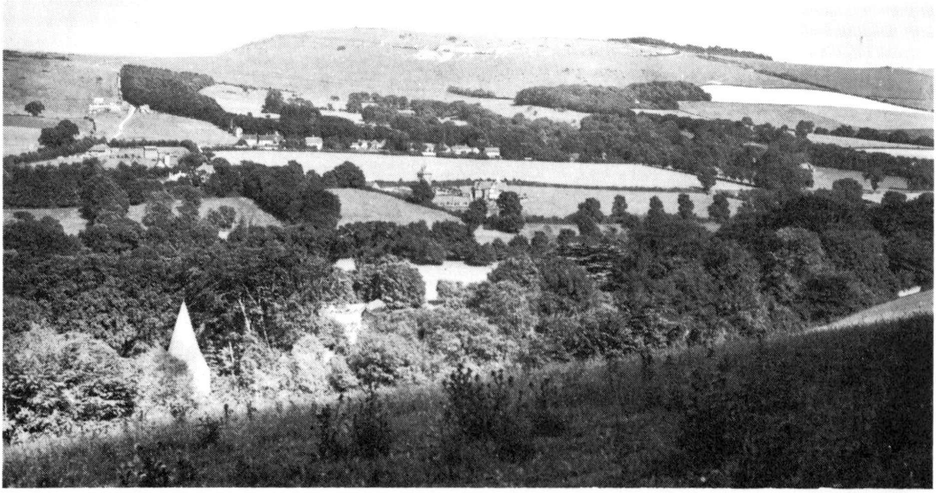

THIS PICTURE SHOWS CISSBURY from near Findon church. Now owned by the National Trust, Cissbury was at one time threatened by the spreading development of Findon Valley. Cissbury is the site of over a hundred flint mine shafts dating to the New Stone Age, c. 3600 BC, and the largest Iron Age hillfort in the area.

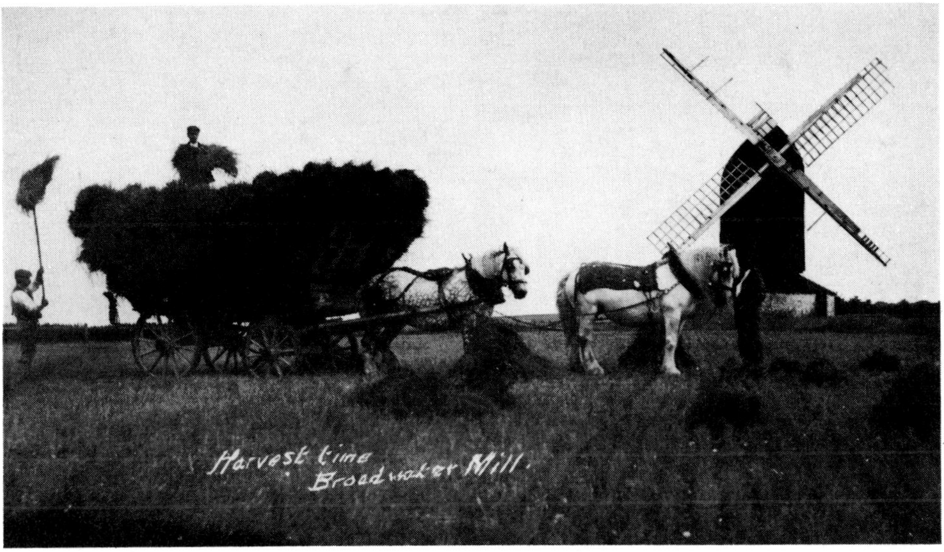


THE HARVEST BEING GATHERED IN nearly a hundred years ago. Behind the harvesters is Broadwater mill. Built c. 1820, it was also called Offington, Cissbury and Ballard's mill and was on the southern slopes of Cissbury, near Mill Plantation. Originally owned by Charles Ballard, it was run by Henry Isted in its last working years, up to 1901. It was finally demolished in 1920.

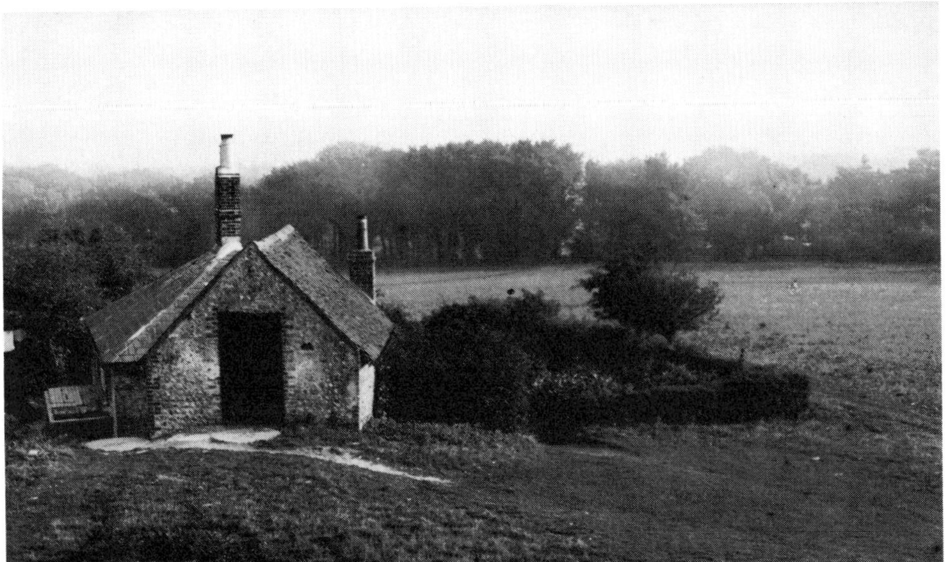

THE COTTAGE where the owner of Broadwater Mill lived, on the southern slopes of Cissbury.

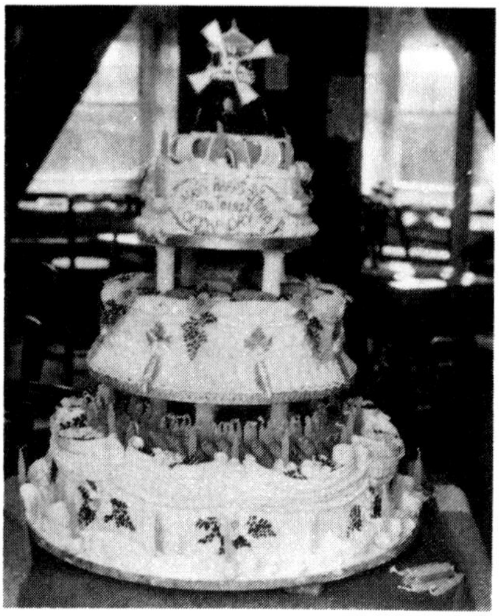

FEW WINDMILLS CAN HAVE HAD THEIR OWN BIRTHDAY CAKE, let alone one with three tiers and a windmill on top. This elaborate cake was baked to celebrate Salvington windmill's 150th anniversary in July 1924 and is shown inside the roundhouse.

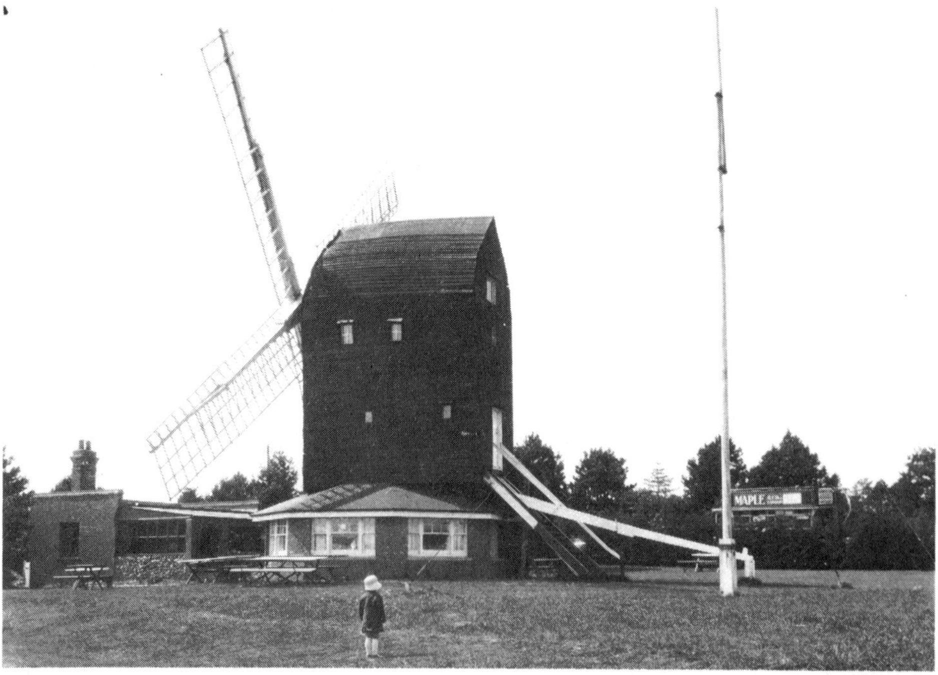


THE ONLY SURVIVING WINDMILL IN THE WORTHING AREA is on the top of Bost Hill at High Salvington. It may have been built as early as 1700, but first appeared on a map in 1724. It is a post mill, built of oak and supported by a huge main post. The roundhouse was converted for use as a tearoom in 1912 and was very popular. This picture was taken in 1925. The mill fell into disrepair, but it is now owned by Worthing Borough Council and is being painstakingly restored to its former glory by a group of dedicated volunteers.

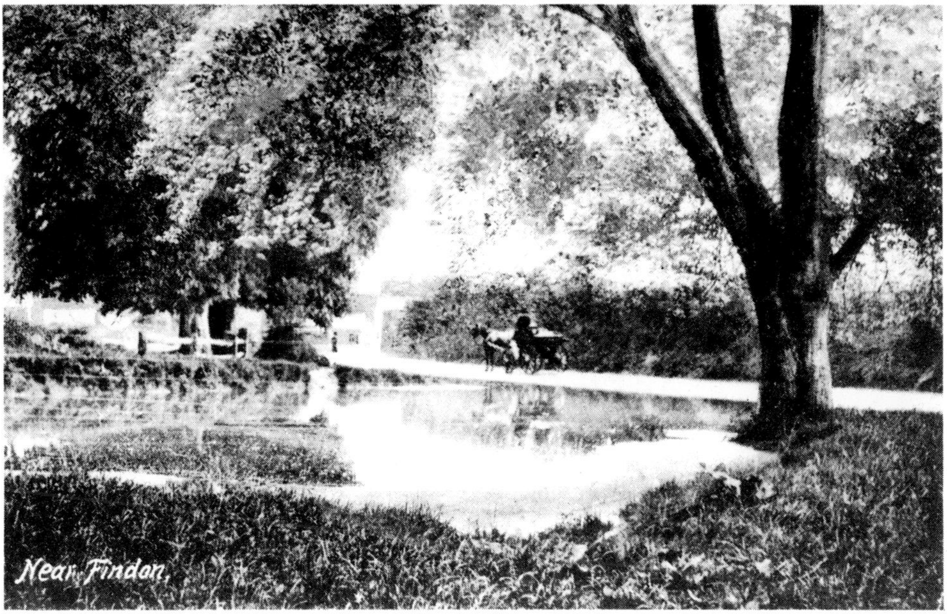


THIS POND WAS AT FINDON. The postcard is a popular type of rather idyllic rural view.

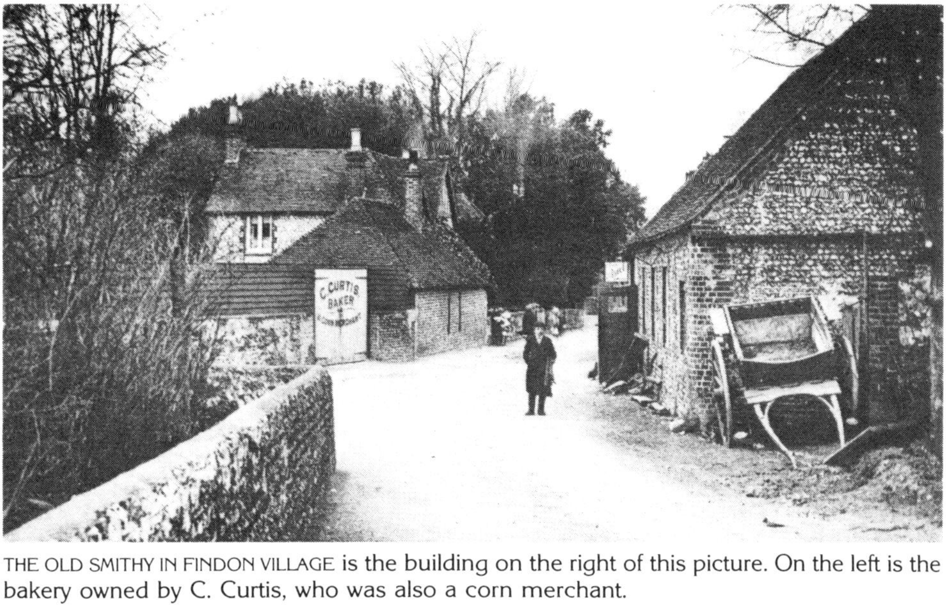


THE OLD SMITHY IN FINDON VILLAGE is the building on the right of this picture. On the left is the bakery owned by C. Curtis, who was also a corn merchant.

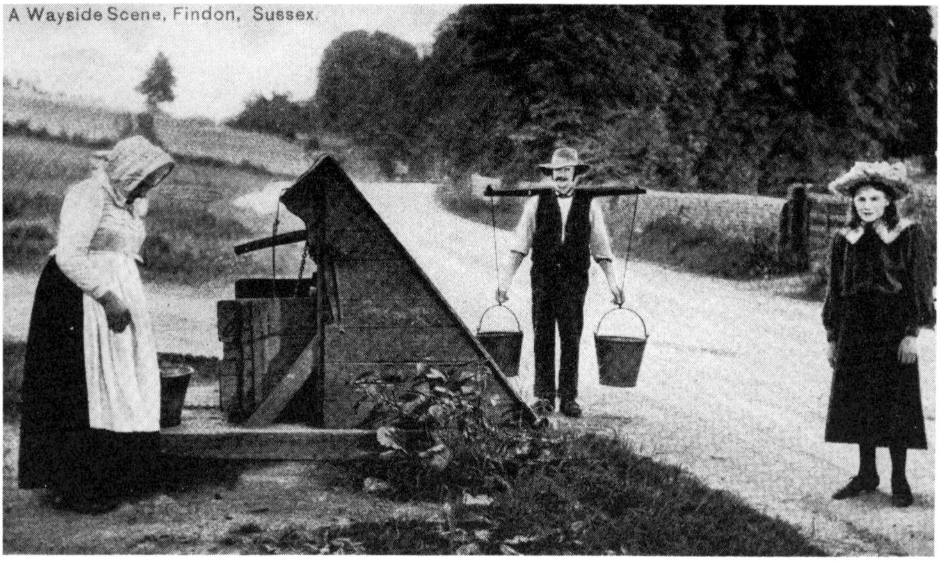


THE WELL AT FINDON was the subject of a number of postcards. This photograph was taken in 1918, although the scene looks much older. Of particular interest are the lady's bonnet and the man's yoke. Country people often had to walk to a well or pump to get water at this time. Mains water was brought to parts of Findon in 1926.

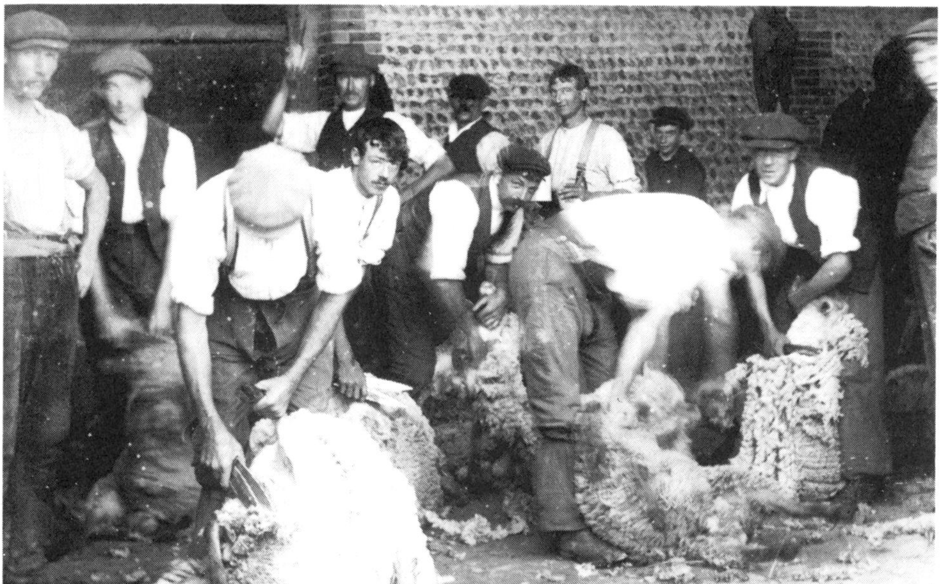

THESE SOUTHDOWN SHEEP are being sheared in a rather cramped shed while several men watch either the camera or the shearers.

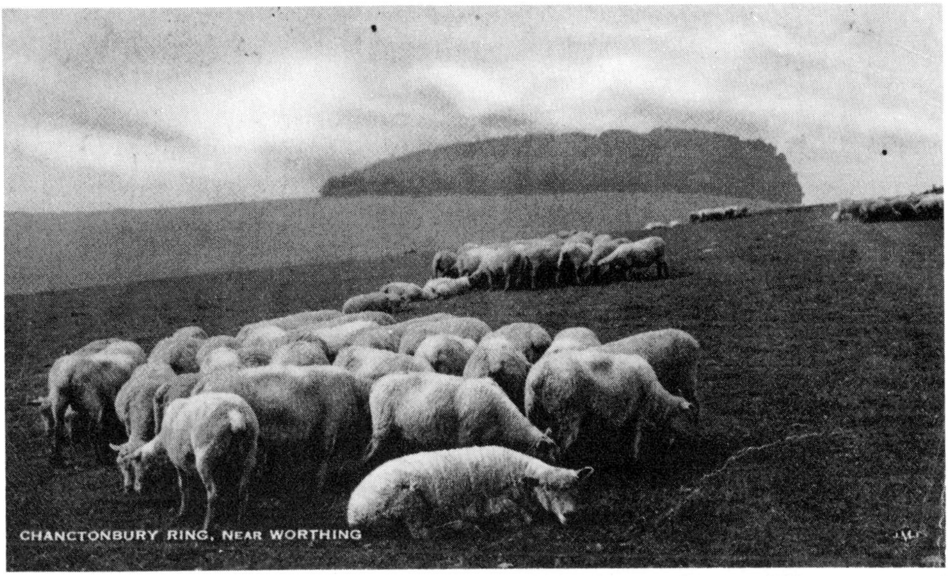


CHANCTONBURY RING, a clump of trees planted in 1760 by Charles Goring of Wiston, is one of the area's best-known and well-loved landmarks. Decimated by storms in 1987 and subsequent years the Ring is a shadow of its former self. It will be replanted, but it will be many years before the new trees reach maturity. Chanctonbury was also the site of a small Iron Age hillfort and a Romano-British temple.

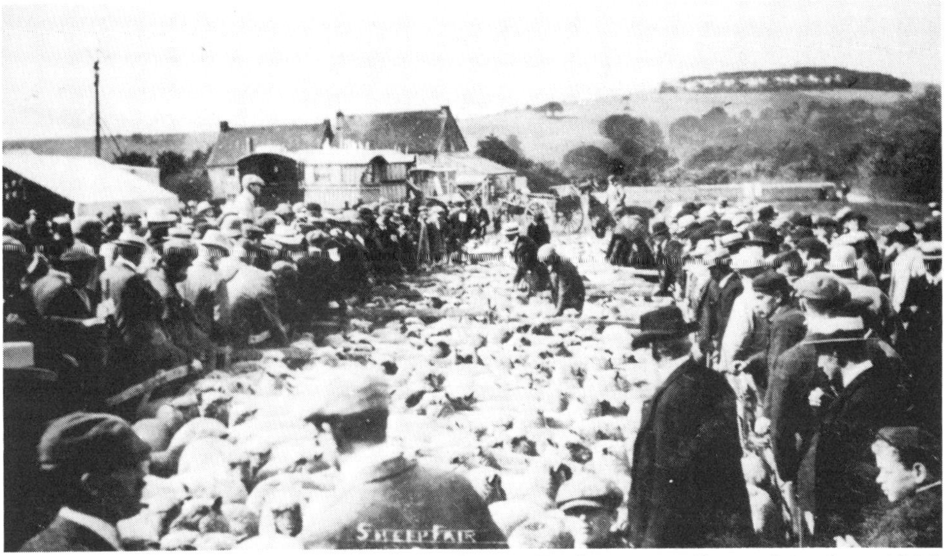


A SHEEP FAIR has been held on Nepcote Green, Findon, every September since 1814. Although large numbers of Southdown sheep were sold there, other breeds were also brought from far and wide for the sales. In 1930 there were 120,000 sheep at the fair. It is still very popular, although the number of sheep has fallen in recent years.

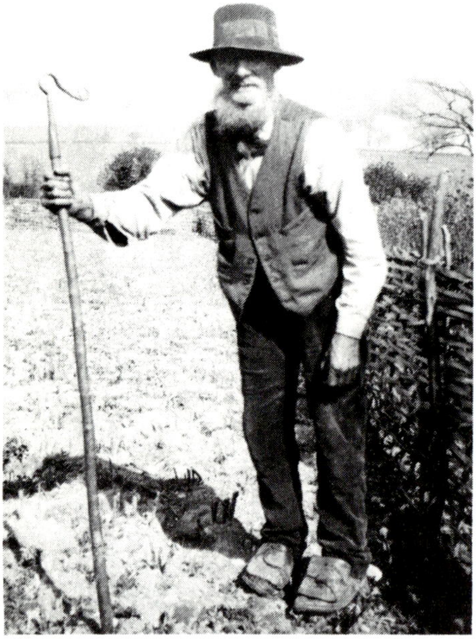

SHEPHERD TOM RUSHBRIDGE OF FINDON, pictured in around 1925. He is standing with his crook beside a sheep pen. His boots have false tongues to keep the mud out.

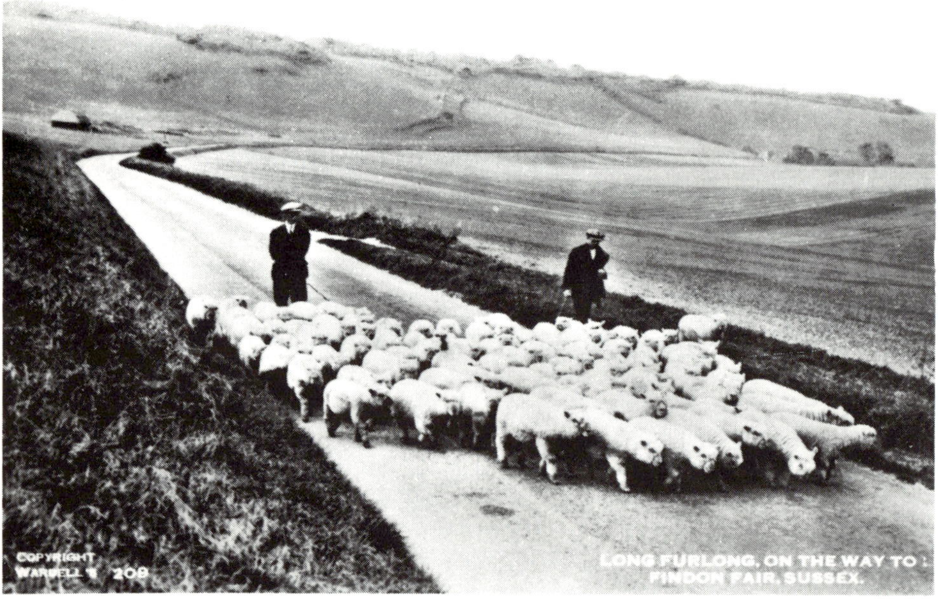


THESE SHEPHERDS AND THEIR FLOCKS of Southdown sheep are on their way to Findon sheep fair. This explains why the shepherds are wearing suits and ties. This picture shows the beautiful sweep of the Downs looking west along Long Furlong from near Church Hill.

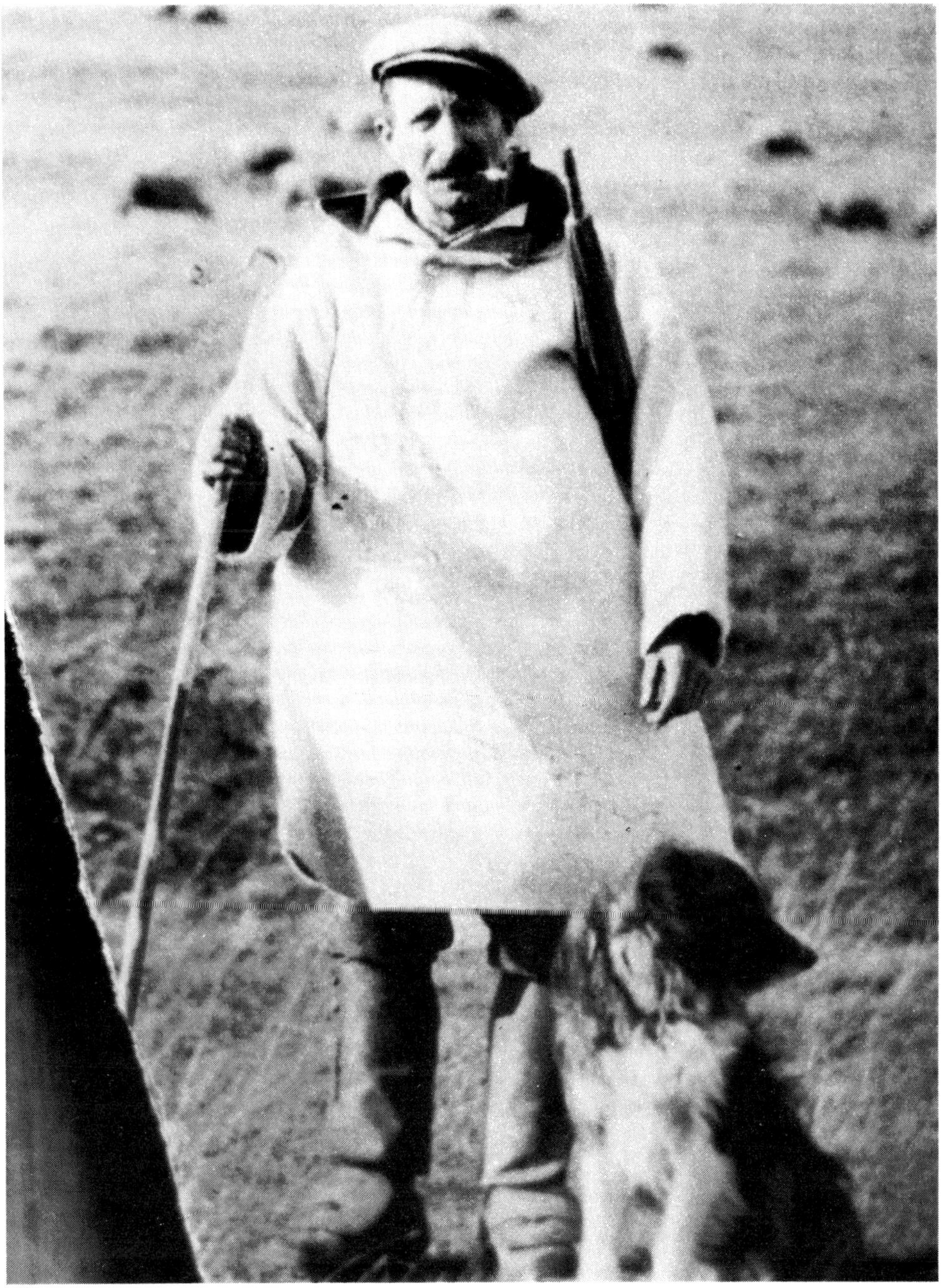

ARTHUR RUSHBRIDGE, like his father Tom, was a shepherd on the South Downs. This picture was taken in the late 1920s and shows him with his dog, crook, umbrella and updated version of the traditional smock.

#### ACKNOWLEDGEMENTS

I would like to thank John Norwood for suggesting that I should do this book, and I would like to thank Ann Wise and my mother for their help.

I am grateful to the following for permission to use photographs:

Terry Child, 21a, 21b, 31a, 41b, 68, 86, 87, 103a, 108b, 109a, 158b
Phyllis Short, 83a • Mrs L. Poston, 108a • Mrs P. Ockenden, 157b
Mr D. Hope, 82 • Worthing Museum and Art Gallery for all the other photographs.